What they told me

For Jamie, who I get to keep. My rainbow after the storm. Consistently consistent, devoted and fiercely caring. I am the luckiest.

Also for my girls, Mia, Zara, Sophie, Heidi and Lacey. No longer little, but always my little women, finding your ways through the forest of life. When the path diverges, and you must take it, may you hold fast until you make it.

Scholastic Australia
An imprint of Scholastic Australia Pty Limited
PO Box 579 Gosford NSW 2250
ABN 11 000 614 577
www.scholastic.com.au

Part of the Scholastic Group
Sydney • Auckland • New York • Toronto • London • Mexico City • New Delhi • Hong Kong • Buenos Aires • Puerto Rico

Published by Scholastic Australia in 2024.

Cover illustration by Astred Hicks, Design Cherry.
Book design by Astred Hicks, Design Cherry.

A catalogue record for this book is available from the National Library of Australia

ISBN: 978-1-76129-170-8

Typeset in Azo Sans and Baskerville.

Printed in China by RR Donnelley.
Scholastic Australia's policy, in association with RR Donnelly, is to use papers that are renewable and made efficiently with wood from responsibly managed sources, so as to minimise its environmental footprint.

24 25 26 27 28 / 2

HAYLEY LAWRENCE

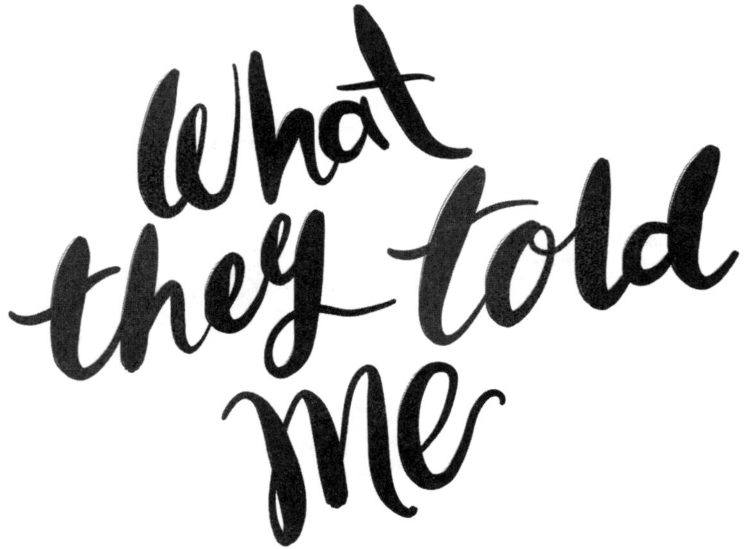

A Scholastic Australia book

The Gillespies

If I could take myself back, right back, to that very last night; if I could squeeze my eyes shut and twist through a portal to then, here's what I would see. Here's what we were.

We were four sets of hands snatching at pegs on the line, clutching at clothes—small, stubby, grubby boy fingers, and long, bony pale ones, and thick, parched calloused ones and mine. Long like Mum's and brown like Dad's. But nobody was looking at our fingers—only at clothes. Wild flapping clothes ready to tear off into the wind. Frantic grasping fingers and eyes darting over shoulders—beyond the house, far beyond—to the looming mound in the sky that was Mount Wilderness. She was not in a gentle mood, that mountain who brought water to the thirsty land and winds that could peel a roof right off a home. Not happy to sit in quiet majesty against a violet sky. No, today Mount Wilderness was brewing a poisonous spell, breathing down over the land, her breath cool against the nape of my neck, whipping my hair into tentacles that wrapped around my face.

'Quick,' Mum muttered, glancing over her shoulder at the jagged stripe of cloud grazing the sky with its teeth. The wind moaned, whipping trees to life and spiralling leaves down from their branches. The windows of the house rattled like prisoners trying to escape.

The first fat splotches hit my shoulders and I smelt the earth open her pores to drink the rain. The world around us turned to milk.

The last sock pinched, we were four heads down, clothing clutched to stomachs, eyes squinting against the spitting rain, running against the wind to the steps of our house, up to the verandah, inside the door. Snow stood on all fours at the doorway like a polar bear, the wind fanning her fur as she stared out at the wild world, dark and confettied.

'Get inside. It's about to hit!' Dad was at the door, beckoning, urging me in.

The first split of light, and a growl from the sky shook the floorboards beneath our feet. Snow barked, but we were safe. Safe inside and looking out across the field to the whitewashed hills, the bendy trees bowing before the wind. The rain came sheeting down in small silver daggers, the hiss of it hitting the earth, turning our footprints at the clothesline into puddles and the dust into mud.

Dad shut the door against the wind, pushing the full weight of his body against it. Then we were four panting, laughing faces. Winners of the storm race. We were hitting kettles, and turning on lights, and setting kindling and striking matches. We were warm mugs in cupped hands and window watchers as the world outside shadowed dark as night, and it was just us in our house of a thousand storms against the clouds that swallowed our light.

Lachy reached inside the hall cupboard, blew dust off a pack of cards. Mum lit the pillar candle on the carved wooden table in the kitchen in case we lost power. Then we were four sets of hands dragging chairs in close around the candlelight. Four sets of hands sliding cards to each other, and clutching cards to our chests.

Mum's hair fell in bleached wisps across her face as she reached for a new card and frowned over her choice, the light from the fire bronzing her face. And I said nothing about injustice when Dad leant across to check Lachy's cards, his thick veined arms resting on the table top, pointing to each card Lachy should use. When Dad helped Lachy win over and over, and Lachy laughed and his ringlets trembled. Because the ring of laughter from our glowing house was a sound that belonged uniquely to us. A sound of happiness.

Dad mussed Lachy's hair and Lachy mussed his back,

and then they were two tumbling rumbling bodies on the floor. Snow pranced around them barking, once, twice, three times. I sat back and watched us. The Gillespies. The lucky ones. Because we were warm, and dry, and steam rose from our chipped mugs, and the fire crackled heartily in the fireplace. When Dad and Lachy collapsed in a panting heap on the floor, Snow settled herself in a ball like a cloud on the rug near the hearth. And I wanted for nothing. Because that night, I knew nothing of need, or want, or pain or grief. I knew only the rain drum-drumming on the roof, the x-ray lightning electrifying the dark, and our house of a thousand storms like a glow worm against the night.

One

A sliver of Crooked River runs between our property and Drake's. Sometimes it's as shallow as a silver film, and during the drought it runs dry. But since the fires came through, followed by the floods, the river has returned. It gargles along the left flank of our land, making the grasses grow thick and the weeds grow tall. I can follow it all the way down to the back of Drake's place. I met him once in the dry river bed at 2:30 am as a dare when Mum and Dad thought I was sleeping.

The dry feels like a long time past, but it was only two summers ago. Back when the land was cracked like an open mouth thirsty for water. I look now at the twigs floating downriver in the murky current. Last night, the rain thundered through my dreams until the early hours of the morning. It fell in sheets against our tin roof until I thought the river would burst its banks and circle our house like an island.

After a summer storm, when the river's belly is swollen from the run off down the hills, Drake and I float on our backs, our faces like round dishes, and let the water carry us down to his place. Drake says when he dies, he wants to be buried by the river, but I just laugh. He's so new. Dad's family have been on this land for generations, back before it was subdivided into the lots Drake and his mum, Bec, are living on. I totally deserve to be buried here before he does.

I pull my phone from my pocket.

Check the river.

No response. No indication that the message has been read.

Doesn't matter.

I tuck my phone into a hollow in the plum tree by the bank of the river. At the base of its trunk, Bridge rests upturned. Her sun-bleached hull has been washed clean by last night's rain. It was Drake who said we should name the kayak when Bec bought her for us from a local online swap page. We settled on Bridge. Because when the river is high and we can't cross between his land and mine, she is our bridge.

I flip Bridge right ways up and pull at her rope. She slides along her belly in the grass like an anaconda, leaving a slick flattened track in her wake.

When I reach the tussocky edge of the bank, I keep my flip-flops on and nose Bridge into the water. Foam has gathered along the banks of the river. I push Bridge deeper into the stream, the chill of sepia water biting my feet. She wobbles. I rest one foot in the middle of her hull, then jump aboard, cutting the oar into the soft edge of the bank to push us out into the middle of the river.

We take off at a good pace, the current strong enough to carry us with only a light paddle. As we head downstream, the banks of the river rise up on either side of us, puckered with small holes from the snakes who rely on Crooked River for life itself.

I breathe in the damp earth and tip back my head to the pale blue sky. It looks like a canvas stretched above me, the delicate sort of colour Mum might once have spent a week blending on a palette to get exactly right. I trap the image in my mind like a snapshot because I want to describe it to her when I get back. It might inspire her to paint again. Winter is knocking on the door of autumn, and before long the sky will be the colour of ice, the earth white and crunchy with frost.

The river rounds a bend and the banks either side plateau out. Over the rush of water, finches flit and swoop, out of one tree, dipping towards the river, then back into the high branches. A rumbling noise grows, and to my right there's a flash of mottled grey at the top of the bank, followed by a throaty bark.

Ronnie gallops along the bank of the river like a horse, with his broad monstrous head, droopy lips pushed back by the wind, tongue lolling out one side. He runs back and forth, stopping every now and again to whimper like he wants to leap off the edge of the river and into Bridge. I row hard towards him, towards the bank, wedging Bridge's belly into the mud. Ronnie leaps down the embankment, tufts of dirt flying out beneath his paws. When he reaches Bridge, he's panting hard. I give him a pat on the head as I climb out. Ronnie nudges against me, his body wagging and frantic, his weight almost knocking me back into the hull. He shakes his dark coat and flecks of mud spatter my jeans, my shirt.

'Well, thanks,' I say, brushing off my shirt. 'Thanks a lot, boy.'

Ronnie looks up at the top of the bank and barks, but his bark is blown away by the breeze and wouldn't be heard over the rumbling above anyway.

I reach for the rope we leave tied to the she-oak trunk and secure Bridge with a trucker's knot. Then, using the same rope, I pull myself up the bank, Ronnie scrambling effortlessly alongside me.

On the embankment, spears of afternoon sun shine against Drake's bare back. His sun-tipped hair is tied in a rough ponytail as he motors along the front field of his house away from us, grass clippings spraying out one side of the ride-on mower like a waterfall. I watch as Drake arcs the ride-on around, sipping from a thermos which glints in the sun. He pushes his black thick-framed glasses back up his nose and sweeps his fringe off his forehead. Drake has the worst vision of anyone I know, so his glasses are pretty much a permanent fixture. I kinda like them. They tame the wild in Drake. Make him look almost . . . sophisticated.

Drake raises one hand when he sees me and starts heading my way on the mower. Ronnie sits by my feet whining, his tail whipping the grass clippings as Drake rides towards us.

He cuts the engine a couple of metres shy of us and pulls out his ear plugs. Ronnie takes that as his cue and runs forwards, paws up on Drake's lap, his entire body wagging.

'That's right. Greet the dog first,' I say.

'Ooooh.' Drake flashes me a smile, and his pale eyes, the colour of a winter sky, meet mine. He pushes at his glasses again and wipes the sweat from his upper lip, his face grimy. Then he looks back down at Ronnie. 'She's a jealous one, isn't she, boy?'

Ronnie looks into his eyes and barks once, as if he's agreeing.

'Yes, Elliott here,' he says, scruffing Ronnie's neck, 'is jealous of all the attention you get.'

'Hardly.'

'Oh, yes, she is.'

Ronnie barks again.

'I have nothing to be jealous of. You think *I* want your attention? You look half wild, by the way.'

'Am half wild,' he says, brushing grass blades off his pants.

Bec calls Drake a giant pup. Big hands, big feet, big nose; all need growing into.

'So what's up?' he says. 'Or did you come here just to observe my rugged good looks?'

'Please,' I scoff. 'I'm actually bored.'

'And that's my problem how?'

'Because boredom-busting is one of your few talents.' I say. 'But you're clearly too busy for my boredom today.'

Drake looks down at Ronnie, who stares longingly back into Drake's eyes. 'Now she's even jealous of my busy-ness,' he says. 'Someone has to mow these lawns, though, don't they, boy? And I don't see her volunteering.'

Having thrown the bait, he grins over at me to see if he's gotten a reaction.

'You can get over yourself,' I say. 'And I *have* mown these lawns before. You seem to conveniently forget about last summer when you were sick with the flu.'

Ronnie is loyal and just wags his tail at Drake, like Drake is his king and anything he says is utterly and completely one hundred percent correct. He huffs his doggy breath, big smile across his monster face.

'Alright, point taken. I'll be done in, like, fifteen,' Drake says. 'What's the plan?'

'Turtle hunting,' I say. 'You and me. An old-fashioned race.'

It's something we've done since we were kids. Find a turtle

each in the creek and pair them up on the bank to race back in. The slowest race in human history. Also possibly the funniest. And turtles will soon be in hibernation.

Now that I've spoken the words though, the idea of turtle hunting sounds cringey. Childish. We're not eight anymore. We're almost double that.

'Or we could do something else,' I add.

It will hurt if he's lost interest. I don't want to live in a world where we're too old for turtle hunting, but at some point I suppose we'll both have to grow up.

'Sounds more fun than mowing,' Drake says. 'Let me finish up and we'll head.'

He puts his ear plugs back in and restarts the mower. It roars to life. Ronnie runs to my side and Drake salutes us both as he turns the ride-on around to head downfield again.

'Come on, boy.' I pat my flank as I jog towards Drake's house.

His place is newer than ours. Which isn't hard, since our house is over a hundred years old. Where Gillespie House is crooked, his is all straight edges. A one-storey sandstone lodge with a white wrap-around verandah and a porch swing we kick back on with a glass of lemonade, watching the sun disappear behind the mountain ranges.

As I near the house, I notice Bec doubled over on the roof, brushing leaves out of the gutter. Her checked shirt is rolled to her elbows, wavy hair pulled up in a messy bun.

'Hey, Bec,' I call over the noise of the mower.

She straightens and turns around, broom in one hand. 'Elliott. I didn't see you come in.'

'I rowed.'

'Ah.' She wipes her forearm across her forehead and squints towards the creek. 'Glad you kids get so much use out of that kayak.'

'Need any help?' I nod at the ladder resting against the guttering.

'Nope, almost done. You might want to watch out though.' She sweeps a shower of leaves off the edge.

Ronnie pounces on the freshly fallen foliage and rolls over onto his back, rubbing himself into the pile. He sneezes and I laugh.

'Scoundrel, he is,' Bec says. 'Speaking of which, if you're planning to take that boy of mine off on some wild adventure, you make sure he finishes those lawns!'

'Always do!'

Bec sweeps off the last of the leaves near the edge of the roof, drops the broom to the grass below and makes her way to the top of the ladder. I press my foot onto the lowest rung to hold it steady as she climbs down.

'Well, aren't you a keeper?' she says, dismounting the ladder and folding it flat. 'Looking after an old lady.'

I laugh. 'Last I checked, you weren't old.'

'Ah, yes.' She dusts leaf debris off her pants with her hands. 'Sometimes we feel older than we are! Now, are you coming in for a quick cuppa? Give Drakey boy time to finish up.'

She rests the ladder under the window of their living room and we take the stairs up to the verandah. Ronnie follows us and sits next to the front door where he whines.

'Not now, boy,' Bec says. 'Daytime is for outdoors. Go frolic in the sun.'

I shut the screen door on poor old Ronnie and follow Bec into the kitchen, where she hits the kettle.

'How was that storm last night?' she says. 'Mother Nature knows how to turn it on. Drake and I pulled up the blinds, turned out the lights and sat in the dark watching the show.'

I grab three enamel mugs from their hooks under the kitchen cupboard. 'I love the storms here the most,' I say.

'And you probably always will,' Bec says. 'You came into the world with a storm, from what I hear.'

I nod.

'Then storms will always hold magic for you. Even if they're sheer terror for others,' Bec laughs. Her laughter is high-pitched and gentle, the tinkle of bells. 'I tell you, rain is a very good thing, but the way it's been coming down . . .' She throws up her hands. 'I mean, who would have guessed, right? Two years ago we were doing rain dances, begging for the stuff. Now I'm having to sweep the roof to stop the water backflushing in. And the weeds—the weeds!' She opens a sealed glass jar and removes three tea bags from it. 'They're out of control. I'm thinking of hiring a few head of goat just to give the poor ride-on a break. A small bit of land takes a big bit of looking after, doesn't it? Your dad would know it well.'

I nod. 'He wouldn't have it any other way, though.'

'I guess your family doesn't know anything *but* the land.'

'Yep. Five generations of it. This is what Gillespies do.'

The truth is, I can't imagine living anywhere else. I've never had to. Nor has Dad. This is where the Gillespies have always lived. Like the very earth is in our DNA. Even one of the streets in the new estate is named after us.

Bec hangs the tags over the lip of each of our mugs and heaps in spoonfuls of sugar. She pours from the kettle and steam wisps to the ceiling as she bobs the tea bags. I watch the dark tannin seep into the water in ribbons.

'What about your mum?' she says.

'What about her?'

Bec pours a small amount of milk into each mug, stirring it in slowly. 'She's not fifth generation, is she?'

'No, but she's been part of it since she married Dad. They haven't lived anywhere else.'

'Mmm.' She looks up at me from stirring. 'I wonder if she gets tired of the work?'

She seems to expect an answer, so I shrug. 'Maybe sometimes, I guess. But she loves it here.'

My words sound a little bit defensive and they feel sour in my mouth, because Bec's question has triggered a memory. When I heard Mum complaining about the rotten old house that's falling down around us. The white ants gnawing at the back deck. Going to eat the house hollow if we don't stop them, she'd told Dad.

Then there was that terrible time, two years ago when the floods came. When we became indoor people in a world of sudden heavy wet. When the rain shushed in a tireless torrent around our house, turning the window panes to a frosty blur and creeping in through the gaps under the door and through the cracks of the windows. And the water seemed to be coming not just from the sky, but from the trees, and the ground, and the roof and everywhere.

There had been no warning. A microburst, they called it later. No warning about the deluge of rain or the flooding that followed it.

Lachy and I were thrilled. An unexpected adventure! *You can't go to school*, Mum'd said, *not in this.* Roads were blocked off, creeks swollen and about to burst. Lachy and I had looked at each other, our eyes shining. A day off!

We'd run out onto the verandah in gum boots and watched the rain cascading over the gutters like a waterfall, the land wet and haggard. We heard the river gushing, moaning, gargling, alive with life. Not like after an ordinary rain. We could see from where we stood that the water in the river was rising. A dark, swirling foamy mass, moving like a thick dirty ribbon downstream.

'You kids stay here,' Mum had said. 'Don't you go down there.' And I'd heard the tremor in her voice.

Mum has always feared this place in a way the rest of us haven't. I think it's because she wasn't born here. She didn't grow up learning to map the path of storms. She didn't know the drought cycle and couldn't read the flow of the river. It was like she'd missed out on a favourite childhood book that Dad, Lachy and I all knew back to front.

So we weren't scared, Lachy and I. We were never scared. Not of droughts, or floods or fires. Because this was our place, and in it we were beyond harm. We still weren't scared when a wall of water roared down the river like a jet engine, carrying whole trees with it, tearing at the edges of the bank before rising and spilling out across the field. We weren't even scared when the muddy water swirled right up to our verandah steps and Dad had to use a broom to push off a snake who'd tried to swim to safety in our house.

I'd helped Mum count tins and dried food in the cupboard, and when the lights sputtered out, we'd sent Lachy to look for candles. And even though Mum snapped at Dad that she wanted us to start over fresh someplace new, someplace where things like this didn't happen, I'd known it was just scared talk, because we'd never seen a flood like that before. But deep down, Mum felt the same as us about Gillespie House. Of course she did.

I realise Bec's still talking.

'Everywhere I look, there's work! Weed this, prune that, fix this, fence that, clean this, manage that. Sometimes I think we'd be better off selling. Move into a neat little house on a flat grassy block in town.'

'*Move*?' I repeat, as she passes me my tea.

'Don't look so ghastly, Elliott dear, I wouldn't do it. I'm a sucker for this place. Those mountains . . .' She clicks her tongue. 'Our burnt sunsets in the west, and I say *ours* because we own the sky out here. It feels like ours, doesn't it? And the big black storms that tear over from Mount Wilderness in the summer. Terrifying and powerful. This place is indeed enchanted. It has a sort of ancient magic that weaves its way into your blood. Very different to some hum-drum unit block in town without a whisper of wind or a single tree to sit under for company. No, I'm not trading this place in. No matter how many storms Mount Wilderness throws at us.'

'Well, good,' I say. 'Because don't forget, Drake wants to be buried by the bank of the river one day.'

'How could I forget?' she says wryly. 'I hate it when you kids are morbid like that. You're young, you have forever. Plan for that instead. Plan for where your dreams will take you.'

I sip my tea. 'My plans won't take me too far. I'm a Gillespie, after all,' I laugh. 'We like to stay where we were born. Our old house needs some work, but besides that I'm happy for everything to stay as it is. Me included.'

Bec sips her tea and grimaces, like it tastes bitter. 'Yeah, well, nothing stays the same too long. Seems that's the way of life. And change isn't always a bad thing.'

'Never cared much for it myself,' I say, jokingly.

Bec wasn't in our glowing little house last night, watching Dad wrestle Lachy on the floor, sipping tea with us as the rain overflowed from the gutters. She can be forgiven for not understanding.

'Seasons will change,' she says softly, looking out the kitchen window at Drake, riding the mower back to the shed.

Bec and Drake have not been Gillespies, the lucky ones, as Dad says. But I'm not stupid. I realise not everyone gets so lucky.

Drake doesn't have a dad whose safe footsteps are heard in the night when there's a crash. Someone to check the fences and tuck him in at night with thick split fingertips. He had a dad once. I suppose he still does have a dad, somewhere. One day, Drake had said, his dad was there, work shirts hanging in the wardrobe, big shoes by the front door, tools in the garage, electric shaver by the vanity in the bathroom. The next day, Drake had come home from school and the shoes, the clothes, the tools, the shaver were gone.

'Life sure knows how to dish out surprises,' Bec says, her eyes fluttering. 'Some are terrible surprises and some are wonderful. Crooked River has been one of the gifts.' She smiles at me, her eyes studded with tears that she blinks away.

I sit in the front of Bridge because I'm lighter, Drake in the back. Bridge's oar slices through the rippled river as we head upstream, dipping and pulling as we surge around the bend. Ronnie follows along the edge of the bank to Drake's fence line, ears up, forehead furrowed, barking down at us.

'He really hates us being in the water, doesn't he?' I say to Drake.

'Yeah. Poor Ronnie is a bit old-fashioned. He believes humans should walk on two legs. Anything funky, like, say, gliding in a capsule through the water, he's not really into.'

Ronnie barks again.

'He wants us to stop being weird,' Drake says.

'Well, old Ronnie boy's going to be waiting a long time,' I say. 'Our weirdness is going nowhere fast.'

Halfway back to my place, when Drake's shoulders are

burning, I take over the rowing, getting into a rhythm with the oar. Paddle left, paddle right. Left, right.

We pull up to the shallows on my side of the river and Drake leaps out onto the bank. He extends his hand to help me.

'What's this?' I say, looking at his hand. 'You pretending to be a gentleman now?'

'*Am* a gentleman,' he says, mocking offence. 'No need to pretend.'

The hand is a new thing. A very new, older-us thing. I like the hand, even though I also mock it every time he does it, which has only been a few times. The truth is, I don't just like the helping hand, I like *Drake's* hands. Have always liked his hands. Drake has good-looking hands, if such a thing exists. They are generous, brown and broad and well-proportioned, about twice the size of mine. They look capable, feel safe, so I take hold of his hand in case he decides to stop offering it, and let Drake pretend to be a gentleman as he helps me out of the kayak. A strange energy runs from his hand to mine. Not like the storm from last night, but a gentle warm buzz. He holds my hand just a moment longer than I think he really needs to, then he lets go.

I don't dare to make eye contact with Drake. The buzz is still inside my hand. Trapped. Like he passed a secret to me without either of us speaking a word. I use those same buzzing hands to drag Bridge up onto the gritty sand, putting all my energy into the job, until we wedge her high for safekeeping. It's only when we head back down to the water that I sneak a glance at Drake's face. His hair is still pulled back in the same ponytail from earlier in the afternoon, loose bits shooting out like stray sparks from his head. His face tells me nothing, but my cheeks are hot, which I'm sure means they are red. Did he feel it too? Whatever that was?

We wade into the cool water, mud squelching beneath our soles. As we get deeper, the mud turns to river stones. Soft flip-flops against sharp rock edges. The water bites at our ankles, our calves, the murky current swirling around our knees.

I point at the willow tree ahead, its low sweeping tendrils caressing the dimpled surface of the water. Drake lifts a branch and I watch his hand holding it like I haven't seen him do this a thousand times before. I lean forward, scanning the shallow water beneath the willow for the curved hump of a shell with its scratched geometrical markings, but I can't see anything resembling a turtle.

'I think they're a bit spoilt for hiding places,' I say.

In the dry, when the river shrank to a rock bed with a few stagnant water holes, turtles were an easy find, and we'd pluck their mossy shells from the water like lucky dip prizes. Not anymore.

'No good?' he says.

I shake my head. 'Too murky.'

We head further upriver, the water growing shallower, warmer. Drake nudges logs with sticks, I lift branches.

I keep thinking of his hand. Holding my hand. The tingle between us. Did I imagine it?

'Not a shell in sight,' he says.

After a half hour of fruitless searching, Drake says, 'How far do you want to go?'

'To World's End,' I say.

He laughs, but I mean it. The river runs almost forever, fed down from World's End and cascading into the mighty Cudgegong Dam. Nobody is allowed to own the river. So we can walk as far upstream as we like without trespassing on anyone else's land. It makes our hundred acres feel bigger. Once upon a time, the Gillespies owned the land all the way along Crooked River on both sides. Thousands of acres and our one house. It seems selfish. Too much for one family, but back then the Gillespies were farmers and cattle need land. Now there are no big farms, no cattle, just housing estates and our land. And a lot of debt. Because making money in a land of drought and flood is no quick way to get rich, Dad says.

Further upstream, small rocky waterfalls gush, soaking the edges of our shorts.

'Well, this here is not going to find us any reptiles,' Drake declares. Turtles don't like fast currents any more than flooding rain. They prefer nature to be slow and gentle. They like their water calm and their rain light.

We move to the edge of the creek where the flow is gentler and the bank flatter.

That's when I see it, wedged against a crevice in the dirt. Overturned. Bleached almost white. Black markings faded. I bend down and pick up the sad empty shell. It's cracked along one side. Lifeless.

An ache pangs in my stomach. Death is not what I was looking for.

'Washed down in the heavy rains maybe,' Drake says, coming close to examine the shell. 'Poor girl.'

The U shape at the base of the shell tells us she is a female. *Was* a female. But she will house no more eggs inside that curved protective shell, lay no more, swim no more. I clutch the shell in my hand.

'Why don't you set her down in the water?' Drake suggests. 'Give her a river burial?'

I look at the fast flow of the creek that was first her home. She wouldn't like the current.

'Let's put her under the Pa Tree,' I say.

We head back downstream until we reach Bridge and the well-worn track up to my place.

We stop under the Pa Tree. Which is really a plum tree. But ever since Dad told me the story about Pa, it's been the Pa Tree to me. Which doesn't make me sad, because I never knew my Pa.

It's just that when Dad tells me of that day, the one where he stood before the plum tree, at fifteen, almost exactly my age, after Pa died, and emptied what was left of his own dad at the base of that tree, his eyes water and his voice wobbles. And even though I didn't know Pa, my throat burns with sadness. Because I can't imagine having to do that. Empty out my dad or my mum. I want them both here, forever. All four of us, forever.

We use sticks to dig a small hole into the spongey earth and bury the shell. Drake lays a rock on the spot, I pull wildflowers from the nearby grass and rest them on top. It feels childish, but also somehow right. Turtles have given us so much joy.

Afterwards, I pull a blade of wheatgrass and twirl it between my thumb and forefinger. It pirouettes, a little dancer. Then I lie back in the long grass under the dappled shade of the plum tree, whose wide trunk and scraggy branches have weathered years of our climbing.

Drake lies down beside me, his elbow touching mine. That touch sends a zing all the way from my elbow to the pit of my stomach. My body is suddenly alive with heat, my heart beating a little faster.

'Can we go turtle hunting again tomorrow?' Drake says, grinning. 'I like turtle hunting.'

'Maybe.' My heart beats a frantic little tune at the thought of being like this with him again tomorrow.

We lie there together, and the birds twitter in the branches above us. I watch a blue wren bob its tail before darting off again. A dance of its own.

Drake props himself up on one elbow so that he's facing me. I try not to tense up. To stay relaxed. But he is so close, we're breathing the same air. The sun is shining through the lenses of his glasses into his eyes, illuminating the different flecks of colour. His hair is a tangled halo around his head. I remind myself he's just Drake. The same old Drake I've known forever, but something about him is different. Or something about *us* maybe.

It's that strange electricity again. Buzzing over us, between us, like our very own electromagnetic field. Am I the only one of us who feels it?

Drake tucks a strand of loose hair behind my ear. Then he does something he has never, ever done before. He leans forward and kisses me softly on the forehead. His lips are warm, trembling. And I feel something unearthly, like the very ground beneath us is cracking open, a beam of light shining up from its depths, straight into the sky.

The Pa Tree's branches ruffle lightly in the breeze like it's no big deal that Drake just kissed me.

But I'm trying to catch my thoughts. To figure out what this means. Was that just a friendly kiss? A more-than-friendly kiss? What is happening to Drake and me?

As Drake pulls away, our eyes meet briefly. 'I'm sorry,' he says. 'I didn't mean to do that . . . I mean, was that okay?'

I nod and when I try to smile, my smile doesn't work right. It comes out stiff. My heart is still beating hard in my chest. It knows something has changed. That this is not a normal Drake and Elliott kind of afternoon.

'How ridiculous that we're being so weird,' Drake says. 'It's just us, right?'

I nod again. Just us. Just Elliott and Drake. In an entirely new way.

For the next few minutes, we lie side by side in silence, until I take a deep breath and reach for his hand. Just to test that feeling. And then his hand is holding mine again. The buzzy zapping seeps back from my hand all the way up to my heart. To hold someone else's hand is sacred, and deeply private. I want to protect this feeling.

Drake lifts our joined hands towards the sky in front of us, examining them. 'These fit pretty nicely. I think they like it. Just saying.'

Then we are two hands entwined against the golden light. Two bodies lying in the tall grass. Hidden. A secret between us. We are old friends, but we are also new. All of this, completely new.

'Ever wonder how much longer we'll be here?' Drake says. He's staring past the branches to the wide blue sky beyond.

'You mean alive?' I ask.

He laughs. 'No, morbid, I mean *here*. Living here.'

'What do you mean? In my family, we stay forever.'

He looks at me with raised eyebrows. 'I'm being serious.'

'So am I.'

'I mean, like, when we finish school.' He examines our entwined hands again. But this time he frowns lightly at them. 'It's only a couple years away. When we go to uni or . . . whatever.'

This is the first time he has ever mentioned the word 'uni' to me.

I sit up, breaking our hands apart.

'Have you not thought about it?' he says. 'I know you're a year younger than me, but you must be thinking about it?'

I try to imagine Drake in a university in some big town or city, but it feels a little bit toxic. Like a foul drink. My heart is beating sickeningly. I know it's a very normal thing, to go and study after school, but the idea of Drake leaving here to do it *repulses* me. Especially right now.

'So what would you do? At this *uni*?'

He laughs and sits up, drawing his knees to his chest and wrapping his bare arms around them. The golden tips of his hair kick up the light. 'You make it sound like a disease.'

I try to laugh, but my laughter is strangled. The thought of Drake in some place far away, somewhere that's not here, is ridiculous. He's been downstream since I can remember. Drake's been at school since the day I started, and he guided me around because he was a whole year older and wiser than me, being in Year One. A kid with broad hands, and thick-lensed glasses and mud-stained knees. I've held those broad hands now. I never knew I would do that, but I have, and I like the way they felt. Secure as a promise. But this? This doesn't feel secure.

'So what would you do?' I repeat. 'At uni?' I hear my own voice waver on the word 'uni'. Feel a bitter sting in my throat.

'Don't know exactly.' He picks at some blades of grass in the earth. 'I was thinking maybe medicine. Or engineering.'

I frown at Drake, examining him for any trace of a grim-faced doctor or a serious engineer. No, I won't allow it. I like Drake the way he is now.

'What?'

I shake my head. I'm not even sure he's serious. 'You don't look like a doctor. You'd need a haircut, for one.'

He smirks. 'And what's a doctor meant to look like?'

'I don't know . . . serious, clean cut. Not like *you*.'

He sits up straighter, dusts his hands on his knees, looks away. 'Well, maybe I'll be a different kind of doctor. Or maybe I'll change and *get* serious.'

'No,' I say quickly. Drake has already changed enough to me this afternoon. 'Don't you change.'

'Or maybe I'll just be an engineer.'

'Whatever,' I say. 'Let me know when you decide.'

'Okay, I will.'

He must know as well as I do that the idea is wrong. He can't leave. Not ever. This is where we belong. What's the point of this place without us in it? And how *dare* he kiss me on the forehead and hold my hand, then talk to me about leaving? Who does that?

Drake is pushing to his feet now, dusting his hands against his shorts, looking down the river, away from me, like he's not even here anymore. Like he can see this uni he'll attend far away and the doctor he'll one day be, with a neat ponytail tied back and a stethoscope around his neck, treating patients we don't even know yet. Maybe his mind is already made up.

'I'd better head back,' he says.

I squint up at him. 'Alright then.'

He really is pathetic if he thinks I'm going to beg him to stay here with me, next to the stupid empty shell we just buried, with the grass that's still pressed warm from us lying in it. Well if that's what he wants, he picked the wrong girl. I don't beg for anyone.

'Mind if I take Bridge?'

I shrug, not bothering to stand. 'Go for it.'

A pain starts throbbing sharply in my chest, but I turn my head away from him. I don't watch as he walks down to the edge of the river, or as he flips Bridge over and takes the oar. I don't watch him pull her towards the water by her rope. I just hear the sliding and scraping of her belly against the gritty bank, like a dead body. I don't go down to wave Drake off like I usually would. Or tell him I'll catch him later.

What a disaster of a first kiss that was! If you could even call it that. If he's planning to leave this place, why start something with us? Why change what was working?

But then a thought comes to me. 'Wait,' I say, standing up. A shiver ripples across my shoulder blades, making my skin goose fleshed.

Drake stops, looks over his shoulder at me, one foot in Bridge, one hand shielding his eyes. 'What?'

'How will you be buried by the river then?'

'What?' He frowns.

'If you're leaving for the city.'

A small smile crosses his face. 'I won't be gone forever. And Mum's never leaving. So I'll be back to annoy you all the time, don't worry.'

I shrug. Pretend I don't feel the tiniest bit better. 'Well, maybe I won't be here . . . And there'll *be* nobody left to visit.'

Mean, I know, but I'm churned up at his talk of leaving. I don't know why he even brought it up, except that if Drake says he's thinking of doing anything, he usually goes and does it. Even if it's stupid, like that time he spent a solid week building a fence across the river to stop Ronnie getting out and the fence got washed away in the very next flood.

'You'll never leave,' Drake calls back, pushing off into the water in Bridge. 'Unless you're dragged off by earth-moving machines . . .'

I smile, because it's true. But the smile only helps a bit. He's stirred something up in my stomach and it feels like muck at the bottom of a very deep well.

Three

As a little girl with swollen eyes, I would come and sit beneath the Pa Tree, its big arms stretched over me like a hug, covering me in whispered shadows. And I would ask questions of the universe about all sorts of things. Nothing too big or small.

I'm older now and I should have outgrown this habit, but I haven't. And so I sit here, cuddled up to myself, asking questions again.

I don't want Drake to move away, universe. I want him downriver to hang out with. I want him swinging on the porch chair with me on his verandah as the sunset edges the mountain ridges in gold. I don't want him to grow up and leave me behind.

Drake is as much why I love this place as the river is. As Mum, and Dad and Lachy are. And now I've hurt him, haven't I? I should have been supportive, should have told him he could do anything he set his mind to. Should have said I could totally see him as a doctor, or an engineer or even an astronaut if that's what he wanted. But I only want him dreaming things that will dig his roots into the earth here, dig them as deep as the roots of the Pa Tree.

Tell me how to fix this, universe, please tell me.

I listen for answers in the gargle of the river. I listen and listen.

Okay, I'll apologise. Drake, I was a brat about you moving away. You'd make a cool doctor exactly the way you are. You don't need to get all serious and cut off your hair. I don't want you to change yourself for anything. And doctors are needed in our town, so medicine isn't even the worst thing you could do! I was being selfish. Totally childish. I'm sorry.

I rehearse it in my head until I almost mean it and the churning in my stomach is softer.

I think of Drake's warm hand in mine only minutes ago. He said our hands fitted nicely. Warmth trickles into my stomach at the thought. Drake and I will be good again. We'll be okay. One of the best things about Drake is that he doesn't hold a grudge. I'm not as good at forgiveness as him. I've been known to hold grudges for weeks, but Drake never lasts more than a day. Even if I'm being a complete brat, Drake will forgive me. This is how I know we'll be okay. Always, we'll be okay.

I survey our double-storey white-slatted house on the hill, brilliant in the last rays of the day. The picket fence running around it is leaning in places where it shouldn't and is spattered in muddy chicken pox from the heavy rain. Flakes of paint on the slats of the house glisten in the amber light. It's not the perfect house. Not modern like Drake's. It has so many nooks in it full of dusty old things. It needs painting and polishing. But it's ours, and it's safe and it holds the people I love inside it. Even if everything's a bit old and tired, it's home, it's us. And we're all allowed to get a bit old and tired, aren't we?

Mum and Dad are tired, much like our house. But I'm grateful that they're not the type for loud screaming matches or smashing of plates. Their kind of fighting is quiet. Icy. It's words not said, and kettles turned on too hard and veggies left uneaten on dinner plates. But it's only a matter of days before Mum and Dad make up. It's never longer than a week. They don't hold grudges like me.

The first wisps of smoke are rising from the chimney of our house. The sun pierces the ridgeline of the far-off hills, shooting golden shafts of light into the sky, leaving the wheatgrass in shadow. I can already feel the evening chill descending. Mum and Dad will be calling for me, texting me to come home before it's dark. I grab my phone from out of the knot in the Pa Tree and head up the hill.

The climb from the river used to feel like Mount Everest when my legs were shorter. Now it's just a stroll. I push through the front gate. As it squeaks, Snow scrambles out from beneath the house and pelts towards me. Her tail whisks furiously as she nuzzles her nose into my legs.

'Hi, girl,' I say, giving her a rub around the ears. 'Whatcha been doing?'

Snow doesn't realise she's meant to be old. She still thinks she's a puppy, even though she's almost a hundred in dog years. Both our dog and our house, ancient. Nobody has told her how ancient she is though, so Snow gets around like she's three. But lately, her fluffy coat has grown a bit dull and patchy. And she spends most of her days asleep under the house.

Snow follows me up the stairs to our verandah and sits by the front door, head cocked hopefully to one side. I don't invite her in because it's almost dinnertime. The deck creaks beneath my weight as I open the door. In the living room, the fire is crackling in the hearth, but nobody's there. My tummy grumbles, aching for food. There are none of the usual dinner sounds or smells—onion frying, meat sizzling, the thick gurgle of a stew. Our timber-panelled kitchen is dark in the after light. The sun has dipped behind the mountains now, the house silent.

A breadboard sits beside the sink. Alongside it a lone knife, an apple, Mum's chipped mug saying 'Princess of the Palace'. The slab bench has been wiped clean of crumbs. I pick up the breadboard, the knife. Put a piece of bread in the toaster, take the butter dish out of the fridge. Find a half-eaten avocado in the fruit bowl. Hit the kettle.

I hear the deck creak, the front door open. Dad's heavy footsteps across the floorboards. The clunk of something solid hitting the floor. No more footsteps.

The kettle boils, so I grab two mugs. Mine and the cornflour blue mug I bought for Dad at a Father's Day school stall that says 'Stress Less'. My toast pops, so I butter it on the breadboard. Spread the rest of the avocado across it, add a sprinkle of salt. I take a bite and head into the lounge room, toast in one hand, two mugs balanced in the other.

Dad is slumped in the armchair recliner, a pile of wood on the floor alongside him. He's staring at the fire, which licks up the sides of a new log. The log cracks, sending out a spark that hits the floorboards and dies.

'Tough day?' I say.

Dad looks up as I pass him a mug. In the firelight, his face is older, darker, more lined. He takes hold of the mug with both hands.

'Thanks, sweetheart.' He looks back at the fire. I have another bite of my toast.

Dad's been quiet the last few days. It's more than just the fight with Mum. With all the rain and the rivers rising, I think he's worried about another flood cutting us off. Come to think of it, that's probably what he and Mum have been fighting about.

'Want to talk about it?' I ask, my mouth full. I mean about the fight with Mum. The river. Life. Any of those things. I've lived a bit. He can tell me.

But then Mum appears in the hallway beside the fireplace, Lachy standing behind her.

'What is it?' Lachy says, looking from Dad, to Mum, to me.

I swallow my mouthful. 'What's what?'

'El, Lachy.' Mum tugs down the cuffs of her stretchy, apricot knitted jumper so they almost cover her hands. 'Why don't you kids take a seat?'

She gestures to the three-seater lounge with her covered hands, so I sit. Sip my tea, crunch down on another bite of my toast. Lachy slinks into the lounge room behind Mum, his frizzy mop of dark hair half covering his eyes as he edges down beside me on the lounge.

'We need to talk to you both for a minute. Need to tell you both something.'

'Okay.' I look from one of them to the other.

That's when I notice Mum's eyes are swollen and blotchy. She appears to be trembling as she eases herself down on the other side of me. I stop chewing. Put down my mug of tea.

Mum takes hold of my free hand lightly in her knitted one. Her hand is shivering like a frightened bird. This is exactly how her hand felt when she told me Nanna had died. It was this same awful quiet. But there are no more Nannas left to die. Or Pas. They're all gone.

The toast catches in my throat like cement. 'Is it Snow?'

'What's wong with Snow?' Lachy says.

The day we have the talk about Snow is a day I refuse to be part of.

'No, honey, there's nothing wrong with Snow,' Mum soothes.

The tight feeling in my stomach loosens, but only a little. 'What then?'

I'm looking from Mum to Dad frantically. I notice Lachy doing the same. Watching us all. Waiting. What else could be this horrific? Someone has clearly died. A cold chill works through my body like a bad omen. Did Drake get home okay? I haven't heard from him since he left.

Dad clears his throat as if to speak, but nothing comes out.

'What is it?' My hands are cold as frost, like all the blood has been sucked out of them. 'Tell us.'

Dad turns around to face both me and Lachy. He looks at us, tea still steaming from his 'Stress Less' mug. He has not taken a sip. His face is a ghastly colourless sort of grey.

'What?!' I'm angry now, because my heart is thudding at me: *danger, danger.*

'Your mother and I . . .' Dad starts.

Your mother? My heart thuds harder, beating to a strange new pattern.

'Your mother and I have . . .' His face contorts, eyes filling with tears. 'I'm sorry.' He clutches the mug in his fist. His knuckles are white lines bursting through his olive skin. He reaches over to clutch Lachy's knee with his other hand.

‘We’ve decided to separate,’ Mum says coolly, rubbing a small vigorous circle on the palm of my hand.

‘Sorry?’ I say.

Mum takes a deep breath. ‘We’ve decided to separate,’ she repeats gently.

‘Sepawate what?’ Lachy’s haunted eyes are searching Dad’s for an answer. A simple explanation.

I feel my own eyes searching Mum’s for the same thing. It feels like we’re speaking different languages. Like she is trying to explain something to me in a dialect I don’t understand.

Mum keeps rubbing the circular motion on my hand, her knitwear exfoliating my palm.

Silence is what we both get. A heavy weeping silence that feels like it stretches on, until Lachy says, ‘What ah we sepawating?’

Mum and Dad don’t look at each other, or at me.

‘We’ve tried, kids. I’ve tried.’ Dad’s voice breaks. ‘Mum wants out.’

‘Out of what?’ Lachy says. ‘I don’t undastand.’

But I understand. In a gush, I understand everything. Blood rushes to my face, pounding up from my stomach, my chest, all the way to my face, my ears. The blood that binds all four of us together, thumping heavily through me.

‘What?’ I hear myself saying. ‘*What*?!’

‘Don’t you dare,’ Mum says to Dad, pointing one long bony

finger at him. 'Don't you damn well *dare*. This takes *two*.'

Dad inhales sharply, looks away.

I feel prickly all over, like I'm an actor in a series. None of this is real. I'm just watching myself playing Elliott in this room, hearing these words.

'Ah you guys splitting up?' Lachy whispers, and a whimper comes out of him, like an injured animal.

'It'll be okay, little man,' Dad says, pulling him close.

Lachy's face is pale. Even his lips have lost their pink. 'Ah you weally?' Lachy says, looking over at Mum.

Mum nods, once. And once is enough.

I watch as Lachy's eyes grow big and fill with tears. I watch them spill over his cheeks, as Dad stands and pulls him to his chest. I watch Lachy bury his face in Dad, looking for cuddles, for it to be okay. Dad holds him tight.

'El, honey,' Mum says, bending her head to make me look her in the eye. 'We're so tired. Of trying. Pretending we're okay. It's not getting any better. I'm not any happier here. It's getting worse. When two people fall out of love . . .'

I gasp. *Out of love?* We're not *out of love*. Love doesn't just *run out*. Our family barely even fights.

But Mum's eyes keep pleading with me. 'We'll be happier apart, I promise you, my sweet girl. We'll all be happier.'

Dad doesn't say anything. He doesn't agree with her. How could he? Her words are impossible.

‘No,’ I say hollowly. ‘No, we won’t be.’

I know this for a fact. There is no way the Gillespies can be happier apart. The muck at the bottom of the well churns wildly again in my stomach.

I realise suddenly that I don’t get a say in this. I don’t get to tell them to fix this up right now, like when they tell me to clean the mess in my room. Stop making excuses, get in there and tidy it. Make it pretty again. I don’t get to tell them that. Even though Mum’s eyes are pleading with me like I do, like she wants my permission to leave.

The truth is, this isn’t a family decision we all get to vote on. Mum is an adult. Dad is an adult. If they call it quits, I can’t change that. If she decides to leave, I can’t make her stay. With me, with us.

A chill creeps from my scalp down to my spine. I begin shaking in a strange and uncontrollable way.

‘Oh, honey,’ Mum whispers. She rubs my shoulders vigorously as if that might stop my shaking. Warm me up. Change anything at all about this.

‘I told you it would destroy them,’ Dad says to her. His voice dead, defeated. ‘You’re destroying them.’

And she quite literally is. I feel like I’m not here anymore, not in this house, not with this family, not by this river. I am not even inside my own body.

‘Stop it,’ Mum hisses at Dad. ‘Stop making this worse.’

Then she turns back to me, rubbing my shoulders, trying to defibrillate me back to life.

'El, I need you to understand. I can't keep going,' she whispers. 'Inside, this is killing me.' She taps her chest with her index finger as tears begin running down both her cheeks, running like the river. 'I wouldn't do this if there was any other way.'

'What's killing you?' I say, my voice wavering and unfamiliar. 'Don't you love us? Don't you love the river, and the hills, and Dad and us?'

Mum shakes her head, pulls me close, but I am a rag doll in her arms.

'Of course, of course, I do. I love you all. This has nothing to do with you kids. I'll always love you. I'd do anything for you. And I still love your dad. We're just not . . . *in* love anymore.'

Lachy raises his swollen sweaty face from Dad's jumper. He is looking at Mum, his eyes like two small pits of fire.

'Well, get in love again,' he hiccups. 'Don't split up.'

'Yes,' I say, my voice barely more than a whisper. 'Please. Please love us enough to stay.'

And now I *am* begging. The girl who doesn't beg for anyone is begging for love. From my own mother. Something I have been taught all my life never to do. Love should be freely given. And yet here we are pleading pathetically. We are begging our mum not to leave us.

'Stop. Please, stop,' Mum whimpers, holding up a hand like a stop sign. She looks at Dad, tears running down her face.

But I hear my voice rising like it belongs to someone else. 'Is it *that* horrible being our mum?'

'No, Elliot, goodness no,' she says sharply. 'This has nothing to do with you and Lachy. This is about me. Me and Dad, and how we're not making each other happy anymore.'

'Mum loves you both,' Dad says. 'It's me she doesn't love anymore.'

He says it like that will hurt less, but it hurts more. Why doesn't she love him anymore? He's part of us. Not loving Dad means not loving all of us. We're four parts of the same whole.

'Of course I still love you. I love you all,' Mum says, her voice shrill. 'I just can't *live* like this anymore.'

'I don't believe you,' I say, my voice a ghost.

The trembling has moved to my stomach. No matter how hard I clench my teeth, my stomach is shivering and it makes my arms, my ribs, every bone in my body shake.

'This isn't a sudden decision, El. It's something I've spent the last two years thinking about.'

Two years? Flashes run through my mind. Photos, like a film clip, flashes of moments, memories, beach days, Christmases, birthdays, all rewritten in a matter of seconds. She's been thinking this for *two years*? I don't believe her.

The holiday in that bungalow by the sand dunes, us walking

the long salt-hazy beach at sunset. Mum and Dad holding hands like young kids, Lachy and I throwing the ball to Snow as she ran up and down the beach, up and down, up and down. Snow rolling in the sand and us all laughing at her. Mum and Dad waking us from sleep and taking us down through the dunes under a full moon to swim in its rippled silvery path.

Dad's last birthday. Our cards calling him the best dad ever, saying we are the luckiest, singing 'Happy Birthday' around his small chocolate cake. Mum kissing him on the cheek. We meant it. We all did. Didn't we? We didn't need anyone else. Just us.

Dad surprising Mum with a new easel, a set of paints and brushes, promising her for the thousandth time a room of her own one day, to make her art in.

Mum telling me and Lachy, 'You kids are my world.' Us believing her. We believed her. She meant it. Didn't she?

Am I remembering it wrong? Am I remembering lies?

Where did Mum find time to think of leaving for *two years*?

Mum takes a deep breath and when she speaks, her words are calm. Almost like she's rehearsed them. Maybe she's been thinking of these words too.

'I need some time on my own. I've been sacrificing myself for this family for a long time, and in the process, Dad and I have fallen out of love. We can't continue like this, pretending it's okay. I need you all to understand.'

She looks sternly from me, to Dad, to Lachy. That look she

gets when we've done something wrong and she is not about to make amends or apologise to us.

The only difference is that Mum is still clutching my limp, cold sweaty hand. Clutching it hard, like if it slips from her grasp, I will fall.

'No.' I shake my head. 'I won't. I can't understand this at *all.*' I rip my hand out of her grasp as a big fat tear slips off the end of my cheek and soaks into my shirt.

I refuse to let her leave. Or make it easy for her. Absolutely not.

Besides, I don't care about what she wants. What she needs. What about what *we* need? This family is a 'we'. It has always been a 'we'. How dare she change that? How dare she think she can become an 'I'. On her own.

And leave us? We're family. We share the same bloodline. Like they both taught us. And family is everything. It's generations. Families stick together. Nobody in a family *leaves*.

I can't see anymore. Just an abstract blur of woody colours and the apricot smudge of Mum's knitted jumper. Her words have blinded me. Even when the tears drip over the edge of my eyes, I can't see. Can't hear through the thumping in my ears. Can't breathe.

What is a family without the mum?

If someone cut my heart out, nobody would expect me to go on walking, and living and breathing. It doesn't work like that.

We need all our parts to exist.

I've changed my mind. Nobody is allowed to get old or tired. And nobody is allowed to leave. Not Drake, not Mum, not Snow. Not now, not ever.

The Gillespies

'When Pa died, I was fifteen years old,' Dad said, sitting down on the edge of my bed. 'Fifteen and fatherless.' He tucked the blankets in around my body. 'That's almost double your age, and still much too young. So I said to myself, it's up to me now. I need to take care of things around here, and I did that. But sometimes, when the wind is howling round the eaves, I almost forget he's not here. It reminds me of being a kid again, like you, and hearing my dad rush inside, shaking the rain off his jacket, the floorboards groaning beneath his feet as he secures the house.'

Dad took a big breath and his whole chest swelled with it.

'Since Pa left, floods have drunk from the roots of that tree, and storms have pummelled the earth with their fat drops, and great gusts of wind have snatched your Pa's ashes away.' Dad held me tight against his chest. So tight, my world became the steady thudding of his heart in my ear.

'I was lonely for a while,' he said, 'but only for a little while.' Dad pulled away to look at me. 'Because when I was still very young, I met the most incredible lady in the world. Any idea who that might have been?'

'Mum!' I said, my eyes shining.

'You are exactly right. She was a little bit wild, and unruly and artistic, your mum.' Dad looked off into the distance. 'Like a brumby, untamed and beautiful. She made me question everything I thought I knew about the world. And she painted. Boy, could she paint! She painted pictures and told me that I inspired her to make art. She completely and utterly rocked my world, your mum did. Turned me inside out and upside down, until she was my first thought every morning, my last thought every night and every thought in between. She drove me near mad!'

I laughed. 'Did you want to marry her?'

'Only the very first minute I met her. She had this energy about her, your mum. It came bubbling up from inside her. The first time I saw her, she was teaching art to your Nan Gillespie, and she came over to talk to me but I could barely speak. Who was this exotic creature with her coloured scarf and jangly bangles? She wasn't from around here, I knew that much. I had to know her. And once I got to know her, I had to keep her. We were still very young when I planned a little surprise for your mum and took her trekking up to the summit of Mount Wilderness. The track up there was tougher than I'd expected, but the weather was warm and clear. I'd packed us a picnic with cheese, and wine and strawberries, and I laid it all out on a blanket for us. Afterwards, I walked her to the highest peak of the summit, where we looked down like two gods upon a world that we had made. The sky was cornflour blue and cloudless, and the horizon stretched forever. We looked over the velvety mountains and the valleys carved far below, and I pointed out our house by the bend in Crooked River, which was nothing more than a silvery snail trail. And then I held her close to me and I whispered in her ear, "I want you to share my world. I want you forever." I pulled a box from my pocket, with a shiny ring inside it, and I knelt down on the crumbly earth with the box in my hand and I asked your mum to marry me.'

My eyes gleamed and even though I already knew, obviously knew, the answer, I wanted to hear it again, so I said, 'And what did Mum say?'

'She said, "Yes, Dan. Yes, I want to be with you forever." And I slid that shiny ring onto her finger, then I picked her up in the air and spun her around on the top of Mount Wilderness. She laughed, and I cried a little bit. We were literally on top of the world.'

'And then what?' I said.

'Well that, dear Elliott, was just the beginning. And now it's the very end of a very long day, and it's time for you to go to sleep.'

'I want you to tell me more,' I said.

'Another night, sweetheart. This story will be continued.'

I snuggled under the covers, and Dad pulled them up under my chin. And I smiled to myself. The Gillespies were the luckiest people alive. And I was lucky enough to be one of them.

Four

I run to the river, my breaths small white puffs in the dusk. Snow pants as she runs alongside me, tongue lolling out one side, smiley eyes watching me. She loves a night run and thinks this is any other night. Only I don't pat her, not even when I get to the Pa Tree and she nudges me with her wet snout.

I round the tree looking for Bridge. I need to row, as fast as possible. Downstream, upstream, I don't care. Row until my arms burn and then keep rowing. All the way to Drake. Not the Drake from this afternoon who wants different things. Not the Drake who held my hand. I want the everyday Drake. The Drake who will sit with me on his swing in the wine yellow glow of the porch light and tell me I'm being a complete doofus. Tell me this isn't real. I've imagined it. I can hear exactly what he'd say.

Your folks are splitting? I think I just saw a cow jumping over the moon and a dish running off with a spoon.

And Bec would come out, sigh up at the stars and give us hot tea and biscuits. And we would swing, and talk and laugh on the porch until the mosquitoes revved in our ears.

My body aches with wanting that. But Bridge isn't there; all that's left of her is the slide she made in the earth when Drake left.

I look back up at the house. Same as always, dull white in the dying light. A lone shaft from the porchlight shooting towards Mount Wilderness. How many nights have I followed that porchlight safely back home in the dark, like the guiding beam from a lighthouse? But tonight our house looks more like a shipwreck sending out a flare. An SOS message to the universe.

Help.

The earth beneath the Pa Tree isn't steady. So I keep moving, one foot after the next, until I'm leaning over the riverbank, watching the swollen water rush by, my shoulders heaving with each breath. My chest is heavy, like metal plates are pressing my lungs between them. I need air, but deep breaths don't help. The plates squeeze tighter.

I can't even row. Can't get out. Trapped by the river, the words, the faces of Mum, and Dad and Lachy, their tears. Trapped by the feelings too big and too many to fit inside my body.

The river, the rain, they're meant to bring life, help things grow. I listen to the rush of it, so much promise after years of drought and silent dry stones. But what was the point of life coming back if Mum doesn't want to be here anymore? Be with *us* anymore?

A squeeze on my shoulder makes me flinch.

'Sorry,' Mum says. She has a blanket in her hand, which she wraps around my shoulders. 'It's getting so cold out. Won't you come in by the fire?'

I used to love those words. *Come in by the fire, it's cold out.* Those words meant warmth, and showers and a nice thick smell of dinner. Now I step away from her, holding her at bay with my outstretched hand.

'Can I hug you?' she says. Her words are as wounded as her eyes, which are wet and swollen like the river.

'No.' She's causing all of this. She's making this happen.

Beneath the blanket, I'm still shivering, but I can't feel the cold. Just the tremors.

'Come inside and let me get you warm, honey. We'll talk about it.'

I shake my head. Take another step away. Unless it's talking about her and Dad working it out, I have no interest.

'You can't stay out here all night.'

I turn my back on her, walk back to the Pa Tree. Yes, I can. I can stay out here with the stars and the great big universe if

I want to, can't I? The universe is for everyone. She is timeless and immortal. She's always there.

You can stay, Elliott, I imagine the universe would say. *You're always welcome here. I'll keep you safe. I'll never, ever abandon you.*

The earth crunches as Mum's footsteps retreat.

She gives up too easily, I tell the universe.

Snow whines as she watches Mum's silhouette shrink up the hill, but she stays by my side. Snow is loyal like that.

I sink down on the damp earth, the blanket falling around me like a dress. Snow drops down beside me, nuzzles her soft white snout into my lap. I rest one hand on her head and let my tears drip onto her fur. I run my other fingers over the rock Drake and I placed on the turtle's grave, next to us. Its flowers are wilting already, but the shell is safe in her blanket of earth.

Universe, I whisper. *Universe?*

The wind tickles the leaves of the Pa Tree, but the universe is silent.

Make her change her mind, I think. *Please, make her change her mind.*

My hands are clenched. I need this more than anything I've needed in my entire life.

Make her stay. Please. It's all I ask. I'll never ask for anything again. Just this, please give me this one thing.

Things can't be that bad for Mum, I know they can't be. Mum and Dad don't even fight that much. It's not like they hate each other. She even said she still loves us all.

But then snatches of conversation replay in my mind.

Last Easter, Mum took herself for a walk along the river and when she came back, Dad was waiting for her on the back porch. I peeked out of my bedroom curtains, and I saw them hugging and heard Mum say in the saddest voice, 'I can't remember the last time I laughed.'

That fight Mum and Dad had when we had to cancel our holiday because the fences needed replacing where Mum said, 'Did you ever ask what *I* wanted? This place has always been yours. Not mine. Not ours. *Yours.* Forget family holidays. This place takes everything.'

Or the time I came home early from school and Mum was on the phone to Aunty Lisa. She was crying and she took the phone into her room and shut the bedroom door, but not before I heard her say, 'I feel lost. Somewhere along the way, I've lost myself.'

When did Mum stop wearing the bright, swirly hippy skirts I've seen in old photos? When did she stop going to art classes at night? When, exactly, did she stop laughing, and dancing and painting?

Still, it's not that bad. It can't be that bad. It can all be fixed.

A faraway noise drifts through the dark, above the soft gargle of the river. It sounds like glass breaking.

Snow lifts her head in the direction of the noise, then bolts towards the house. I bolt after her.

Five

Dad is on his knees in the kitchen, blue shards scattered around him in a pool of muddy water. I can still make out the broken words through the pieces of china: 'Stress Less'. Dad is gathering them in a pile through the slush of tea on the floor with his hands.

'I dropped it,' he says.

A small thread of blood tracks down the edge of his hand.

'Did you cut yourself?'

He shakes his head. 'I'm fine.'

'Let me see that.' I take Dad's hand in mine and examine it. His palm is tough and bumpy, like old snake skin. But his hand is shaking. I grip firmer to steady it.

I've got this, Dad. That's what I want him to feel as I open his wound, a small red mouth. Hold it this way and that in the light.

'I can't see anything inside it. You go clean it out. I'll get the dustpan and broom.'

I've got this, Dad. I've got you. I love you.

Dad goes to the sink and flicks on the tap as I get the dustpan from the pantry.

'Where's Mum?' I ask hoarsely.

Mum is our first-aid person. The one who puts sticking plasters on cuts and kisses things better.

'She's with Lachy. He's feeling a bit sick.'

'Is he vomiting?'

'Yes,' Dad says, without looking at me.

I sweep up the spreading tea and the thousand little islands of shards. One mug, shattered into so many pieces.

'He'll be okay,' Dad says.

My little brother is vomiting. Dad is smashing mugs. I am numb. How will any of us be okay?

I brush the pieces into the bin where no-one can see them, mop down the floor with a dish towel, get Dad a sticking plaster to cover the cut.

Dinner is late. It is quiet and polite. It's eggs on slightly burnt toast with tomatoes. It's forks moving with mouths closed. It's 'Pass the salt, please.' It's 'Juice, El? Lachy?' It's thoughts heavy as storm clouds over the table. It's Snow whining at the door.

Snow, who knows something is dislocated, the same way she knows when we're packing for a holiday. Except this is almost exactly the opposite. Still, Snow knows. The air is different. The way we hold our bodies. The thoughts that steam off our skin.

Dad doesn't eat. He sits in his spot on one side of the table, Mum in her spot next to him. His head is bowed, face colourless. There's a silent sickening stream of tears down his cheeks that no-one talks about. Tears I can't fix. Only Mum can. And she doesn't want to.

I study her face. Blank as a mask. No expression at all written on it. Mum doesn't look at any of us. Her hair hangs in one long limp ponytail over her shoulder. She eats in small measured mouthfuls, her dainty wrists resting against the edge of the table as she dissects her toast.

Aren't mums meant to be selfless? Aren't they meant to give everything they have to their families? Aren't they meant to lay down their lives to protect their kids?

Well, not our mum. This is the most selfish thing anyone in our family has ever done. The most painful, hurtful, destructive thing. But she is sitting here, across from me at the table now, without any tears, without any pain on her face, without any feelings about this at all.

I look away from her in disgust. I want to kick back my chair, go over and shake her awake by her shoulders. Shake it out of her, whatever it is making her want to leave. I want to hurt her, the way I'm hurting, Lachy's hurting, Dad's hurting. Why isn't *she* hurting enough to fix this?

Lachy whimpers next to me. I squeeze his leg under the table. When he looks at me, I give him a brief tight smile. It's the best I can do.

After dinner, I leave my plate by the sink, go to my room, lie on my bed and stare at the ceiling, listless as a rag. Listen to the silence in the house. Until the silence makes way for other noises. Instead of music, crickets. Instead of laughter, beams creaking in the roof.

Hundred-year-old house, what have you seen? What tears, what fights, what storms have you stood through?

When Great-great-grandfather Gillespie first built this house, he wasn't sure of its strength. Then the first big storm blew over from Mount Wilderness, rattling the house, raining hail down on its roof, trembling its floorboards, and he told his kids to shelter beneath the solid hardwood dining table, in case the roof came down. Now a hundred years of storms have passed, and still the roof has not come down.

I thought Mum felt the same as the rest of us. That in this house, we are indestructible. This house protects us, and we protect each other.

The sun seems to have been shining on all the happy families this weekend as I scroll through my socials. They're eating at cafes, star jumping on mountaintops, riding horses at sunset. Here a happy family, there a happy family, everywhere a happy family. Captions from mums and dads like, 'Love you guys', 'My whole world', 'Best fam ever', 'Hanging with the kids'.

Until this afternoon, I felt like we were one of the happy families.

I look up Mum's socials. Nothing for weeks. Before nothing, just a few single random photos I hadn't noticed on my feed. A wine glass against the dying sky, 'Goodbye Sunday'. A haunting image of a she-oak against a stormy sky, 'Strength'. A swallow from last spring who built her nest in the eaves of our house. The swallow is mid-flight, her wings pointed like an arrow. The swallow is flying away from her nest, away from the house, into a big, empty blue sky. 'Freedom', Mum writes.

I dig back further. A year ago, two years. Back to when there were family pictures in her feed. Lachy leaning sideways on Dad's stocky shoulders, his smile gappy, his grubby hand clutching at a piece of quartz crystal he'd found in the creek. Me beside Dad, grinning up at Lachy, our house as the backdrop. We look happy. I thought we were. 'My world. Love you.' Mum has written these words with a heart wrapped in a bow. I didn't even bother to like her post. Didn't notice it.

Was she telling the truth? Do the other parents posting pictures of their perfect families mean the words they've typed? Is everybody online lying? Pretending to be happy and perfect?

Mum must have been lying. If we were her world, she wouldn't think of leaving us. And to go where? For what? I can't imagine her life without us. Or our lives without her. We're a unit. Like a cheese toastie, fused together. You can't un-fuse the parts afterwards.

My eyes sting with tears. I'd give up this house *and* Crooked River just to have Mum post a picture of us with words like that again. I'd heart it and write back, 'I love you too, Mum. I love our family. We are the luckiest.'

When did we stop being the luckiest?

I click on my message thread with Drake. The cursor blinks.

Mum's leaving us.

Too harsh.

Just letting you know, Mum and Dad are splitting up.

Too soft. Too okay.

Mum and Dad are finished. Over. Done. Getting a divorce.

Wrong.

I delete all my tries. There's no way to make it sound right. My insides are crushed eggshells, stabbing at me with their sharp edges. Too sharp to speak about.

Maybe I don't need to tell anyone. Lots of kids' parents split up. Lots of *other* kids' parents. Not mine. It doesn't happen in my family. It hasn't happened in most of my friend's families either.

Sienna's dad is away more than half the year and her mum hasn't left. Amy's dad is horrible to her and her mum and they're still together. Dad doesn't do anything like that. Dad is fun, and kind and hard working. He's home night, after night, after night. There's no reason for Mum to fall out of love with him. She has no right to go and do that.

There's also no reason I have to tell the people outside these walls that inside we're collapsing. That Mum doesn't love Dad anymore. That our own mum is leaving us. Whose mum leaves them? It's not natural. Bears look after their cubs. So do wild boars, foxes, dogs, cats—all mammals do it. Lambs die without their mums. It's not right for the mum to abandon her kids. It's a big, huge dark wrong. If Mum leaves us, she's quitting. Can't she see? It's so shameful I can barely breathe.

I force myself to take a deep lungful of air. Slow long breaths. Maybe Mum will change her mind. Maybe they've just had a fight and tomorrow, when I wake up, I'll find them in the kitchen, Dad holding Mum from behind, whispering in her ear, and Mum smiling into his cheek. Who couldn't love my dad? He's kind of like a big grizzly bear. Cuddly, and furry, and kind and funny. Mum can't have fallen out of love with him.

The thought makes me feel better. I replay the morning scene over and over, of him whispering in her ear, of her smiling sideways at him, until it seems a certainty. Of course this isn't happening. Not to *my* parents. Not to *our* family. This stuff doesn't happen in our family. Splitting up has never been an option for the Gillespies.

But then I remember the faraway look in Drake's eyes today. His talk of leaving. He wasn't my everyday Drake. He was a strange older version of my best friend. The touch of his hand on mine still burns my palm. I can feel the impression from his lips on my forehead. Is everyone changing? If I try to talk to Drake, tell him what's happening with Mum and Dad, I might shatter like Dad's mug. Too many pieces to fix.

I want to hide under the hardwood dining table. Wait for the storm to pass. Come out when the old Mum and the regular Drake are back.

Maybe I can do that.

I choose a photo. One I took this morning by the Pa Tree.

Sunnies on, cool as a lizard. I add a warm filter to the picture, making the sky deep blue and Bridge behind me canary yellow. Everything bright, easy, breezy.

I post it. Online, we can be whoever. This was a real moment. Nobody needs to know what happened after. My life can be happy snappy like the perfect families. And one of my friends might see my post and want my life too.

My bedroom door creaks open. I pop my phone under my pillow.

Mum slips inside. I turn over in the bed, away from her, but she sits beside me anyway. The weight of her is like a small egg. Her hand is on my hair.

'I love you so much, El,' she says.

I lift her limp hand off my hair and give it back without looking at her.

'I love you, honey. That will never, ever change. Dad loves you. That will never change either. You have a mum and a dad who both love you so, so much.' Her voice is a whisper.

'Wow. Did you rehearse that?' My voice is deadpan.

I look around my room. At the pictures of us stuck to my wall from when I was little, even before Lachy was born. Mum, Dad and me. Each of them holding one of my chubby little hands when I was learning to walk. The holiday to the coast. Mum brushing my hair for a dance recital. Then I look at all my trinkets gathered over the years. My special jar of river rocks from the millions of walks we've done in the drought. This room, my safe space. Holding so many parts of me. My history. Our history. This room holding Mum, and Dad and Lachy too. They make me who I am. I don't know how to be any other way. I don't want to learn. I like us exactly as we are.

'I'm still your mum. *Always* your mum,' Mum whispers, reaching for my hair again and stroking it.

I stay turned away from her. Don't let her see the tears soaking into my pillow.

It won't be the same if they split up. I'm not stupid. I know how this works. A part-time mum is not the same.

'I am,' she says. 'You'll see. When I find a place, you can come stay with me and we'll have fun like we used to.'

'Find a place?' I repeat. The thought strikes me like an arrow through the heart.

'Of course I want Dad and you kids to keep the house—it belongs to Dad. In a million years, I couldn't look after a place like this. And you're all happy here.'

She doesn't say 'we're'. She says 'you're'. Like she's already something separate from the rest of us. A bubble of panic rises in my throat.

'I don't want you to find a place,' I say, the words choked up in my throat. 'I like you here.'

'Oh, sweetie.' Mum falls silent for a while, stroking my hair. Then she sniffs. Probably crying. Which she knows I hate, because she barely ever does it. I imagine her dabbing at her face with the crushed tissue in her hand.

'I'm not having a part-time mum,' I say after a while.

'No,' Mum says. 'I don't want that either, no way. Being a mum isn't a part-time job. No matter where I'm living or where you're living, and no matter how old you get, I'm always one hundred percent your mum.'

Yeah, right. More lies.

'I'm going to make a promise to you.' Mum squeezes my shoulder. 'I promise you everything will work out. We'll find a new way. You, me, Lachy and Dad. Okay?'

I don't respond.

'Parents separate every day, all around the world, all around our country. And people survive. Things will be different, but we'll be okay. We might even be better. You just have to trust me, okay?'

My bedroom wall is blurry. Her words don't make me feel better. They dissolve the image I had in my head just moments ago. Of her, Dad, the kitchen, the morning, smiling at each other. Maybe I'll never see that again as long as I live. The thought makes me catch my breath. 'We've made up, honey, it's all okay.' The image is melting away. I want to plant it back sharply in my mind.

'You said we were your world,' I say. 'You still love Dad. You said that.'

'You *are* my world.'

'Well, you don't leave your world. You make it *work*,' I spit.

'I'm not leaving my world, El,' she says. 'I'm leaving my relationship. This isn't about a fight Dad and I have had that can be made up. This is about something much deeper and more adult than you can understand.'

I screw up my nose. Too *adult* for me to understand? But she wants me to deal with it. Clearly I'm adult enough for that part.

'I have had to make a very difficult choice,' Mum continues. 'It's taken a lot of time and a lot of courage to think things through. I've spent the last twenty years putting others first, but this time I've had to choose myself and put me first. People are allowed to do that. To choose themselves when it means saving themselves. To leave a relationship that isn't serving them anymore.'

'But you and Dad are married. That's forever,' I say. It sounds like something out of some silly childhood fairytale, but this is what we've been raised on. The foreverness of family. Love. Marriage.

'You're right, honey. It's meant to be. And I meant it to be forever when I married Dad. So did he. But over years and years, things change, El. People change. Our needs change. And sometimes, two people stop meeting each other's needs, or wanting to. Or trying to. Sometimes, two people turn out to be so incredibly different and to want such different things, there's no possible way to meet in the middle. And it's nobody's fault, really. Even when we have the very best of intentions, things don't always work out the way we'd hoped.'

'You can *make* it work out. If you want it badly enough, you make it happen.'

'I've tried, El. I know you don't understand, but I've tried so hard,' she says, and her sigh is long, sad, empty.

'Try harder.'

Mum takes a deep breath in and holds it. 'I'll be involved in every possible way in your life. That won't change.'

'No, thanks.'

'What do you mean?' Her voice is thin as a cobweb.

'I don't want a sideline mum.'

'No, no, that's not what I mean. Did it sound like that? I'll be everything I can be, El.' The desperation in her voice, the pleading in it, kills me, but I refuse to show her how much it hurts me to know she's scared.

'Right.' My voice is deadpan. *Talk away, Mum. Your words are hollow.*

'I'll still be calling you,' she says. 'Every day, calling, and facetiming, and texting, and waiting for you, and loving you and spending every spare minute with you and Lachy. I love you kids more than life itself. More than you could possibly know. Well, one day if you ever have your own kids, then you'll know how much I love you. How hard this was to tell you.

But I was withering to nothing inside,' she whispers. 'That's how serious it was.'

Mum breaks down then. Shaking my bed with her cries.

I want to cuddle her. Tell her it's okay, I forgive her. I don't want her to wither away. But it's *not* okay and I *don't* forgive her. Not for one second. If she leaves, I've lost her. So that's what makes me say the horrible words biting at my tongue.

'If you go, you're dead to me.'

I feel Mum flinch beside me, but I don't care. All I have inside me is pain and fear. They, my only weapons. The only things that might change her mind. She will lose me. If she leaves, I'm gone. It's her choice and she is free to make it.

Mum takes a deep breath, and her shuddering quiets.

'I'll call both your schools Monday morning.' Her voice is weak and croaky. 'I'll ask the school counsellor to see you. I want you to have someone you can talk to.'

'No!' I say in horror.

'Why not?'

I would rather be publicly poisoned than be pulled out of class to see the school counsellor. That happened to a girl at school after her dad died suddenly in a car accident. It's a red light above your head that tells everyone something really tragic is happening in your life. It starts the talking. And that doesn't even cover the actual talks I'd have to have with the school counsellor. Who doesn't even know my name. Who would expect me to tell her about this awfully private and painful thing growing inside my family like a cancer. I don't know anything about the school counsellor except her last name. She may as well ask me to slice my own stomach open and spill my intestines onto her desk.

'I don't want my friends knowing,' I say in disgust. How humiliating having everyone know what a failure my family is, especially while theirs are all busy being perfect.

'Honey, heaps of people see counsellors. I've been seeing one myself the last year.'

'And look what you're doing now!' I say. 'It's obviously not helped!'

'Actually, it's helped a lot.' Mum touches my hair gently, sweeping it off my forehead. 'I think you should talk to someone, El. Someone professional.'

'No.'

As if talking to a professional can change anything. Or how it feels.

No, no, no.

I am not going to make this easier for her by being okay about it. Stitching up the gash and pretending I'm not still bleeding internally.

Mum raises her hands in surrender. 'I can help you if you'll let me.'

I scoff in disgust. She can help me. There is one thing

Mum can do that would very much help me. One very simple thing. But she won't do it. Instead, she wants me to see some overworked and underpaid school counsellor to fix the damage she's done.

'I don't suppose you've texted Drake?' she asks softly. 'It might be helpful to talk to someone who has been through—'

'No.'

'What about Tamar or Frankie?'

'No.'

'Anyone?'

I shake my head. 'It's not something I'm bursting to share.' My voice chokes up. It feels like Mum is committing a murder. 'I'll tell them when you're . . .'

I can't say that awful empty word. *Gone*.

Mum is planning to go away. Forever. Nothing will be the same again. She will never be in the kitchen making breakfast and packing our lunches in the morning. She won't be here to kiss us goodbye as we walk down the driveway to the bus stop for school. Won't be sitting across the wooden table playing cards with us by candlelight. Having dinner with us. Calling my name down by the river when it gets dark.

She won't live here anymore. Instead, we'll have a whole list of never-agains. If I'd known there was a time limit on any of those things, I'd have loved them better. I'd have noticed them. Treasured them.

How dare she? How dare Mum leave us, then tell us what to say and to who? How damn well *dare* she?!

'I love you, honey.'

Her hand slides off my shoulder. I listen to the padding of her feet on the floorboards as she leaves. The clicking shut of the door behind her.

I could cry out with the pain of it, a knife twisting circles in my stomach.

Lights are out early in our little house. Gone is the glow worm standing strong against the storm. Now we're just a dark blot on the landscape.

Soft footsteps sound down the hall, then two sets go up the creaky stairs. To their room in the loft. The lighthouse room. Are they still going to sleep in the same bed? How does that work? I guess one of them could sleep on the lounge, but that would be worse, far worse.

Please let them sleep in the same bed, universe, like normal, just for tonight. Let them talk it through, let them love each other and not hate each other. Let it still be their *room.*

I turn off my lamp and lie in bed, blinking back tears. Staring at the intricate cornices in the ceiling, the cracks running through them. In the dark, Mum leaving feels as big as an elephant sitting on my chest. So heavy, I can't breathe. I sit up, gasping for air.

Then a gash of light into my room, a wedge, a creak.

The door opens and Lachy creeps in, his hair a tangle against the hall light. I brush my eyes dry.

Lachy stands a foot from my bed, twisting his boxer shorts in his hand. His eyes are swollen. His nose snotty.

'Can I sleep in yoah bed?' he sniffs.

I pull back the covers and he crawls in. His skin is clammy as he clutches onto me. Am I meant to be the mum now? The one to make him better?

'Did you do a wee?' I say. It might sound mean, but Lachy still wets the bed occasionally. And the last thing either of us need tonight is to wake up shivering and wet in a puddle of his pee.

'I got a pull-up.'

Lachy stopped wearing pull-ups a year ago, but I just nod.

'You think Mum and Dad will weally split?' he whispers into my back.

His voice is hopeful, but I won't lie to him the way Mum lied to me.

'Honestly, I think Mum *will* leave,' I say. 'I think she'll try it.'

Lachy clenches harder against my side and I wrap one arm around him.

'But then, who knows? She might come back,' I say. 'She just might.'

And I like the sound of the words. They make sense.

After a little while, Lachy's grip on me turns limp, then drops.

His little body is tired, his breathing, heavy. I lie alongside him, my eyes wide open like an owl's.

What on earth is Mum thinking? When she leaves our warm yellow windows, and our crackling fire in the hearth that Dad always lights for us, and the smell of my pancakes in the kitchen on a Sunday morning, and the sound of Lachy giggling and the softness of his boyish cuddles, and cups of tea the way only I can make them, she'll be so achy with loneliness, she'll realise she made the biggest mistake of her life. And she'll come back, of course she will.

The Gillespies

'One very special night, exactly seven years ago, a fierce westerly was blowing off the back of Mount Wilderness, a bit like it is tonight,' Dad said, tucking the blankets tighter around me. 'It was bringing with it all the ice from its teeth and a tearing wind that could cut a person in half.'

This was my favourite story. The one I never tired of. The one that got me climbing my newly seven-year-old bones into bed just to hear it.

'The fire was blazing inside, chocked with red embers to keep the walls warm and the wind out. Because the wind, it was tearing around the house, looking for cracks and gaps to rush through, and our house, it had enough of them. So the wind whistled inside the house and raged outside it, sending twigs skittering across the roof.

'I know, because I was outside. Gathering armfuls of wood

in the last light of the day. The sky above Mount Wilderness was an eerie ashen haze. Black ragged clouds gathered, magical and terrifying, like the razorback of a wild beast. The wind was fierce and unforgiving. It was a night for rattling rooftops and thunderbolts. A night for staying indoors, safe and warm. Which is exactly what we planned to do, your mum and me.

'Your mum was already tucked up inside the house, cosy by the fire. She asked if I needed help carrying in the wood. I was carrying it in loads so that we'd have enough dry wood to last us all night and the next few days after it rained. I wouldn't let your mum help though. Not because of the cruel wind or the storm that was almost upon us. And not because the wood was heavy as an ox, because your mum might be little, but she's strong. There was another reason I said no to her help that night.'

'Me?'

He tucked my hair behind my ears. 'Because inside your mum's tummy was something very special. Something we had been secretly growing for months. Her tummy was so big, your little mum looked like she'd swallowed a beachball, and we didn't want anything hurting our little beachball.'

I laughed.

'Oh, but this was no laughing matter, because outside—CRACK!' I snuggled deeper beneath the blankets as he continued. 'The first shot of lightning hit the ground, illuminating the trees on the hills like soldiers. The thunder outside was an angry god, rumbling the earth beneath my feet. It made me feel protective to know your mum was curled up warm in a blanket before the fire with you snuggled up inside her, both of you safe.

'But then a noise came, carried on the wind. A sort of wailing. It sounded a bit like your mum. And a bit like my name. I ran against the wind to our front door, clutching the bundle of wood still in my arms. I pushed the door open and it slammed against the wall from the force of the wind.'

'That's when you saw her,' I said.

'Yes. Standing in the middle of the living room, blanket wrapped around her, trembling and white. I said, "What's wrong, honey?" She was standing kind of funny. Legs apart, like this.' Dad stood with his feet waist width apart, his knees halfway bent, like he was straddling an imaginary horse.

'That's when I noticed the small puddle of water on the floor beneath her. "My waters just broke," she said. "I think the baby's coming." I dropped my bundle of wood on the floorboards. "Okay," I said, and I went to her, put my hand on the small of her back. But she shook her head. "No, not okay."

'Your mum doubled over then, pressing one hand into the lounge and clutching at her stomach with the other. She groaned. I didn't know what to do. I went to touch her, but she held me at bay with one hand. Started rocking side to side.

'When her pain was over, she stood up again. Breathing, but trembling like a wet kitten. "It's too soon," she said. "The baby isn't due for three weeks."

'"I'll call the hospital," I said. Your mum nodded.

'The rain was hammering on the roof, lightning bolting around the house, windows flashing white. Thunder roared, the floor shook beneath us. I fumbled through my phone for the hospital's number and began dialling. I pressed the wrong buttons, so I had to start over. Then your mum was doubled over against the lounge again, gritting her teeth and whimpering. The phone was gripped hard in my hand and still I was shaking. The thunder growled so loudly I could barely hear the voice on the other end.

'"My wife's in labour," I said. "Should we come in? Her waters just broke." The midwife asked, "Is this her first baby?" And I said, "Yes."

'"First babies usually take a little while. What's her name?" the midwife replied. "Naomi Gillespie," I said. Then your mum moaned again with the pain.

'"Is that her I can hear?" the midwife asked. "Yes," I said. I didn't like the way your mum looked. Her face was tight and white from pain or shock, I couldn't tell which.

'"How far are you from the hospital?" the midwife asked. "About an hour," I answered. "Hmm," she said. Your mum kept moaning. "Those sound like strong contractions. If you're an hour away, you may have left your run too late to make it to hospital."

'"Sorry?" I asked. My heart was thumping so hard I could barely hear myself speak, but I said, "What do you mean, *too late*?" The midwife said, "Well, that sounds to me like well-established labour. I can't know without seeing her, but those sound like serious contractions."

'"But this has only just started!" I protested. The midwife sounded apologetic. "I can only go by what I'm hearing," she said. "The trouble is, if you risk driving an hour . . . with this weather system, there are trees down over roads. You could end up delivering your baby roadside." I felt the colour drain from my face.

'"What are they saying?" Mum asked. "Ahhhhhh!" She clutched at her stomach as another pain took hold. I did *not* want to be delivering our baby roadside.

'"I think it's safer if we send out an ambulance; let them bring you in, okay? They are well trained in delivering babies." The midwife sounded so calm. "I'll stay on the line and tell you what to do while you wait for them to arrive."

'"Okay," I said. "Okay, help's on the way, Nomes," I said to your mum.

'"Just to be safe, we're going to try and slow this labour down," the midwife said. "So I want you to run your wife a bath." Your mum was moaning again. Rocking, holding her stomach. "I can't leave her to run a bath, not like this," I said. "The bath is upstairs."

'"What about a shower?" the midwife suggested. "Nomes, honey, I'm going to run you a shower." Your mum shook her head, breathing fiercely. "Ahh, that's a firm no to the idea of a shower," I reported back.

'"Okay," the midwife said, "I want you to go get some towels, dark-coloured if you have them, a pair of scissors and a bucket of water. Can you do that for me? This is just a precaution. Just in case this baby wants to come fast."

'I could not believe this was happening. But, of course, I did that. I lined up everything the midwife told me to. Like your life depended on me following her instructions.

'For the next half-hour, your mum rocked and swayed through the pains. She was so brave. Then the rocking, and swaying and whimpering turned to grunting, and panting and pushing. Next thing I knew, a baby shot out onto the towels in our very own living room in front of the fire. It was you, El, all slippery, and pink and naked. Your mum was crying and you were crying. But as I picked you up, you stopped crying and you looked at me with these big dark eyes, blinking in the firelight, wondering where on earth you were. You looked right into my eyes, I'll never forget it. Like you understood now where you belonged. That we were your people.

'"Welcome to our world, little Gillespie," I said, and then I was crying. I couldn't stop. You were a whole, real, miniature little person. And we had done it ourselves. Just me, Mum and you. I kissed you on your forehead and I kissed your mum on hers. "We're a family," I said, still crying. "Our own little family."

'"Congratulations, Dad," the midwife said on the phone. She sounded like she was smiling too. Nobody had ever called me that word before. And when I looked down at your face, my precious little Elliott, I saw glimpses of the dad I'd lost and the dad I'd just become. And I wanted nothing more than us: the Gillespies. We were the luckiest. We are still the luckiest.

'And now, my sweetheart, it's time for the luckiest girl on the planet to close her eyes and go to sleep for her first night as a seven-year-old.'

Seven

'Can you make pancakes now?' A whisper in my ear.

Lachy.

Sunday is pancakes. The Elliott Special. My secret recipe guarded like the Colonel's secret spices. Nobody can make them like me.

Lachy's in bed beside me, playing with my hair. I taught him to plait recently, and I'm not sure it was the wisest thing I could have done, because now he's always tangling my hair trying to plait it. I sit up, extricating my hair from Lachy's knobbly fingers. Sunlight is bursting through the edges of my curtain.

Something's not right, but I can't quite remember—oh. It drops like an anchor in my stomach.

'I'm weally hungwy,' Lachy says.

He still hasn't mastered the r sound. Mum and Dad should really take him to a speech pathologist. But Dad's been too busy at work and at home, fixing things that are broken. And Mum's just never gotten to it. She's been kind of quiet lately, if I think about it. Different to Frankie's mum, who runs every weekend with her running group, is on the P&C board at school and keeps inviting Mum to join book club. Mum isn't a joiner. She doesn't seem to get out much, except to do the grocery shopping. I can't remember the last time we went to a doctor or a dentist, so I guess Lachy can forget about seeing a speech pathologist. He might have to say his r sound like a w forever.

'It's rrrreally, not weally,' I say irritably. 'Rrrrrr, like a lion.'

'Gwwwww,' Lachy says.

'Try rrrrrrumble.'

'Wwwwwwumble.'

'Rrrrrraiin.'

'Wwwwwwain.'

Forget it. Now isn't the time.

'So can you make pancakes?' he says hopefully.

Has Lachy forgotten that quickly? How could he even be thinking about pancakes, or food or his stomach? Maybe one of the good things about being eight is that you just accept things. Shrug and accept your fate, like you have no say in it at all, which is true. Only I can't just shrug my shoulders and deal with it. Not this. That's a firm 'no' from me. I will never accept Mum leaving Dad. And the very last thing in the world I feel like doing is making cheery pancakes.

Then again, pancakes are what we do. The Gillespies. On a Sunday morning. It's what *I* do. What Mum and Dad have loved me doing the last five years . . . so *maybe* I should keep on doing it. Play smarter, not harder. Play a game of strategy. Remind Mum what she loves about being a Gillespie.

'Sure, I can make pancakes,' I say. I give Lachy a light ruffle across his tangled mop of hair and push back my sheets. 'Maybe you can even help me pour the batter.'

His eyes brighten. 'Will you give me the wecipe?'

'Not a chance, kid. But I'll let you lick the bowl.'

He scrambles out of bed behind me. 'Deal.'

Our warm bare feet pad across the cool floorboards and into the kitchen. It's empty. There is no Dad cuddling Mum from behind, whispering things we can't hear into her ear until she smiles. Not that I really expected to see it, but I am still clinging, clinging hard, to the hope that they might have sorted it out overnight. Talked it out, found a solution. The way they make us do after an argument. Don't walk away until you've kissed and made up.

The house is quiet, no shower running, no kettle boiling, no floorboards creaking. It's okay, though. Mum and Dad are both still here in the house. We still have that. Maybe they're both still sleeping. In the same bed.

Lachy is busy setting the table while I scoop the flour, crack the eggs, add my secret ingredients into the bowl and blend it all up with the mixer. Then I pull a chair up to the stove for Lachy and we get into a routine. Butter sizzles in the frypan as he pours the batter. I wait until the pancakes bubble, then one big flip, one more minute and they're onto the serving plate.

I hear the pipes in the wall shudder upstairs, the *shush* of running water. Lachy catches my eye.

Then the stairs are creaking, and a soft padding noise moves down the hall towards us. I turn around. Mum's eyes are dark underneath and her eyelids are swollen. Her whole face looks puffy. She looks old, even though she not long turned thirty-seven.

A little ember of hope grows inside me. It means she didn't sleep much last night. It means she might be having second thoughts.

'The mornings are getting chilly, aren't they?' she says to us, pulling her dressing gown around her small frame and securing it with a sash.

I don't say anything back. Return my attention to the pancakes.

Mum's slippered feet pad across the kitchen floor to the back door, which she pulls open, spilling a beam of morning light across the floor. I feel the air move as the space between us shrinks and the slippered feet move closer, ever closer, until the soft barely-there fabric of her dressing gown is brushing my forearm.

'Elliott let me paw,' Lachy says to Mum, wrapping his arms around her waist from behind.

I bow my head into my pancakes. The vision is wrong. It's meant to be Dad wrapping Mum up.

'You did the pouring?' Mum turns around to face Lachy, crouches down to his level and holds his face between her long hands.

He nods solemnly.

Mum kisses Lachy on the top of the head. 'They'll be extra tasty then, won't they?' As I flip the last pancake, I hear Mum say, very faintly, to Lachy, 'Love you, sweetie.'

The pancakes are getting cold as we sit at the table. Mum is chatty. A bit too chatty.

'I think it might be time to run the fire all night,' Mum says. 'Just to take the edge off the mornings.'

Does she still get to decide things like this? And since when did we sit around discussing the cold weather?

Heavy footsteps sound down the stairs and suddenly nobody is talking about the weather anymore. Nobody is talking at all, not even Mum.

Dad walks into the kitchen, grey-flecked hair roughly dishevelled and sticking out at weird angles. He stops still for a half second when he sees us. All sitting at the table waiting for him. Did he think Sunday breakfasts were finished? Does he remember it's a Sunday?

'This looks . . . good. Thanks, El.'

Our eyes meet for a fleeting second, then he drags back his chair and sits beside Mum. They don't look at each other. They give all their attention to the pancakes.

'The Elliott Special,' Dad says, blinking a few times.

'Lachy poured the batter,' Mum says, slicing a sliver off her pancake and making a show of chewing. Raising her eyebrows. 'Hey, these are good.'

Except they're not. Not at all. When I lift a forkful of pancake to my mouth, I can't taste a thing. And when I look across at Dad, he hasn't even lifted his fork.

That's when the tiny spark of hope inside me sputters out and I want to cry. I know now. There was no talking it out. No changing of minds.

We eat quietly. Lachy chatters on a few times, but he's the only one and even his chatter is stilted. Like he's aware that it's not right to be talking about trivial things when so many bigger things hang unspoken above our heads. Like *why*? *Why*, Mum?

I look at her, the question burning in my eyes, but Mum has stopped talking. And eating. She's beyond faking it. Here in body but her mind is somewhere outside, out the open back door, where she's looking towards Mount Wilderness beyond our wrap-around verandah. What is she thinking? Is she thinking she'll miss it?

Universe, please let her think how much she'll miss it.

I'd rather die than leave. Our fiery sunsets over the hills, the smell of the damp earth in the rain, the safe sound of a storm hammering against our dry roof, the twittering of finches, the caw of the green-black ravens, the gurgle of the river. I can barely swallow at the thought of what she'll miss.

Mum gets up from the table and opens the screen door. Snow's tail swishes.

'Come on in, girl,' she says. 'Come and join us.'

Snow follows her inside, panting her happy Maremma smile. She sits obediently by Mum's feet, looking up with imploring eyes, drool gathering along her lower black lip.

Mum dissects her pancake. Feeds the rest of it to Snow, slice by slice, as Snow mouths it gently from Mum's hand.

I look at the mountainous stack of pancakes on the table. Usually Dad and Lachy are fighting over who gets the last one.

Lachy and I gather up the dishes, and I take the uneaten pancakes to Snow. Snow eats well for breakfast. Happily, gratefully. What will Snow think if Mum disappears from her life? Here one minute, gone the next, like a magician's trick, minus the fun. Like she died. How do we explain to Snow that Mum, who has been her mum since she was a pup, is not going to live here anymore?

I leave Snow to her pancakes and head off by myself for a walk upriver. Water is soothing. Walking is soothing. Both together should be soothing.

Except even with the icy rush of the river around my ankles, my shins, my knees, the fluttery panic in my tummy won't go away. My heart is beating faster than it should. Like it knows to be scared. *Everything will be okay*, Mum says. How can it possibly be if we're divided into parts? It's so wrong. We're meant to be together to the end. All of us.

I head back downstream, pulling myself up onto the bank, where I hide beneath the cool shade of the Pa Tree. I sit under its branches taking deep breaths. The way Ms Myers at school teaches us. She's big on meditation, so we do it before the start of every English class.

I sit cross-legged now, hands open and relaxed on my knees. And I breathe. In slowly, out slowly. Shutting my mind to the racing swirl of thoughts clamouring for entry at its door. No thoughts. Only breaths. It feels better not to think. Not to let the chaos in.

But when I finish meditating, the door bursts open, and with it the fluttery feeling, the swirling chaos is back. This is not going to go away. Even if I meditate, Mum is leaving us.

Universe, what do I do? Please tell me.

Nothing comes. I pick at blades of grass. Pick, and pick and pick. There must be something. Has to be.

What, universe?

Silence.

Tell me. Tell me right now.

If I sound angry, it's because I am. Angry, and desperate and demanding. There has to be some adult who knows a way out of this boggy pit.

All of this is Mum's fault. *She wants out*, Dad said.

Deep down, I know Mum's not been happy for a long time. How long? I can't say. I just remember that the mum when I was little, who wanted to paint, and do craft, and go on walks and river adventures with us is very different to the mum who's been living with us the last couple of years. The one who likes to sit by herself with a cup of tea, with her phone, staring out at the mountains or talking to her sister.

Something is wrong, but I don't know what. How long can a person live like a ghost? I wanted it to be forever. I thought she would just fix it, whatever it is making her sad, and we'd keep going. Get back to the way it used to be. At least till Lachy and I were grown up. At some stage in the future, Mum would figure out what the problem was and fix it.

But it seems like Mum can't. Has she really been withering away inside like she said? She doesn't look like she's withering. She still showers and dresses, so it can't be that bad. Is it possible for a person to be disappearing and for those who love them not to even notice? Surely one of us would have noticed. Dad would definitely have noticed. He would notice that she'd fallen out of love with him too. Wouldn't he?

She needs to stay and figure it out. That's what people do in families, right, universe?

The thing I usually like about talking to the universe is that she never gets mad at me. Just listens patiently. I can yell, and rant and swear and the universe never loses her cool. She stays wise and silent. But today, her silence is maddening.

I need answers, universe. Give them to me RIGHT NOW.

Of course, the universe doesn't give me anything. She holds all her answers to herself.

I get up and scowl at the branches of the Pa Tree, all stiff, and knobbly and scraggy. Then I turn my back and walk away in disgust.

Thanks for nothing, universe.

Eight

The world has been shattered for one day, three hours and forty minutes. Which means only two days ago, life was perfect. As we eat dinner, I think, *two days isn't that far back. It was only Friday.* Two days ago is close enough in time that if I reach out, I can probably still touch it. Claw back the happiness.

But after dinner, Mum asks Lachy and I to follow her into the living room. Dad is there already, adding a log to the fire.

'Take a seat, El, Lachy.' She gestures politely to our cracked leather lounge. Like we're acquaintances she hasn't seen in years. 'You too, Dan. If you don't mind, I'd like you all to sit.'

Not this again.

Dad sits down one side of Lachy, I sit the other. Mum stands awkwardly in front of us. She fiddles with the bracelet on her wrist. The one with the heart dangling from it that Dad, Lachy and I bought her for Mother's Day a couple of years ago.

She looks the way Frankie did when she had to give a speech to our English class. Her knees look like they're shivering.

'I want to be upfront about this with all of you.' She holds her own hands, then takes a gulp of air. 'I received a phone call this morning.'

I don't think Dad is breathing beside me. I don't think any of us are. Mum smooths her skirt over her hips. I notice her hands are trembling like her knees.

'I found out I've been accepted into a place.' Her voice is the same as that time she told us she'd been accepted into an artist's residency, where she got to stay in this desolate little cottage in the mountains and paint with other artists.

'What sort of place?' Lachy says.

My heart is numb. I wish I was like Lachy. I wish I didn't know what she meant.

Mum clasps her fingers together again. 'Well, it's the place I was really hoping for, actually.' She sounds excited. Maybe she is.

Dad's cheeks are flushed. My heart starts thudding like a drummer is beating on my chest wall. I don't want to know this. Any of it. The where, or what or when. I can't imagine my little artistic mum being transplanted into a different home. My imagination doesn't stretch that far.

Besides, if you're going to operate on someone, cut them open and rearrange their parts, I'm sure it's best not to tell the patient the details. Don't describe every little incision you're going to make. Just put the patient to sleep and cut them up. Wake them when it's over. But Mum is no surgeon. She doesn't know not to tell us.

'It's a lovely little unit in town,' Mum says.

Clearly she wants us to be awake for this. For every incision. Slice by small slice. No anaesthetic, no sleep.

'Part of a bigger complex, actually, with a heated pool and tropical gardens. It even has a pond with ducks in it and a bird aviary, Lachy.' She looks hopefully at him.

I stare at her without blinking. An aviary. Is she serious? This is as helpful as offering someone a carrot while they're falling from a cliff.

'I think you kids will really like it there,' she continues. 'The pool is heated all year round and you'll have a bedroom each, I made sure of that. We'll make it really homely.'

I suddenly remember Dad. The one she is really completely leaving. I look across at him.

Dad has this faraway glazed look in his eyes, like he's trying to imagine us all—without him—in this unit with tropical grounds, and a heated pool and a bird aviary. Somewhere homely—without him.

When he catches me looking at him, Dad looks back at Mum and clears his throat. 'Well, that sounds good, doesn't it, kids?' His voice is shaky, like an old man's. He clears his throat again. 'Sounds like you found a good place.' His face is ghost grey, and when he swallows, his big Adam's apple disappears down his throat to hide.

I can see the fear swimming just beneath his skin. Behind the whites of his eyes. In the sheen of sweat which sparkles like glitter on his top lip. I've not seen fear in Dad's face before. Not when we found that brown snake living under the house, not when a wild pig came charging at us downriver, not even when that electrical storm blew in off the back of Mount Wilderness and tore sheets of tin off our verandah roof.

'. . . nice little barbecue area . . .' Mum is still chirping away.

My skin is goose-fleshed. If Dad is scared, then this is bad. Very, very *bad*. Much worse than I thought. My little mum—the scariest thing my dad has ever faced.

'I wanted to show you some pictures, just so you can see what it's like for yourselves. So you don't have to be worried about what it might look like.' She pulls out her phone.

I shut my eyes.

'El, please,' Mum says softly. 'Just a little look.'

I open my eyes as she begins flicking through a real estate slideshow. Compact white kitchen. Empty bedrooms with pale walls and carpets. Hollowed-out lounge room. Caged-in balcony. A tiny soulless box without a drop of enchantment, or magic or memories. The pool at the unit is shaped like a lagoon and edged in palm trees. A fake imitation of a waterhole.

Nothing on our wild and humble Crooked River or our old white house high on the hill with the enchanting backdrop of Mount Wilderness.

Mum does not belong in those perfect stale walls. Lachy and I sure don't belong there. I can't see any of us laughing in that pool or cooking pancakes in that kitchen. None of it is stamped with the Gillespie magic. None of it is meant to be part of our story. In our blood, or in our lives.

'I'd like to take you kids to see it with me, after school tomorrow,' Mum says.

'Do we get to swim?' Lachy says. 'And see the ducks and the biwds?'

Little traitor. One lot of home-baked cookies in that bleach-white kitchen and Mum'll probably win him over. He'll be fine about it. Well, not me. Not ever.

'It might be a bit soon to swim there, but absolutely we can see the ducks and the birds.' She leans across and touches Lachy's cheek. Smiles at him. Then turns to me. 'El?'

'Um, no. No, thanks.' I fold my arms across my chest. I feel yucky inside, like I'm in someone else's skin, with someone else's skeleton inside me.

'No, you won't see it, or no, you don't like it?'

'Both.' Venomous things leap to my mouth. I bite my lip to trap them, and even though I don't say any more of the awful words I'm thinking, I'm shocked by how much I want to.

I want to hurt her.

Maybe it's because Mum is acting like a completely spoilt and selfish brat, thinking only of herself. And she needs to stop it. Right now. Stop this nonsense, like she used to tell me when I chucked a tantrum because she wouldn't let me eat an ice-cream right before dinner. She needs to get rid of these silly ideas and go back to being our mum. Dad's wife.

'Honey, I need to sign the lease this week, what with how hard rentals are to get.' Mum touches my arm. 'I'd rather know it's somewhere you'll be comfortable staying. I won't take it if you don't like it.'

'I don't,' I say.

'El—'

'I only like it here. If you cared, you'd know that.'

Mum looks down at her bracelet.

I can feel steam billowing up inside my throat the way it rises in a boiled kettle. 'When did you have time to look for this place anyway?' I say.

'Last week,' Mum says gently.

Last week is before two days ago. My idea of the happiness we had two days ago twists.

'You didn't even tell us you were doing this last week,' I say.

'I did it when you were at school,' Mum says. 'I looked at a few places, actually. There weren't many on the market.'

I nod, taking in this new information. 'So while we were

busy at school, you were just, like, planning out your new life? Lying to us and sneaking around looking for new places to live like you were having a secret other life?'

Why isn't Dad angrier about this?

'I'm telling you all now,' Mum says. 'I'm not hiding anything. I just needed to be sure. This was not something I could tell you kids unless I was certain.'

'So you're *certain*?' Now I hear my own voice shaking like an old lady's.

That one word cuts me a new wound. Fresh blood gushes out. Certain means *definite*. It means *no doubt*. It means this is happening.

'The last thing I ever wanted to do was hurt any of you,' Mum says, her voice raspy, her eyes glassy. 'The very last thing.'

'Well, you failed. A very big fail.'

Mum's eyes wince, like I just stabbed her, but I'm not sorry. She's the one doing this. Choosing this.

'Believe it or not, El, this is the hardest decision I've ever had to make in my life.' Her voice cracks. 'The very hardest,' she whispers.

'How long have you been making this plan to leave us?' I say coldly.

While I was happily rowing downriver to Drake's yesterday, Mum was figuring out which new home she wanted to make her own. How to break the news to us. She's been saving up the details of her other life, piece by piece, so we might handle it better. But that doesn't make it better. It only makes her a liar.

Mum looks at me with sad, pleading half-desperate eyes. 'I need both of you kids,' she says quietly.

There is breathing now. Lachy's shallow fast breaths and Dad's heavy ones. We are all breathing the same panicky air.

'You'll come and stay, won't you, El?' Tears are slipping carelessly over the rim of Mum's eyes and down her cheeks. 'Help me set up when I move in?'

She sounds so sad and desperate, I want to hug her. Tell her of course I'll help. I've always been the helper. The reliable kid. The big one. The responsible one. And I love her, the mum who brought me into life on the wooden floor of this very room. She got me here safely. Has loved me always. But then I remember what she's doing. This mum saying she wants to leave us doesn't match the mum I've always known and been loved by. The two are as opposite as night and day. Wolf and sheep. Angel and devil. I can't help her leave us. She is sucking the breath out of my lungs and I won't help her take away everything I know.

'Of course she'll help,' Dad says. And he reaches out his big-knuckled brown hand to hold her thin mouse-like one, smothering it entirely.

I look at Dad. No way. I'm not playing pretend.

But Dad shoots me a stern glance over their hands.

Does he know something I don't? Is it possible Mum is more

fragile than she's letting on? If I push her away the way I want to, if I hurt her as much as she's hurting me, throw all my hate at her to make her stop this . . . will she wither finally down to nothing?

'I'll think about it,' I say to Mum.

It's the best I can do.

The Gillespies

'Tell me a story,' I said, flicking my legs over the edge of the bed.

'Not until you stop fidgeting and get into bed,' Dad said.

So I scrambled under the sheets and lay stiff as a nail beneath them.

'That's better,' Dad said. 'Now, which story would my girl like to hear?'

'The Snow story,' I said.

'You've heard this one so many times,' Dad moaned.

'Yep, and I want it again.'

'Okay.' Dad settled himself down on the bed beside me, pinning the sheets against me with his weight and making me cosy.

'Back when you were a baby . . .' I prompted.

'Ah yes, back when you were a baby, your mum would push

you in your stroller around town, her cheeks flushed, her eyes all soft and smiley. She was so proud of you. And I'd say to myself, "*I* gave her that baby. We made her *together*." You were the one gift I could give your mum when we didn't have much else; the gift of motherhood. A beautiful little girl for us to love. Half mine, half hers. But sometimes, secretly, I felt like you were just your mum's, she loved you so completely. When I felt like that though, I would remind myself that I'd made you too. This little baby who was so perfect. Nobody else in the world could have made exactly you. And we both loved you like there was nothing else in the world worth loving more. Because to us, there wasn't.

'There were still farms around here then. And farms, of course, mean dogs. One day, your mum was pushing you in a stroller through the supermarket. You were a toddler and your hair was soft, and golden and wispy, sticking up like a porcupine. Your eyes were big, and dark and shiny. We used to say that when we looked into your eyes, we could see all the way to the other side of the world in them. Old people were often leaning into your stroller and cooing at you.

'This particular day it was Farmer Max who peered in and gave you a smile. "She'll melt the toughest of hearts, that one," he said to your mum. "Say, you're not looking for a playmate for her by any chance, are you? I've got a litter of pups at home. Cute little things, but time for a litter of pups is something I don't have." "Oh," your mum said. "What sort of pups?" "Maremma," Max told her. "Guardians of the flock, but not a bit aggressive. They're white as chalk. Little missy here would look good with one."

'So your mum came home and told me about the pups. "We already have one little menace," I said to her, picking you up in my arms. "Do we really need another?"

'Your mum was quiet as she unpacked the groceries. "It would be nice for her to have a playmate," she said softly. She was thinking of the baby we'd lost. The one that would have made you a big sister that year. We'd been so busy, I hadn't had much time to think about that baby and I felt guilty that I hadn't. Especially since your mum still cried sometimes about that lost baby. "I'll leave it up to you, honey," I said. "Whatever you want."

'A week went by, and we didn't speak of it again. But one day between jobs, I went round to Max's to visit the pups on my own, even held them in my arms. They were balls of cotton with pencil-sharp teeth. They made me laugh. I didn't tell your mum I'd gone. I went to the other side of town to finish fencing and thought about the lost baby brother or sister you should have been playing with. I thought about the pups again. I imagined how they'd make your mum laugh. How you'd have someone to grow up with. When I finished the last picket, I called your mum. She answered right away. "I've been thinking," I said. "About those pups."

'There was a pause on the other end of the phone. "Dan," your mum said. I could hear her smiling through the phone. I was going to make her so happy. But then she said, "Dan, I couldn't help myself. I couldn't let them go to someone else. I picked a little girl. She's sitting right here on my lap now." And your mum laughed. "I'm sorry, I should've called to check with you. I just couldn't resist. When you see her, I know you'll feel the same. Max wouldn't even take any money for her."

'I jumped into my car and blew twin trails of dust behind me all the way home. When I came through the door, your mum was on the lounge, holding a finger to her lips at me. You were curled up asleep, your head resting on your mum's thigh, a smile on your lips. A shaft of afternoon light streamed in from the window, lighting you up like a little angel. And head-locked in the crook of your elbow, also sleeping, was a white cloud. Both of you snoring.

'"Snow," your mum said quietly as I crept forward. "We're calling her Snow." And from that day, Snow's been like your guardian angel.'

'Dad,' I said, looking up at the ceiling. 'Does everyone think their dog is the best?'

'Sadly, no, sweetheart. Not all dogs are as loved or as lucky as our Snow.'

'Well, for the record, I don't just think she's the best,

I *know* she is.'

And that night, after Dad went to bed, I snuck Snow into my room, right up onto my bed. I let her sleep curled up beside me all night long.

Nine

Monday is just like every other morning. Except that I'm not here. I'm floating high above myself, somewhere around the ceiling. Watching this copy of me going about her routine. The artificial intelligence Elliott.

Fridge open, lunch out, fridge closed.

Drink bottle under the tap. Fill to the brim. Screw lid on.

Pack bag.

Skirt on, shirt on, socks and shoes.

Brush teeth, hair, check phone.

It imitates me, it looks exactly like me. It just has no soul.

Mum is in the kitchen making Lachy's lunch. Lachy is eating cereal at the bench, still in his pyjamas. Dad is out at an early fencing job. All of us, robots. Playing our part in a game.

I kiss Lachy on the head, say a faint goodbye to Mum. The screen door bangs shut behind me and Snow runs to greet me, her tail sweeping the air with its white feathery tendrils. As I give her a head scratch, I feel it. First a prickle, then a rash creeping over my body, over my heart, over my brain, into each and every organ. It's like a sickness.

Nothing will ever be the same. The earth beneath my feet is cracking up the way it did in the drought, splitting open in one long jagged crack. Mum on one side, us on the other. Except droughts are seasonal. Rain can fix droughts.

I push my feet to move. I don't want to stay home. I want to get away, far away.

I take long striding steps down our gravel drive out to the main road where I turn left to the high school bus stop. The trees lining the road are afire with autumn. Usually I love their flaming leaves waving and drifting from their naked branches, but today they feel show-offy. Indifferent. The trees will go on doing their thing. They don't care that my heart is beating so hard it hurts my chest. That my breaths are so full they hurt my lungs.

The bus sails past me, before hissing on the brakes last minute just after my stop. Maybe the driver didn't even notice me. If I'm lucky, I've become a ghost. None of this matters.

I climb the steps inside the bus, flash my pass, which Angry Andrew the bus driver has a thing about. Even though he knows exactly which school all the kids attend and has been driving me to school for more than two years. He's a stickler for rules. Order, quiet and rules.

Still, he doesn't apologise for breaking the rules by missing my stop and pulling up outside of the bus zone. Or for making me half-run after the bus. Which would normally be enough to make me want to die with embarrassment—the desperation of chasing down the school bus—but there it is again. Numbness. I can't seem to feel anything.

I take a seat by the window, near to the back, wishing I really was a ghost who could drift through my day with nobody noticing me. But at the next stop, Drake gets on. As I knew he would. And he sits beside me, like he always does.

His jacket brushes my arm, and I feel the swish of it. His right knee is resting against my left, and it's warm. Drake's hair is brushed back into a bun. I can smell that he's washed it too, as it has that after-the-shower smell I know from his house. I want to close my eyes and breathe it in, that smell. I want him to never, ever change whatever shampoo it is he uses, because that smell is cosy evenings, and sunshiny mornings and happiness. Now I do close my eyes, because tears are coming into them.

I sit beside Drake, being bumped along gently by the bus, aware of the shape of him beside me. Wanting to have him back as my friend, wanting to erase all the silly immature things I said to him by the river. Wanting to cuddle him, really cuddle him, without any words.

'Did you not sleep?' he says.

I flutter my eyelids to get rid of the water and then look at him. 'A little bit.'

Drake gives me a weird crooked grin. A sorry grin.

'Am I forgiven yet?' He cocks his head to one side. 'For committing the sin of wanting an education? Will you ever find it in your heart to forgive me?'

How immature, how pathetic I was only days ago. Back when that was my big sickening problem. Heat rushes to my cheeks. It seemed so awful at the time. But that was a different time, when I was a different me, operating under a different set of laws. Drake wanting to go to uni is not a crisis. It's a nothing. A less than nothing. Part of growing up. A very normal and natural nothing.

'Consider yourself forgiven,' I say.

'Everything okay with you?' Drake asks, studying me a moment.

I shrug. 'Why wouldn't it be?'

I look out the window, away from him, to the blur of fiery maple trees passing by. I ignore the vomity feeling in my stomach.

I want Drake to stay by my side at school today. Which is not normal. Which is not something we ever do. He hangs out with his year level friends, I hang out with mine. He would do it if I asked. If I just said, 'I need you.' Three words and he would stick to me like glue. But I can't say them, or explain them. I don't even know why I'm feeling so clingy. Like a piece of sticky grass. It's not a good look for me. I want to shake myself back to normal.

It's just one day at school. Everything will be okay. Everything will be fine. Except for this one little catastrophic thing exploding inside my house.

Ten

At school, I say goodbye to Drake and head for the bricked edge of the garden. Tamar waves at me from where she sits next to Frankie. The morning light catches in Frankie's hair, lighting it into a mess of fiery curls down her back.

'Someone was quiet on the weekend,' Tamar says as I join them. She checks her hair in her phone, which is slicked back into a perfect bun.

I did see their group chats. I'd missed one hundred and fifty-eight messages at last count. Funny, last week there were no secrets. They wouldn't expect there could be any now.

'I was with Drake,' I say.

They exchange a knowing look.

'Uh-huh,' Tamar says. 'I'd be swimming down my river every weekend too, if I had a cute guy best friend living on the other side of it.'

'I rowed,' I say. 'And Drake's not *cute*. He's just Drake.'

'Cute', isn't the right word. It doesn't touch the edges of what I feel about Drake. The safety of him. The way he feels like home. It's not like Tamar's mad crush on that random guy with a million social media followers. I don't have Drake's photos all saved in a special folder on my phone. I don't daydream about him commenting on my posts or asking me out on a date. It feels more private than that. Like a precious stone I want to protect in my hand, and not let people see, or touch or ruin. I think of Drake's hand in mine. Did he really hold my hand? Did he really lace his fingers in mine and hold our hands up to the light, twisting them this way and that? *These fit pretty nicely.* A flush creeps up my cheeks.

'I can pretend I believe you.' Frankie shakes her head and her curls rattle. 'But there's this energy between you and Drake. He watches you at school.'

'No, he doesn't!' I say. Oh, I hope he does. 'He was just mowing the lawns on the weekend, so we hung out.'

'Oh, and you watched *him*, did you?' Tamar says, one combed eyebrow raised. 'I bet he was shirtless too. Not that you had *any* interest in that, of course.'

'Can I come and watch him next weekend?' Frankie presses her hands together like she's praying. Pleading.

My heart stabs at my chest. How will I ever have friends over again?

'You two are pathetic,' I say.

Tamar clicks her tongue. 'Ah, she's jealous too. Wants him all to herself, I think, Frankie! Why do I surround myself with jealous individuals?'

Frankie laughs at that, and I laugh too. There is nobody more possessive over her crush than Tamar.

'I might just start saving Skater180's pictures to a special folder on my phone,' Frankie says.

'Me too,' I joke.

'Your lives are worth more than that,' Tamar says in mock seriousness. 'You know they are.'

Yes, school is exactly where I need to be. With my friends who know me.

When the bell goes, I link arms with the girls, one on each side, and we head to English, filing in with the rest of the class.

Ms Myers paces the room in her floral happy pants that swish when she walks. 'You know the drill,' she says.

Frankie, Tamar and I sit cross-legged together and the other kids all find spots in the room to do the same. There is no order; never is. The heavy smell of spice-scented candles wafts from Ms Myers' desk. That scent takes me away from school, to shops full of tarot cards, and healing crystals and sorcery. Somewhere magical and other worldly.

'Okay, closing eyes now.' Ms Myers voice is soothing as music chants softly from her speakers. 'And, breathing,' she says. 'Slowly in . . .' Her footsteps slow as she paces around us. 'Hold . . . and out. Good, keep going. In . . . hold . . . out. Good rhythm, Elliott, Tamar.'

Nobody in Ms Myers' class is a rebel. She tells them to leave if they don't want to be there. She doesn't need the negative energy. So everyone stays. Not because they have to, but because they want to. Unlike in Maths, where I don't want to be there but I'm never invited to leave. I can't say whether it's the calming effect of the meditation, or the music, or the candles or her voice that flutters around the room like a butterfly, but whatever Ms Myers does, it works. Not only does it work, she is the brightest, cheeriest, most colourful teacher in the entire school. And she never talks down to us, even though I'm sure sometimes she wants to.

When I get up off the floor and find my desk, my bones feel looser, my mind clearer. On each desk is a sheet of paper, face down.

'My ex-husband was over for dinner with his wife on Saturday night,' Ms Myers says. 'Don't look so shocked . . .' She holds up her hands in defence. '. . . I'm fifty years old—I've lived.'

Wait. What?

'Now don't get me wrong, I love my ex-husband. He's a total nerd, but he's a loveable nerd.'

I don't hear the rest of her words because my eyes are

sweating. Ms Myers paces the room, laughing as she tells her story. Something he told her, something she told him. Something else that must be funny because the rest of the class is laughing too. The rest of the class, but me.

Candle-burning, meditating sparkly-smiled Ms Myers has been through a *divorce*? Even the word sounds nasty. Ms Myers, who teaches us Shakespeare, and Sylvia Plath and John Steinbeck. How does she do that? How, when her life has been brutally axed in two? Does the world expect you to just pick up and carry on as if it's no big deal your family has been torn in half? No excuses, no sympathy—swallow some concrete, move on?

Jude was a kid at school in our grade. Everyone knew his parents hated each other. Not just the kids knew, but the teachers and the front office ladies. There were some court orders and the orders meant that Jude's dad wasn't allowed anywhere near Jude. He wasn't even allowed to come to school to collect him. So when Jude's dad tried to pick him up early, the school called the police. The cops came, red and blue blinders blocking off the front entrance to the school. Kids don't forget shows like that. I remember as we were watching from the office, Frankie said to me, 'When parents split up, the mum and the dad hate each other. They fight, and curse and cry. I feel sorry for Jude. How humiliating.'

And I felt sorry for Jude too. How awful. I felt both sorry

for him and incredibly safe for me. I thought nothing like that would ever happen in my family. I thought we really were the lucky ones.

Then Jude's mum arrived at the school. She came running inside, wrapping Jude up in her arms. And she did all three of the things Frankie had said. She cried holding Jude, then she yelled and cursed at Jude's dad with so much venom in her voice I thought he'd die of poison. But Jude's dad didn't die. He yelled back at Jude's mum and didn't stop until the police handcuffed him and put him in the back of a paddy wagon.

Ms Myers is *divorced*. She has been through this same awful thing? She isn't even an awful person! She can't be, not with that flowery voice and all the candle burning. I can't imagine her crying, or yelling or swearing. She even has her ex-husband over to dinner with his new wife. Maybe that means Ms Myers' ex-husband isn't horrible either. Why would two people get a divorce if one of them isn't rotten in some way? Good people work through problems, they don't quit.

It's Mum's fault. She must be the rotten one. But Mum's a good person. The two facts don't match. And Dad isn't rotten, he's one of the best. They both are. It makes absolutely no sense why two good people wouldn't stay together.

Ms Myers flicks on the whiteboard and an image blurs into focus. 'Munch was a famous Norwegian painter.' She gestures to the screen, which has a painting of a skeletal figure halfway across a bridge. Behind it, a burning mottled sunset. The figure is looking directly out of the painting at us, eyes big and wide hands pressed to its cheeks, mouth open in a creepy scream. Other people are crossing the bridge too, arm in arm, dressed in dark drab clothes, chatting carelessly.

'Munch believed our outlook on the world was coloured by our experiences, by how we see things, by our emotions. So he painted *The Scream*. What secret horror do you think this person might be feeling, as these other people pass them by? What is *The Scream* seeing that others aren't? The image arrests us because we are desperate to know. What? Where? Why?' She paces the front of the room. 'Have any of you ever felt a sudden chill down your spine that nobody else can feel? It's a terrifying, isolated lonely feeling.'

Goosebumps dust my forearms.

'How we are feeling in any one moment changes the way we see the world around us. The way we look at a room, or a friend, or a river or a sunset . . . a hundred people can look at the same scene and feel something different about it. Now I want you to turn over the sheet of paper on your desks.'

I turn the paper over. It's a photograph. The silhouette of a tree on a barren hill, bare branches reaching to an empty sky the colour of chalk, a raven perched on the lowest branch, the faintest smudge of a sunset in one corner. One sentence is written below the photo.

It was an accident that brought me here.

'Now, without talking,' Ms Myers says, 'and while your minds are clear, I want you to use the prompt on the table to tell me a story. Entertain me. Invite me in. Tell your story through the lens of whatever feeling you have in your gut right this minute.' She clasps her hands together. 'Go.'

Tamar chews the end of her pen, bends her head and starts scribbling with fury. A few kids murmur, then the class falls quiet. Everyone, heads down, buried in their imaginations. My heart stutters. My imagination is not such a healthy place to dwell right now. But I close my eyes until I hear the voice of a story whispering in my ear.

It was an accident that brought her here, they'll say. Beneath the stark-limbed tree. A terrible tragic accident. They'll whisper the words, because nobody will want to say how it really happened. What even is an accident? A mistake. Something not meant to happen.

Some people mean to do things. They plan. Just like the mother meant to leave the girl. She'll say she didn't mean to, not in the beginning, but what does it matter in the end?

Now instead of a mother to clothe her, the girl has a raven to pick her skin clean.

This is the burial place of her people. Now it is her turn to rest her broken body. How many days will it take for them to find her here, alone? Will they caress her brittle bones with their soft hands? Make her a shroud from a stiff heirloom blanket passed down through generations?

She lies in wait. She has forever. There is no time where she is. Just the tree, the raven, the beast and the thin river sliding by. The sun is downed for the last time. It will not rise for her again.

Long ago it was that the mother left her. Alone, in the wilderness, where the wild things play. Did nobody tell the mother it was wrong to leave? That children do not survive long out there?

The water was gasp cold as the girl crossed the river. Toe-curling ice. But her teeth were gritted, fingers clenched. She pushed on. Deeper now. So much fury in one small body. Fury and fear. It comes back to her like a faint breeze. She remembers the sensation in wisps.

The fear is all burnt out of her now. It went with her breaths.

It was the beast who found her, meaty head on mottled fur. Locking onto her and dragging her from the riverbank to the tree. And now her body is a husk. The beast lay down beside the husk and kept vigil through the dark night. No moonlight, only stars. And they were quiet, those two. Beauty and the beast. Two bodies, one breath, one heartbeat.

My fingers tremble as I drop the pen. The power of words, of thought, my own, scare me. Doesn't my mother know I will not survive in the world without her?

The Gillespies

Acoustic songs had been playing that afternoon when I'd arrived home from school. Amber light speared into the living room, illuminating Mum's profile as she stood by the window in a long-sleeved floor-length gown, a brush in one paint-flecked hand, a palette of colour in the other, before her easel. Dad stood behind her, his arms wrapped around her front, cradling the base of her tummy, which was full of baby Lachy, big as a balloon.

Dab, dab, went Mum's paintbrush on the canvas, adding splotches of periwinkle here and coral there. She was an artist, intent on her work. And Dad, tickling her tummy, had been intent on distracting her. Neither of them had heard me come in over the music. As it picked up tempo, Mum had turned to face Dad. She'd painted the end of his nose coral with her brush, striped his cheeks periwinkle with her fingertips.

'Mess is an artist's work,' she'd teased. 'And I intend to make as much mess here as I can until you build me that studio. From this day until that, I will be as messy as possible. If *that* doesn't inspire you, nothing will!' she laughed.

'Ooh, she's blackmailing me!' Dad had said, playfully snatching at Mum's brush. 'Well, two can play that game!'

But Mum's narrow fingers had been too nimble for Dad's thick ones, and when he couldn't get the paintbrush, he'd wrapped Mum's arms around his neck instead, and said, 'I promise you, honey, one day I'm going to build you the most beautiful studio by the banks of Crooked River. It will be the studio of studios, the envy of all, with great big windows to let the light pour in. And you can make as much mess as you like there—splash the walls with colour for all I care!'

Mum had pressed her paint-spattered fingers to Dad's cheeks, stood up on her tippy-toes and kissed him. 'Oh, I love you, I really do. How did I ever get so lucky?'

They'd swayed together to the music and neither of them had noticed me sneak down the hall into the kitchen and help myself to a whole handful of cookies.

A few afternoons later, Lachy had been born. He'd spent his days curled up like a caterpillar in our arms, frowning in his sleep and pouting his lips. He had fingers like tiny worms and feet that could fit inside a matchbox.

I guess we just got busy with Lachy, busy being four instead of three. I didn't hear Dad talk about building Mum an art studio again. And Mum just kind of stopped asking.

Eleven

The baked bricks are warm against my bare legs as I sit on the garden wall with Tamar and Frankie for first lunch. I pull out the two plain slices of bread I threw into my lunch box this morning. I had no energy to make an actual sandwich, no appetite to eat one.

'What on earth do you call *that*?' Tamar says, scrunching up her nose.

I'm about to invent an explanation for my plain bread, when Frankie says, 'Sorry, it smells gross, I know.' She is digging inside a screw-top container with a fork. Baby spinach leaves, onion rings, chopped avocado, sliced tomatoes, pine nuts, capsicum, shredded carrot, alfalfa sprouts and tofu.

'Wow,' I say. 'Mumma went to a lot of effort for you today.'

Frankie's mum is Mumma to everyone. We call her that, because Frankie didn't ever make the transition from Mumma, or Mummy, to Mum like the rest of us did as we grew up.

'It looks pukeworthy,' Tamar says. 'Sorry, but I think I'd rather starve.'

'Don't listen to someone who eats Frankfurt sausages,' I say. 'She's not exactly an authority on good food.'

'Mumma's latest craze is to put us all on this funky diet,' Frankie sighs. 'I wish she'd just kill us and be done with it. Why do we always have to be the weird ones?'

'Because Mumma likes both words: funky and weird,' Tamar says.

'Yeah, well, now we're apparently all vegan. Even though she didn't ask me if I actually want to be a vegan. But all of a sudden, there's no meat in the house, no junk food to sneak out of the cupboards at midnight, not even a slice of cheese or a single drop of cow's milk in the fridge.'

'Wow,' I say.

'You would, in fact, die,' Frankie tells me matter-of-factly, 'since cheese is your thing. And now we live off almond milk and flaxseed. I'm just lucky she hasn't thrown out the salt, because it's the only thing I have that gives flavour to my tragic life. Apologies in advance for the stinky salads and the sour-milk breath they give me. This phase is gonna last a while, I can tell.'

'Eventually Mumma's going to realise she's criminalising you,' Tamar says.

‘Is *criminalising* even a word?’ I ask.

‘It means “turning you into a criminal”. Which Frankie will, in fact, become—when she starts stealing food out of desperation.’ Tamar shrugs. ‘People have been killed for less. You don’t have to turn the history books back too far to know that.’ She pulls a half-squashed blueberry muffin from her lunch box. Regards it for a moment. ‘Here,’ she says, holding it out to Frankie. ‘Because I don’t want a criminal for a friend. Consider it an act of charity.’

‘Oh, love of my life, my hero,’ Frankie says, taking the muffin from Tamar and shoving it into her mouth like she hasn’t eaten in a week. Frankie tosses her salad into the bin behind us. All of Mumma’s effort, gone.

I try to forget about my own mum, but she keeps creeping her way from the back of my mind to the front. Dinner last night was two-minute noodles with a side of tomatoes added out of guilt. Nobody is talking about special diets at our place. We’re struggling to do the basics. Eat. Shower. Sleep. Dress. I don’t think Dad has actually showered since Saturday. I don’t have the heart to tell him he’s starting to smell.

‘Right, El?’ Tamar nudges me with her elbow. She and Frankie are laughing so hard, their faces are as bright and shiny as a clown’s nose. Frankie snorts and Tamar laughs even harder. I laugh along, pretending I didn’t miss the joke.

I just want Mum and Dad to stay together. I don’t want

Mum to go. I blink ten times to hold the tears back.

I could tell the girls. They would be so good to me. They'd put their arms around me like a shield. Make sure nobody and nothing could hurt me. They'd be careful with their words. Would guard and protect my fragile, broken little spirit. But they can't actually stop this. They're as powerless as I am.

Besides, where to start? How to say the words to them? There are certain words that don't fit with me, with my parents. Plenty of kids at school have had their parents split up, but my parents aren't like that. Besides, Mum will probably change her mind. Even if it takes her moving out for a week or something, she'll realise. And she'll come back. It will hurt her too much to be separated from us. So what's the point of making a big pathetic deal about it to my friends?

Last night, I searched 'mothers who leave their families' on the net. I came across loads of articles about something called a 'midlife crisis'. Mum is at exactly the right age for this. Thirty-seven, middle of her life, having some kind of crisis she needs to sort out. I always thought by Mum's age you were old, like, your life was over then, you had it all figured out, no more drama or excitement.

Why is Mum doing this? She's a good kind person. Has always been a good mum. Doesn't yell much or punish us too hard. Always puts us first. I know she's going to wake up from this craziness of wanting to leave and beg to come back, to forget all about it. And as a family, we'll make a decision never to tell anyone about the crime she was planning to commit. I won't have to tell anyone and none of us will have to live through it. We will agree to bury this as a family secret in the graveyard of unspoken things. That's what will happen. I can almost guarantee it. So I push Mum to the back of my mind and focus on what Frankie and Tamar are saying. Which is actually kind of funny.

'So just because he has his licence now, Archie thinks he's all cool,' Frankie says, 'And he was trying to show off in front of me, like "I can drive now, I'm so much older than you," right? But he's learning on a manual, and this driving lesson, Mum had no-one to babysit Lilly, so she chucked her in the back of the car too. When they got home, Archie wasn't with them and Lilly was traumatised, saying "I don't like the lumps, Mummy, I don't like the lumps." Archie kept bunny-hopping the car, until Lilly was screaming "No more lumps, no more lumps!" She was absolutely terrified in the backseat. Mum laughed and Archie took offense, so he got out of the car, slammed the door and walked all the way home.'

Tamar laughs. 'Serves him right. Lilly knows a crap driver when she sees one.'

'When it's my time to learn, I'm not learning on a manual,' Frankie says. 'I'm going straight for an automatic. Why make life any harder than it already is?'

'Can you believe that will actually be us in a year?' Tamar says. 'Just one more year and we're on the roads.'

The sick feeling flushes back into my stomach. One more year. Where will Mum be in a year? What will my family look like? Will she be teaching *me* to drive? Will she be part of my life? There are so many things I still need Mum to teach me before I can get along in life on my own.

'So we're having a big clean-up this weekend,' Tamar says. 'My folks said to ask you guys if you could come help. We're ordering in pizzas and someone is bringing a barbecue so there'll be a sausage sizzle and stuff.'

It was only two weeks ago that the biggest drama in our lives was the river bursting its banks. Our house on the hill was safe and dry, but not Tamar's. Her house became one with the river, water rising right up inside and flowing through her house. Almost everything was destroyed.

'Yeah,' Frankie says. 'Course!'

'You might want to wear old clothes. The mud stinks,' Tamar says. 'But we're hoping we can move back in soon.'

My mouth seems to have seized up. Both girls are looking at me.

Of course my family will help. Tamar's dad was so good to us when Dad had his fencing accident and spent two weeks in hospital. And her mum cooked us dinners and came over to check in on us all. Then she sat with Mum on the verandah and laughed till they cried into their glasses of wine. And when the sheets of tin flew off the roof in the storm that year, Tamar's dad helped nail them back on. Of course we'll help them in return. Their house has had a metre of muddy water running through it. It's what people in our town do. It's what the Gillespies do.

'We'll be there,' I say. 'Of course, we will.' And I fake a smile.

The same way I'll have to fake an excuse later about why we can't be.

Twelve

'Of course we'll be there,' Mum says, phone under her ear as she stirs the soup on the stove. 'It's our turn to help. It's our pleasure.' When she ends the call, Mum catches my eye briefly. 'Tamar's mum,' she says. 'She's having a clean-up on Saturday.'

I grunt.

Mum spoons soup into bowls. Calls everyone to dinner.

Dad is shaggy, unshaven, blank-faced.

Lachy bites his bottom lip as he stares into his bowl of soup. 'I hate soup,' he mumbles.

I feel like snapping at him. We have bigger problems than soup. But Lachy's eyes are red and watery, his hair a matted bird's nest.

This afternoon, Lachy went to see the new apartment. The birds. The pool.

I refused to go. And I haven't asked Lachy how it

went either. But he hasn't exactly come home bursting to tell me all the details. Maybe he's finally realised that he's been duped. Mum's moving out. That's what the new unit really means. And one aviary full of birds won't fix it.

Mum is the last one to join us all at the table. She gives Lachy a forced smile. 'You liked the place, didn't you, Lach?'

Lachy nods into his soup.

'Do you want to talk about it?' she prompts.

A spark of fire catches in my stomach. It feels like a low act from her to try and coach the eight-year-old into being enthusiastic about the split.

Lachy swirls his spoon around in his soup, catching the lumpy bits. 'Maybe latah,' he says.

'Okay, honey, when you're ready. But the ducks were pretty amazing.'

'Yeah.' He gives a little smile that quickly fades.

The fire in my stomach grows. If Mum was once our queen, she is now oblivious to the state of her people. The numbness, the quiet, the shock that makes us incapable of the most basic tasks.

'I told Tamar's mum we'll be there to help out on Saturday,' Mum says to Dad. 'They need us.'

Another mouthful of soup is shovelled into Dad's mouth. He nods. He's surely thinking the same thing I am. How are we going to help Tamar's family when we can't look after ourselves?

'We're not exactly an *us* anymore,' I say. My words with Mum seem to have taken on a hard edge. Like some old bitter cop. I don't like hearing it in myself, I like feeling it even less, but this is what Mum has put inside me. This poison.

'El.' Mum rests her spoon on the table. 'Please don't make this more difficult.'

'*I'm* making things difficult?' I dunk my toast in my soup. Dunk, dunk, dunk. Watch a bit break off and float around in the slick.

Maybe if I'm suddenly making things difficult, there's a good reason for it. Maybe it's because I feel like I'm living inside that Dr Seuss book where windows are in the places doors should be, and cars have feet instead of wheels, and trees have chimneys and tigers are sitting inside strollers.

Surely there is a law against this. What Mum's doing. Someone needs to tell her how wrong it is. Why hasn't Dad told her? Isn't there some higher authority who can come in and put a stop to this? When I was a little kid and I was doing something naughty, I remember Nan Gillespie telling me in her stern voice to stop my 'silly nonsense'. And at the sound of her voice, I was shocked into stopping.

I don't think I've been a difficult kid. Unless Mum and Dad have lied to us, Lachy and I have been pretty good. I've heard them say it a thousand times. *You're good kids. We're so lucky to have easy kids.* Maybe when the kids are good, the adults go crazy and do silly things instead?

'Dad and I still care about each other,' Mum says gently.

She looks at Dad, but I don't think he heard her because he's staring into some unseeable place, spoon paused halfway between his bowl and his mouth. Soup drip, drip, dripping off, making small splashes in his bowl.

I look back down at my own clear soup with lumps of pickled vegetables bobbing in it. Canned soup. What would Mumma think after all the vegan goodness going on at Frankie's house? I bet their plates are adorned with bright colourful foods tonight. Even at Tamar's new emergency rental, with her whole house being flooded, they've been eating decently. Takeaway from the Thai restaurant one night, Italian the next. And her mum still manages to stock cupcakes for her lunch box.

Mum places one hand on the table and looks me squarely in the eye. 'Dad and I still care,' she says, almost like she could read my thoughts. But what exactly does she care about? 'We still care for our friends, don't we, Dan?'

'Sorry?' Dad is still wearing the vacant face. Tuned to a different frequency. Caring about different things.

Mum rubs her eyes.

'Well, you can count me out on Saturday,' I say, laying my spoon down beside my bowl. I can't eat this. Can't swallow it.

'Tamar is one of your best friends,' Mum says.

'Yes,' I say. 'And you can explain to her why I'm not there.'

I want to punish her. *You* tell everyone what *you're* doing. Why should it be my job? Why should I feel embarrassed because of the choices you're making? If you want to leave, *you'll* be the one dealing with it. Not me.

But then it occurs to me. What if Mum *does* tell everyone? My stomach is hollow at the thought.

'Actually, don't explain anything,' I snap. 'Just say I'm sick.'

'That would be a lie,' Mum says. 'Of course I'll explain what's going on.'

Horror strikes me sharp as a sword. 'No, don't.'

'No, El, you're absolutely right.' She wipes her mouth with a tissue and crumples the tissue in her fist. 'It's not fair on you or on anyone else. Our friends need to know sooner or later, and the sooner it's out, the better.'

'No.' I shake my head. 'I don't want anyone to know. It's none of their business.' The horror of it, the fear of having everyone know, is fierce. Mum has no idea what it's like to be me, to be a teen and have everyone talking about it behind your back on socials. She never went through that. Telling everyone makes it real.

'Elliott.' Mum's voice softens as she looks around the dining table at our ashen faces. How can she be so calm? Surely she feels some level of guilt about this. 'We're not the only family to have ever gone through this. A marriage ending isn't a scandal like it used to be. Lots of families are separated, almost half the kids in the country live between two homes.'

I shake my head. 'Not families like us. We don't.'

'We're not the only people going through a difficult time right now, El.'

I push back my chair. 'Are you actually kidding? You're going to tell me to suck it up because other people have had their houses flooded, or whatever? No. Just no. Every single thing about this is unfair.' My bottom lip is quivering in a way I can't control. How dare she tell me I'm not the only one suffering. 'I don't care what anyone else is going through. The fact that Tamar's house got flooded doesn't make this easier. I wish *our* house had flooded. I choose that over this. People actually feel sorry for Tamar. Your house flooding isn't something to gossip about. It's nobody's fault. And if people in this family are all of a sudden allowed to opt out of their commitments whenever they feel like it, I'm opting out of this one.'

I slide the cool canned soup away from me to the centre of the table where it sloshes to the brim of the bowl. I won't be forced into anything that makes this harder. Mum's made her position very clear. There is no more team Gillespie. It's each of us for ourselves now.

Mum bangs her spoon down hard on the table.

Lachy yelps beside me and clutches at my leg. 'El,' he says, his voice pleading.

But it's too late. Mum pushes back her chair and stands up,

two hands pressed against the table. Good. I want her to yell, tell us everything she hates here, everything that's wrong. Yell, and scream, and cry and curse. The way she's meant to if she wants a divorce.

Then we'll know what's wrong. We can get to fixing it.

Mum levels her eyes with mine, holds my gaze, and her eyes are pits of fire. But she does not yell. She does not cry. She does not curse. Instead, her voice is low, quiet, controlled.

'What makes us so special? You think we're somehow different to the rest of the human race, Elliott?'

Yes, we are. We *are* different.

'We're Gillespies,' I say. Built of winters so cold the river freezes over and summers so hot the river runs dry.

'So bloody what?' Mum says.

'Gillespies don't leave,' I say. My voice is shaky and small. My words are childish, like something Lachy might say. I have a sudden urge to run off and hide in my wardrobe, cry into my teddies like I did when I was in kindergarten.

'You think I should go on and on miserably, even if Dad and I have fallen out of love and there is no love left between us?' Mum demands.

I'm about to answer 'yes'. *Yes, I think you should.* But it turns out she wasn't really asking me my opinion because she goes on.

'Until I'm just a shell of myself? Crushed into smaller and

smaller pieces? You think I should keep doing that until there's nothing left of me?' She looks from me, to Lachy, who drops his head, to Dad. 'Does anyone at this table actually care about *me*? About what I want or what I feel? Or do all of you just want me for what I can do for you? Well, damn the lot of you! I'm not the only one responsible for how things have turned out. If you're looking to blame someone here, El, I'm not the only one you should be looking at. A marriage takes two people to work. It takes *two*.'

Mum kicks back her chair and it falls with a clatter.

Dad stands up. He looks at me, unsure. But Mum has already bolted from the kitchen, catching a sob in her hand on the way out.

The Gillespies

'You want to know about the day you were born?' Dad said to Lachy, as I brushed my teeth in the bathroom next door. 'Why would you want to know about that day? It was only the coldest day on record that year. The darkest day too. The kind of day we couldn't let the fire go out, because a blanket of cloud hung low and thick as soup and it wouldn't let a single ray of sun through to warm the earth. Surely you don't want to hear about that day?'

'Yes, yes, I want to heah it,' Lachy implored.

'Are you sure? Because it was a bitter mean old day that you came into the world.'

'Yes, yes, I want to know.'

'Then best you get all tucked in before I begin, my little man. Get nice and warm under those covers, because just hearing this story might be enough to chill you down to your bones.'

I heard a rustle of covers.

'That's better,' Dad said. 'Are you ready now? Are you sure?'

'Yes!'

'Okay, then let's begin. And I'll begin by saying this.' Dad gave a big dramatic pause. 'You were *much* better behaved than your sister.'

Lachy laughed with glee.

'Hey!' I said through a mouth full of toothpaste, poking my head into Lachy's room.

Dad held a hand up to silence me. 'Sadly, it's true. For a start, you came on your due date, and I mean *exactly* on your due date, like you'd plotted it on a little calendar in your head. And I'm no scientist, but your mum tells me that only seven percent of babies are organised enough to arrive on their due date. So we knew already, we knew right from the start, that you were special.'

Lachy's eyes sparkled as he snuggled down further under the covers.

'The second thing is that because El's entrance into the world was so wildly dramatic—' Dad grinned across at me.

'Hey!' I said again, even though, secretly, I loved hearing how unruly I was. I rinsed my mouth out and came back to lean against Lachy's doorway, listening to the rest of the story.

'—this time, we organised a nurse to come straight to us, straight to our place for a homebirth. We had a little pool blown up for you and your mum in the living room. All we had to do when you decided it was time was to fill the pool with warm water and call the nurse. And like something out of an instruction book, your mum woke on the morning of your birth, more pregnant than she'd ever been, and she called out to me. I was in the kitchen with El, helping her make pancakes, before the Elliott Special was a thing. And when your mum yelled, I dropped the spatula and ran to her. Sure enough, you were coming. Now, there *are* reports that I may have run around like an electrified chicken for a little while . . .'

'You did,' I say matter-of-factly. 'I remember.'

'Alright, but I can assure you both, there was time enough to call the nurse *and* fill the bath, which is a whole lot more than we'd had with Elliott. So by comparison, your birth felt almost relaxing—though maybe don't tell your mum I said that, she might kill me—and when the midwifery nurse arrived, the fire was roaring so nobody would be cold: not your mum, who was bobbing around in the pool in her bathers in the living room, and not you, whenever you decided to make yourself known. El was feeding your mum ice cubes to suck on, and I was stacking towels and blankets on the lounge.

'When I let the nurse in, a blast of icy air blew in with her, and I saw that Mount Wilderness was buried in a dense cloud, so thick you could only see her base. But our house was an oven, enough wood to last us three winters straight. I shut the door behind the nurse and the icy air was shut out with it. It was only mid-morning, but it was that dark inside we had all the lights on, and your mum was moaning, hanging over the edge of the blow-up pool, and I was hoping, hoping I'd blown it up well enough. But I didn't have to hope for long, because soon your mum was grunting and pushing you into the world, and El and I were beside her, telling her what a good job she was doing, cheering her to keep going, and then, with one final cry, out you came, swimming into my arms . . .'

I'd stopped listening, Dad's voice fading into the background as I was transported back there to that day. Back to that moment when a real live baby entered the world, when I saw Mum push him out and Dad's hands grab him. And when he came to the surface of the water, Lachy took a deep breath and then he cried. He cried heartily about the injustice of being born. And at the same moment he cried, I cried, tears spilling down my cheeks, because he was here, safely here, my little brother. I was a big sister. A protector.

'I swam?' Lachy said to Dad.

'Yeah, you swam,' Dad said. 'What do you think you'd been doing those last nine months? You were a champion swimmer and you swam right into my arms.'

I didn't remind Dad of the bits he'd left out, because I wanted Lachy to have the nice version. I didn't want Lachy to know about how during the birth his heart rate had gone up, too high, and the nurse spoke about an emergency transfer to the hospital. Dad's story was nicer, and, anyway, just as the nurse was talking about an emergency transfer, Mum gave an almighty push and Lachy shot out into the pool. Caught by Dad's quick hands and lifted out of the water. Dad, whose mouth—like mine, I guess—was hanging open as if it had no hinge.

'I held you to my chest, skin to skin, and the nurse wrapped a blanket around you,' Dad said. 'Such a tiny little man you were, and you were looking right into my eyes. *Where on earth am I?* your eyes asked. The next thing I remember was another blast of arctic air and El's little voice. "It's snowing! It's snowing, it's snowing!"

'Your mum was still in the warm pool, her arms hanging over the back edge. You were in my arms, the fire blazing hard to keep us warm inside. And your menace of a sister had run right out the front door and left it open. We could see her standing in the salt-white air in her slippers, holding out her hands, palms up, turning slowly, as soft flakes of snow drifted down from the sky.'

I closed my eyes at the memory. It had snowed a handful of times for me at Crooked River, but that was the first. Oblivious to the chill air that bit at my cheeks and gnawed at my bare hands, I had stood on the crunchy earth catching soft white snowflakes as they fell.

When I went in to meet my brother properly, he was wrapped in Mum's arms on the lounge, in a soft stripey blanket. And when he was passed into my icy red hands, Lachy looked from one of my eyes to the other, as though he were searching for answers about this bright new world and all of its problems, which I, in my seven-year-old wisdom, would surely know, and share with him.

That day, in my mind, I made a silent vow to my brother, which he never knew but I've never forgotten. *I'm your big sister*, I thought to him. *I'm going to look after you every day of your life and I won't let anyone hurt you, anyone at all.*

Lachy clutched hold of my thumb then, his entire fist wrapped around it, and he'd held on very tightly, like he was securing my promise. Shaking on it. And when I'd looked out the window, the trees and grass were dusted with icing sugar, like a fairy had come along while Lachy was sealing my promise and had sprinkled a pattern of lace over all the earth.

Thirteen

The hateful boxes hide in Mum and Dad's room. They've grown in number during the week. Nine now, of varying sizes, strapped with packing tape. Her scrawl on top of the boxes labelling what's inside looks almost joyful. Like she can't wait to be rid of us. Start her new adventure. I peel back the tape on one of the boxes, open the flaps. I'd never be game enough to be caught caring if Mum were here, but she's not.

She's at the clean-up day with Lachy. Dad stayed behind, in solidarity with me. He's loyal like that. Has always been loyal. And if he feels anything like I do, the last thing he'd want is to be surrounded by people at a social gathering. Especially ones who know us. Team Gillespie, the unbreakables. Four parts of the same puzzle. We slot together to make one picture. Ha! If they only knew! Well, I guess soon they will. There is no such thing as being unbreakable. Look no further than the Titanic.

Dad must be glad someone stayed home with him, even though we're not exactly hanging out. It's the knowing—knowing each other is still here. Hearing other human sounds. We're on the same side. Me staying tells him I don't agree with what Mum is doing either.

Our family is our club, a lifetime membership, a gang. Gang members get tattoos on their skin and matching shirts to show they are bonded forever. Married people get rings. Rings Mum and Dad still wear. Circles that mean forever, because circles have no beginning and no end, they go round and round endlessly. Like love is meant to. Mum and Dad swore on those rings. Made promises before all of our family on their rings. They promised each other forever. I've seen them making their vows in pictures plastered on our walls. I've watched them say the words on their recording of the day. They promised to stay together for richer and poorer, in sickness and in health, for better or for worse. That's what they swore. How *dare* Mum go and break her sacred promise now just because she doesn't feel like they love each other anymore? How dare she.

Then they made me and Lachy. They bound themselves together in our family, forever blended. You can't divide kids in half and give the mum part to her and the dad part to him. We are bonded in blood now. The way it should be. Mum and Dad have spent my life telling me exactly who I am, which family I belong to, which land. How lucky we are.

I am a Gillespie. Five generations in Crooked River. A mum, a dad, a brother, the sweetest dog in the world. Our old white house on the hill that has always felt a little bit haunted by the ghosts of our ancestors, but also a little bit magical, with its treasures hidden beneath years of dust up in the attic and its floorboards that hide things from the old days down in the cellar. Things no hand has touched for maybe fifty or a hundred years. Secrets kept in brittle mould-flecked letters and old toys abandoned by children who have grown up. Black and white photos of the Pa I never got to know, standing on the same verandah I crawled across as a baby.

This is who we are. Where we belong.

Does Mum feel differently because she wasn't born here? Was it all a trick? Did she mean any of it?

It's never crossed my mind that somebody could take these things away from me. My river, our house of a thousand storms, my family. I wouldn't let anyone even try. These are the things I cling to, the things that make me. The thought of my own mother taking these things away from me certainly never crossed my mind.

Lachy's too young to understand how this place and our people in it have made him, but I want to teach him. Dad and I together. Lachy will learn it in time, the way I learnt it, through stories and memories, over cups of tea by the fire and nights under the stars, with a warm blanket tucked to his chin in bed.

But is any of it even true, the stories? Was Dad glossing it all up? Building me a real-life fairytale? Who even am I if Mum leaves? If I have to be divided between two homes, between a mum and a dad who will end up hating each other, crying, and yelling and cursing at each other like Jude's parents?

And how did I ever believe I was safe, or different or special? Nothing is so sacred it cannot be stolen. Even your own mother can pull things out from under you. People can die, like Pa, like Nanna. They can leave, like Mum. Rivers can dry up forever. It's childish that I ever believed I was safe. Until last weekend, though, I really did believe everything they'd told me. I lived securely inside those little stories, in the world Dad had built me. So lucky to be a Gillespie. Lucky to be one of the chosen ones.

What a load of crap.

So bloody what? Mum had said. *So bloody what if we're Gillespies? It doesn't make us special. It doesn't make us immune to pain or suffering.*

I'm brought back by the heavy *thunk, thunk* of the block splitter. Dad is outside, chopping what was once a tall strong tree into splintered pieces we will burn. He's doing what the Gillespies have done for generations. He's chopped enough of it by hand the last week to get us through an entire winter. He's still chopping. Next year's supply maybe.

A whiff of Mum brings me back to the boxes. Her shampoo mingled with the perfume she wears when she's going out.

The smell has seeped into her clothes. And there they are, those clothes. Thrown in on their hangars, half-folded. I pull out the nightie she has worn for years on summer mornings in the kitchen. It's soft and thin as silk. I see her wearing it now, brushing at my mangled hair on a school morning, when Lachy was screeching from his high chair. Telling me I look like a half-wild street urchin. Buttering the bread for my sandwich, cutting my apples, throwing Lachy another slice to keep him happy while she added strawberries to my lunch from our strawberry patch. I don't remember Dad on these mornings, just Mum; a kiss on the forehead and an aching grey mist stretched like floss across the front field. Mist that would bite at my cheeks as Mum waved me goodbye from the front verandah like a narrow white ghost and I made my way down the long drive to the bus stop. She would wave until I was out of sight. I know, because I would turn around to check. It was a test of her love. Was she still waving? Yes, yes, she was. So I would wave one more time, and smile to myself. Secure and safe. Yes, she loved me. Yes, I was a Gillespie. All was well.

Next in the box, Mum's party dress. Frog green and slinky, bought on clearance because it had been altered for someone and not many women could fit a dress that size. When Mum put it on, she was a goddess, her hair fine and wispy around her face. Mum was always a veggie-patch-covered-in-dirt kind of mum. A knee-deep-in-river-water, holding-fence-pickets kind of mum. She was an early morning kiss with bleary eyes at breakfast, a glasses-on-nose, painting, book-reading kind of mum. But when she put on that green dress, she was suddenly royal. Like Cinderella, transformed from cinders to princess. I remember Dad walking into the living room and stopping mid-step at the sight of her. Then he took her in his arms in a way I'd not seen before, holding her gently around the waist, and he spun Mum around the room, murmuring into her ear. Mum laughed and Dad kissed her softly on the neck. He turned to me after the kiss and said that if he ever forgot it, I was to remind him that he was indeed the luckiest man alive.

I have always remembered his words. Held them, ready to use if I should ever need to. I've been saving them for a special occasion. Some explosive fight where Dad said or did something very wrong by Mum, only I've never seen such a thing happen. Didn't think I needed the words.

I remember there was a party they were going to that Cinderella night. Almost the entire town was going. Dad wore the suit he kept for weddings and funerals, and dressed it up with a cream shirt and a green speckled tie. He told me they'd be dancing, so I ran to my room, put on a swirly dress. When I came back to the living room, Dad told me I looked like a princess but this party was only for adults. I cried big hot tears. I was all dressed up with nowhere to go. Dad crouched down and cuddled me. He told me mums and dads need adult time sometimes, just for them. And Bec was coming over with Drake to have fun with me. So Bec brought Drake over and she babysat me. 'We'll have a pyjama party,' she'd said, but I refused. I stayed in my dress all night. I remember saying to Bec, 'How dare Mum and Dad go off dancing and leave me behind? How very dare they?' And she cuddled me close and told me that it was good for adults to have fun by themselves. It was very important.

I'm pretty sure that was the night Lachy was conceived.

The memory makes me shiver. There weren't many parties over the years. Few enough that I can count them on one hand. Did I stop them going out because I got mad at them every time? Did I not let them have enough fun?

I touch the sheer fabric and it almost burns me. This was a happy-days dress. A party-time, laughter and dancing dress. It's been a long time since Mum wore it. I don't even know if it would fit her anymore, because that was when Mum's cheeks still had a shiny pink colour to them. It was before Mum got thinner, before everything began to shrink. The laughter, the adventures, the baking, the art, the dancing.

Why would she pack this dress? My stomach twists sharply. Does she expect to be doing those things again one day? The dancing, the laughing, the partying? With who?

I listen to the steady *thunk*, *thunk* of Dad chopping and I'm glad he's out there. Not in here seeing this dress Mum has packed. Not in here wondering what her plans are for it. I hold the sheer fabric to my face and breathe it in.

Then, before I can stop myself, I'm clutching the dress in my hands, crushing the fabric with my fingers, staining the dress with my tears, making loud noises from my throat that I can't quiet. Shaking and sobbing until it feels like my ribs are being crushed by a set of giant hands.

Mum is leaving us. She actually, really is.

She is taking all her things with her, things that have made her and things that have made me, things that hold my memories. Things that don't only belong to her, but to me too. I feel I have a right to my mother. A right to make her stay.

The entire house—walls, roof, floors—and all of us are holding our breath, waiting for her to leave us. I want the waiting to be over, but I don't, because I don't want her to go, and I'm not sure which is worse. Waiting for Mum to leave or the actual leaving.

Has Mum got any feeling for the walls who have heard her laugh, soft and light as a fairy? Or the stained-glass door which has welcomed her inside each day? The fireplace that has kept her warm? The roof that's kept her dry? The floors who have held her weight as she paced through the nights with me over one shoulder as a baby?

I dig through the rest of the box. I don't even care anymore if she finds me doing it.

Photo frames. She's taking our photos. Her and Dad on their honeymoon, framed by a blood red sunset with the silhouettes of bending palm trees behind them. Her hair haloed white from the dying light. An angel. Dad grinning like he just won a truckload of money.

If I could walk into that photo from that long ago night on the only overseas holiday they ever took, to that desolate part of the island, I might whisper into their happy ears, 'It all ends. In sixteen years, she'll leave.' Maybe if I could go back in time and tell them, I could stop it. I could say to Dad, 'Make sure you keep her happy. Build her that art studio you promised. And take her dancing. Lots of dancing. So she can wear dresses that make her feel beautiful. Buy her flowers to let her know how special she is.' And then I could turn to her and whisper, 'You'll have two kids. One girl, one boy. Then you'll fall out of love. But maybe you won't, if you tell him how to fix it before it's too late. And keep dancing, even if makes your kids rage. Tell them all what you need. They'll do anything to keep you. Literally *anything*.'

I dig further. Photos of me as a baby. Then Mum, Lachy and me when Lachy was a chubby little toddler splashing his legs in the river. That family photo a few years back from our holiday by the seaside when we paid for professional photos. 'It's worth the cost,' Mum had said. 'Time goes so fast and the moments are gone. None of us know when it might end. How long we have.'

At the time, I'd thought she was talking about death. But she says she's been thinking of leaving for years. So she must have known it, deep in her gut like a seed. Knew what she was going to do even then.

When is our last night together as a family? It infests my every thought, makes my heart sick with pain. And the saddest thought: what's keeping Mum here isn't Dad or the house. It isn't me and Lachy. It's not the Pa Tree or our gargling Crooked River. None of us are powerful enough. It's the rental unit keeping her here. The fact it isn't ready for her to move into yet. So Mum lingers like an old dying person, and we wait for her to become our ghost.

My phone buzzes. Once, twice, three times, four.

I've been waiting.

Mum's voice is a murmur in the kitchen. She's been back precisely an hour, but I've stayed tucked away inside the safety of my room, where the afternoon light is gentle. Soft as it streams in through my window, past my desk with its tumbledown papers, and books and half-finished craft. The sick feeling in my chest won't go.

A long snort like a vacuum comes through the gap under my door: Snow. I pull myself up off the bed and ease open my door. She pushes her way in, her whole body wagging. I shut the door again.

Snow jumps up onto my bed and drops down on my doona. It's our secret. She knows she's not allowed to. She knows I always let her. If Mum or Dad come in, she leaps off and lies down on the floor. Innocent as a leaf. But they won't be coming in tonight. I sit cross-legged beside Snow and she rests her big fluffy head on my thigh. I stroke her thick fur and she closes her eyes.

'What are we going to do, girl?' I say to her.

She looks up at me with sad dark eyes, blinks slowly a few times, like she understands. Or at least senses it. Snow licks my hand once, twice, then nudges under my palm with her snout. I pat her again. She's trying to tell me it will be okay. Poor old Snow has no idea that it won't be. Not ever again. That everything in her world is about to change.

My face feels sweaty and swollen. I reach for my phone. Maybe with Snow beside me, I can face the texts.

From Tamar and Frankie. Not hundreds, just a few select careful ones. Which is somehow worse.

Tamar

Mum told me what's happening. I'm so sorry El.

Frankie

Yeah we're both sorry. We're here anytime if you want to talk about it. ❤

Tamar

Tbh we're both in a bit of shock. From the outside your family was like picture perfect. I can't imagine how shocked you must be. It really sucks.

Their messages are rehearsed. They probably did what we always do when something awkward happens: message each other individually to figure out exactly how to put it on the group chat. Or maybe they're still together, lying side by side on what's left of Tamar's lawn, legs crossed behind them in the air, sharing their screens with each other and nodding. *Yeah, that's good. Say that. Maybe lose that part. Yeah, say that instead.* Usually, I'm part of that conversation. Usually, like them, I'm on the outside looking in.

Tamar and Frankie come from regular families. One mum, one dad, same kids. Except for Tamar's older half-brother, but he doesn't live with her, he's already an adult, so it's like he doesn't exist. To all the world, she has a completely regular family. Not one sliding off a cliff for all to see.

There is one glaring question both the girls are not asking . . . *Why didn't you tell us last week, like the exact second you found out?* This is major. This is something we would all dissect. Be shocked about, talk about. They would have discussed this between themselves and decided not to mention it, and this feels more upsetting than anything else, so I type:

It's no big deal. Lots of parents split up.

Frankie

True, but it must be a big deal when it happens to your own parents.

I'm sure when she moves into some pokey little unit, she'll change her mind quick smart and come back. 😆 She'll hate it.

Tamar

She totally will!

Frankie

Of course she will! She won't be able to stand the silence.

Then there's the Elliott Special. She won't be able to live without that.

I am trying so desperately to be all light and casual about this. But after that comment, there's a long pause in the texting. Nobody writing anything. Just Snow's breathe on my thigh, her soft fur beneath my fingers, the weight of her wise head on my lap.

Finally, Tamar types:

Tamar

But if she doesn't change her mind we'll help you through this okay?

I heart the message even though I hate what she means by it. Then I put my phone in my pocket.

I refuse to go through this.

I refuse to wait for Mum to leave.

I refuse to cry any more about it. I hated the sounds my throat made before. They were scary, more animal than human. I don't like my body acting in ways my mind doesn't approve of.

So I inch open my bedroom door, wait till I hear Mum's footsteps head upstairs. More packing, most likely. Then I head out. Through the creaky gate, flattening the soft grass beneath my feet, past the Pa Tree without a word, down to the riverbank.

A breeze is blowing off Mount Wilderness, where clouds have gathered over her jagged peak. I can feel her icy breath creep through my clothes and down my back. The wind carries leaves that twist, and writhe and dive into the moving mass of Crooked River.

It's time to confess.

Fourteen

There has never been anything too awful to tell Drake. Now there is this dark heavy thing to reef out of the mud and dump in his lap. A thing that will dredge up the past for him. The longer it takes Mum to realise the mistake she's making, the more damage she does to everyone.

I text:

Rowing partner required.

The dots flash up instantly to show he's writing back.

Would the lady like to go up or down?

Up.

I want the hard stuff over with. An easy ride back.

Be there in 5.

I give him the thumbs up and stand by the weeping willow to wait. Every passing minute, the pang of sickness in my stomach is sharper.

It will be over in an hour. That's only sixty minutes. Still, my heart *clod-clods* in my chest.

Bridge noses into view, sleek and shining in the sun. And there is Drake, hair out streaming like a mane behind him.

I want to turn back for the house. Tell him we'll do this some other time. Tomorrow or next week. But Drake is already paddling for the bank. And my legs are taking me down to meet him, my brain retreating to the furthest corner of my skull. I put one clunky foot into Bridge's hull, then two. Each movement bringing me closer to the awful words.

Bridge rocks one way, then the other. For a second, I think she will capsize and throw me out. Then I won't have to say the words at all, but Drake grabs hold of my hand to steady me. I close my eyes. Maybe I don't have to tell him now. I can just let him hold my hand and he will feel it through my skin, he will know.

Except a moment later, I'm sitting down, our hands parted before they could pass him the message. Drake pushes us away from the bank, into the middle of the torrent, where it is just us and the rush of water. Then he hands me the oar and I am rowing against the power of the river. Cutting into her skin with the blades of our paddle, one way, then the other. I am fierce, and cruel and brutal.

We pass the giant willow tree, her branches weeping long lines of tears into the current. I brush her tendrils with the oar.

So what if I hurt her? Does anyone care?

Drake is silent behind me. Can he feel the energy running through my blood? Can he feel my heart pumping harder, making my strokes angular and tight?

'There's something I haven't told you,' I say into the wind. 'Something kind of big.'

I keep rowing. Powerful arms to cover my weak heart. The banks rise either side of us so that we are the valley and they are the mountains.

Drake waits for me to continue. One of the good things about Drake is that he listens. Even today, when I don't want him to listen, he'll still do it. But if I don't tell him, someone else will. It's not fair if he hears it from someone else. He wouldn't understand. *But you know everything*, he'd say, *everything about me*. Which is sort of true. I even know about the birthmark on his backside. Except, lately, I'm starting to wonder if we ever really know everything about anybody. Even our own parents.

I take a lungful of air. Keep slicing at the water as I exhale, my muscles warm, alive, burning.

'If it's about the other day—'

'It's about my parents,' I say.

Right cut, left cut.

'Oh. What about them?'

I haven't settled on the right words. Every way I've tried feels like a strange new language. A wren flits from one side of the bank to another, a shimmery shadow. A dark ghost bird . . . or maybe a bad omen? By speaking the awful words aloud, will I make this whole thing real?

The muscles in my arms quiver. Still I row. Digging left, then right, deep into the water, punishing myself. I'm glad for the punishment, the pain. It's the only way I can speak.

I look up at Mount Wilderness, who towers over us, her clouds thickening like a witch's broth above her peak.

'Mum's leaving.' I spit the words up at Mount Wilderness like it's her fault. I think partly it is. If she'd been kinder, hurled us less savage storms, made life a bit easier for us down below, maybe Mum wouldn't be going.

Drake says nothing. I can't be sure he actually heard me, but I can't bear to say it again. So I take a breath and go on, my heart thudding up into my throat.

'She's leaving Dad. The house. Us. Everything.' My words are quick, but my voice is strangled, my mouth making strange contorted shapes.

I push through the burn in my arms, push against the careless gargle of the river. Right and left, I push us onwards and upwards, even though my chest is heaving, and my breaths are gulping and my ribs are sharp with pain.

The river will still flow when Mum leaves. It flowed the day Dad emptied Pa's ashes. It doesn't stop for anyone.

'Geez, El,' Drake says. 'I definitely wasn't expecting that.

That's a bit of a shock.'

I sniff, squinting into the sun, trying to keep my voice level. 'Yeah, well. That's life.'

I keep up my strokes. Left, right. Burn, burn. Harder, harder. Burn, burn.

'I'm really sorry.'

'Yeah.'

With Drake, I can't pretend this is okay. Drake remembers. Every day, he lives life without one parent.

'At least Mum's giving us notice,' I say. Which is more than he got.

'No,' he says sharply. 'Don't do that.'

Another good thing. Drake lets things be. Doesn't try to make them better or worse.

'Pull over,' he says. 'To the bank.'

'No.' I don't want to look into his sorrowful eyes.

So I keep going. Keep him at my back where I don't have to face him.

More rowing. The burn has eaten its way to my chest. Drake puts his hands on my shoulders. I keep going, just for something to do.

Left, right, I dig the oar in. Deeper and harder, I fight the current.

'My turn,' he says, tugging gently at the oar.

I give up and let go, let him take the oar. I can't win against the tide. It's too strong. My arms flop down beside me, quivering and limp. I could cry from the pain.

'When did she tell you this?' he asks.

The oar flicks one way, the next. A nice pattern to follow with my eyes, as we wedge up along some old tree roots embedded in the bank.

'They,' I say. 'And last weekend.'

Drake is quiet for a moment. The air bites my cheeks, my ears ache with it. Birds call to each other, swooping and fluffing to get to their nests before dark, to settle in. They say birds mate for life. I wonder if it's true. How can birds manage to do that when humans can't?

'Did they give a reason?' Drake asks, putting down the oar. We sit together in Bridge, him behind, me in front. Breathing. Thinking.

I haven't heard much about Drake's dad leaving. Just a few things, scattered over the years, that I've pieced into a ragged cloth. Drake's dad found someone else. A new lady to build a new life with. And they got a new house, had new kids, got new pets. Drake found this out afterwards, bit by bit. In phone calls that stopped coming and over visits that dried up.

The reason is important. It doesn't make it better, but it matters. Drake likes reasons.

'Mum isn't happy anymore,' I say. 'Says she hasn't been happy in a long time and they've fallen out of love.'

Drake absorbs this, but I feel him shift behind me like it's not satisfying enough. And it isn't, but it's all I've got.

'Do you know why, though?'

'Do I know why they fell out of love?'

Drake expects things to be logical. Like everything that happens in life follows some scientific formula. X plus Y equals Z. One thing must lead to another. Even when we bake a cake, he is like this. Where I estimate cups and teaspoons, he measures it all out. He likes his world to be precise. But the world isn't always precise or logical. I wonder how he'll manage as a doctor if one of his patients dares to die for no good reason?

'No. I don't know. I don't know why, or when or how. Not everything has a clear-cut reason, Drake.'

But still I try to think. I think of lots of things, and nothing all at once. There are the storms out here, the loneliness, Dad working so much. There's that she stopped painting and Dad didn't get around to building her art studio. There's her mum dying three years ago and the not getting out of bed for months afterwards. There's the losing weight, the loss of laughter and dancing and art. There are all of those things. But none of them add up to leaving. All of them together don't equal what Drake is looking for. An answer that makes sense.

'Nothing makes sense anymore,' I whisper.

The world is a blurry watercolour. A dove grey sky, a murky

riverbank and a bottle-green river. Everything featureless and smudged.

'I have a question,' Drake says. 'If your mum's truly not happy, would you want her to stay married to your dad?'

I glare at Mount Wilderness with her black threatening crown. 'Yes.'

The rain will be on us by nightfall. The rain, and the cruel wind whipping the leaves into a frenzy.

'Yes?'

'They were in love. They promised forever.' My throat feels like a blocked pipe, my words come out thick. 'And it's not just about *her*. What about the rest of us? Dad—' I gasp. The words, too sore to speak.

Tears roll down my cheeks, my nose runs and the cruel icy breeze stings my eyes mercilessly. I breathe until the hot ache in my throat settles.

'Dad's a ghost,' I whisper. 'Lachy's a lost lamb.'

'I know,' Drake says. 'Believe me, I know.'

People say the words 'I know' a lot, when they really don't. But Drake does. He knows better than anyone. He's the only friend who *does* know what this is like. Who has any idea of what the future might look like, months from now and years. The scary unknowable future.

His hand is warm against my shivering back. That hand is all the words he doesn't say.

Instead, he just says, 'You'll be okay. Eventually, you will.'

I wonder if that's what Bec told him all those years ago? But is he okay? Really? Is anyone?

Every Father's Day we invite Drake and Bec to lunch. Drake's had to find new fathers. Ones that don't share his blood. It's my dad who taught him how to shave when he was fourteen, in our bathroom. My dad who took him for his first driving lesson. My dad who taught him how to use a block splitter to chop firewood, how to play the piano. *My* dad has become *our* dad.

'Maybe she's just leaving to sort herself out? Get better, or something?'

'Maybe,' I say.

It's not that she doesn't love us. She said it herself. Maybe the reason she can't make any promises is because she doesn't know if she can fix herself. And if she can, she'll come back. Back with her boxes, and her green slinky dress and her photos.

But then I remember her words.

I've been thinking about it for a long time.

I can't do this life with Dad anymore.

I've found a place, a nice little unit in town. I'll be happier there.

I still love your dad, but we're not life partners anymore.

The shard of hope dies inside me like a shooting star.

'I know it might be selfish of me,' I say to him. 'But I want Mum to stay. She can get happy again. We'll help her get happy.'

It sounds silly that it could be so simple, but there are lots of things we could do to make it better for Mum. Lachy and I could stop having stupid little fights about stupid little things that don't matter, like who didn't hang their towel up after a shower. I could help more around the house, cooking the dinner, or sweeping the floors or folding the baskets of washing. Dad could build Mum her art studio and we could all give her time to paint. Certain hours where she gets to just disappear and do her thing. Splash paint all around the walls of her studio. And we could go in when she was finished and all covered in flecks of paint, and none of us would care because she would be smiling, and we would be laughing and Dad would be holding her in his arms again, and spinning her around the room and whispering in her ear. I could babysit Lachy so that Mum and Dad could start going out again for dinner and dancing.

Why didn't I ever offer to help them out before it got to this? One night a week, they could go out for adult time, just the two of them. They could go dancing and Mum could wear that green dress. She could learn to smile again in that dress, I'm certain. That's why she packed it. And Dad could tell me again never to let him forget how lucky he is as he cuddles her.

'But what if she can't get happy again with your dad?' Drake says.

'She can.' I inhale a deep breath of cool mountain air. Of course she can.

Drake is quiet for a long time.

'My dad was happy once,' he says finally. 'I mean, he must have been. In the pictures they both look really happy. But things change.'

When I turn around and lock onto his wild cat-coloured eyes hiding behind his thick-framed glasses, a shiver of liquid fear passes through me. I feel like he's preparing me to lose Mum. Not to hold her here. I break eye contact and turn back around.

Drake is used to marriages not working out. That's all he knows. But I'm used to them working. They can. Generations before me have proven it.

'Mum used to tell me every split up is different,' Drake says. 'But at the bottom of it, they're all pretty much the same. Nobody dies, but someone you love is gone forever.'

The tears are hot, and unexpected and unwelcome. As unwelcome as his words. I should never have told Drake. He's burying my family while it still has a heartbeat. Mum hasn't left yet.

But I can tell by the way Drake is shifting behind me that he's not finished. There are more uncomfortable words to come. And it would be mean of me to block my ears, even though it's taking every bit of strength I have not to press my fingers into them.

'I was younger than you.' The tremor in his voice is so

slight most people wouldn't pick it up, but I'm not most people. 'I went to school one day. A normal day, so normal I don't actually remember anything about that morning. Only the afternoon. I walked in the door, dumped my bag and found Mum crying on the lounge. Something was wrong. Different. Then I saw the gaps and empty spaces in the living room, in their bedroom, in every room of the house. Dad took his things and didn't come back. No goodbyes. Just a new life that didn't include me and Mum.' His voice cracks.

'Stop,' I whisper, my eyes closed. 'Please, stop.'

'I'm sorry. You know the rest anyway,' he says. 'But what my dad did, leaving the way he did—that's not normal. Or fair. Most parents don't do that.' He clears his throat. 'Your parents won't do that to you, El.'

This is exactly why I felt sick about telling him. Opening up the crypt of old memories. All the pain flying out of him, like black butterflies after years trapped in the dark.

See, Mum? See what you're doing?

'And I'm okay now,' Drake says.

I nod, but he can't even properly talk about it. The circle in Drake's family has been broken. There is no ring on the fourth finger of Bec's hand. Bec changed her name after Drake's dad left. She went back to the surname she was born with. I only know because a few years ago I realised Drake and Bec had different surnames and I asked Bec about it. She said she should never have changed her name when she got married. Said it was a sacrifice, giving up her family name. And so she has taken back her birth name. *If you ever get married, El, think long and hard about whether you want to give up your name. It's no small thing.*

That's when I decided I wouldn't. Not ever. I was born a Gillespie and a Gillespie I'll stay.

Now I wonder about Mum. If she leaves, will she still be a Gillespie? Mum was a Hansen before she got married, like Nanna, but she's been a Gillespie all my life. The life Mum had before she met Dad, before me and Lachy, feels like something out of a novel. Something you read about, but it never really happened. As unreachable as Mars. It was before I breathed and walked on the planet. I have no connection to Mum's other life. If she becomes a Hansen again, she will travel even further away from us.

Universe, please let her stay a Gillespie, please.

Lately, Mum feels like a magic potion, thin as smoke and wispy as air. And I, the apprentice magician, am losing hold of her as she slips from my life.

'C'mon,' Drake says, climbing out onto the muddy river sand. He holds out his hand to me.

I hesitate before taking it. And when I do, there it is again. The warmth, the safety, the shot of heat through my stomach. The electric air buzzing around us. I am terrified, suddenly petrified, of what this is, and what it means. This is an experiment that could go very, very wrong. One without a map or a formula or logic or guarantees.

Drake must feel a change in my magnetic field because he stops to look at me. 'Come here,' he says.

Drake pulls me gently towards him for a cuddle. Right into his arms, he pulls me, and I let myself be pulled. Let his arms come around me to shelter me like tree branches in a storm. His arms make me a promise, only I don't know what that promise is. Just that it is good. So I hang there, clinging to Drake like I'm dangling off a great big cliff.

Until suddenly I'm sobbing. Sobbing and sobbing against him.

'You know I love you,' he says, like it's a totally natural thing to say, even though neither of us have said it before. Yet I do know how he feels, I think I've always known he loves me, and it cuts both ways. Maybe that word 'love' isn't even a feeling but a solid thing. Something you do. And when you do it, it has force, like a strong river running between us, binding us together in years, and tears, and laughter and time.

'You're going to be okay, El,' Drake says into my hair. 'Because you're Elliott the Great. Nothing can destroy Elliot the Great, remember.'

I choke on a laugh, because he's remembering a game we played as kids. Where I was Elliott the Great and he was Drake the Grand, and together we fought the evil spirits trying to invade our castle in the Pa Tree.

'Drake the Grand won't let it happen,' he says in a gruff voice.

We stand there as he holds me, the gurgle of Crooked River carrying away our words, my tears. I think back to us lying in the long grass side by side, holding hands. When I catch Drake's eyes I can see that he's thinking of that moment too. It scares me that we're both growing into something we haven't been before. Experimenting without knowing if it will work out.

I pull away from Drake. Wipe my eyes dry with the heels of my hands.

'We can't get complicated right now,' I say. 'I can't afford for us to mess it up.'

Drake's eyes are a slatey shade behind his glasses. He looks down at his shoes, almost like I just rejected him. Only it's not that, it's not that at all.

I reach for him, and he opens his arms again.

'I can't lose you,' I whisper, and my fingers cling to his shirt.

'Never,' he says into my ear. 'You'll never lose me, El.' Drake squeezes me then, holding my body against his, and we stay that way, two bodies, our hearts beating against each other, my cheek on his shoulder, my chest rising against his. 'I've got you,' he says. 'I promise.'

Nobody has said those words to me before. I guess nobody's ever needed to. And the feeling of being had, being held, of Drake helping me carry the heavy blanket of life for a while, is soft, and buttery and warm. But promises are powerful spells and people should be careful. It only takes the hint of one broken to shatter an entire world.

The Gillespies

It was an afternoon at the beginning of the summer solstice. The kind where the light stretched on endlessly and the sun hung low in the sky, a blow torch crisping the grass, wilting the leaves on the trees, scorching the deck on the front verandah.

Fans in the house blew hot air around slowly, without relief. Snow was hiding in the shade under the house, Lachy was hot and whining, all of us sweaty. Mum stripped Lachy down to a nappy, his soccer-ball tummy round and delicious against his sweaty curls. She laid him down in his cot underneath the fan with a bottle of cool milk and we played a quiet game of cards while Dad snoozed. Mum left the game halfway through, peered into Lachy's room, eased the door shut behind her and gave me the thumbs up.

'Let's get Snow,' Mum whispered. 'Her fur is so thick, poor thing.'

So I went outside, crouched down under the house and called to her. She was panting, her tongue hanging out one side, lying in the hot still shade.

She lifted her head, wriggled out from under the latticework, and we took off. Just her, and Mum and I, down to the riverbed. The river had run dry that summer, so we could walk all the way upstream with Snow, until we reached the waterhole at World's End.

The water was cool and shadowy, green and deep. A circular mirror that reflected the cliffs and the tall she-oaks above it. The whole sky was painted on her surface.

I watched Mum strip off her clothes and lie them on the roots of a nearby tree. She was wearing a pink polka-dot bikini. Her legs had shape to them and her hips were rounded. She had a small tummy like a pouch, left over from where she'd carried Lachy a year before.

I ran to where Mum stood beneath the tree, slipped off my flip-flops and stripped off my dress. The stones of the riverbed were sharp beneath my bare feet and hot as coals, so we hopped, Mum and I. Hopped, hopped, over the stones to the edge of the waterhole.

Mum went first. A shallow dive that broke the sky mirrored on the water. She emerged, slicking her thin hair off her face.

'It's so cool!' she said, smiling. 'Get in!' And she shot a line of water at my feet with her cupped hands. 'Come on, Snow!'

she called. And she took off breast-stroking to the tall limestone rockface on the far side of the waterhole.

She's so brave, my mum, I thought. Not scared of leeches, or eels or whatever other creatures might be hiding beneath the surface. And with her, I could be brave too. So I dived in and swam, head down, towards her. Snow barked once and sloshed in after us, her breath ragged.

Then it was just us three and the big limestone cliff, our echoey voices bouncing off the stone as we tore a long path through the glassy surface. I could hear Snow's chuggy dog breaths and our breaths, panting beneath the trees that towered over us and the murky riverbed that channelled below us.

'Lay on your back,' Mum said. 'Breathe this in, the beauty.'

We both did, floating on our backs, Snow dog-paddling alongside us, only our faces and our tummies bobbing above the water. And I looked up in wide-eyed wonder at the electric blue sky stretched above us.

'Coooeeee!' I called, and my voice echoed back at me. We could have been the only people on the planet.

We swam in the waterhole till we were shivery and our teeth chattered. Swam until we were properly tired. Until Snow had given up, waded to the stony edge and shaken herself dry from her ears all the way to the final quick flick of the end of her tail.

When we dragged ourselves out of the water, our skin was

deliciously cool and we were laughing. Not for any reason—just because we were happy. To be alive, I suppose. To be alone in this wild ancient land.

Snow licked at our hands. She was smiling too. And all the way home along the dry riverbed, the three of us trotted, wet and cool, to where Dad and Lachy were waiting for our return.

Fifteen

When I return from kayaking, dinner is on the table. I take my usual seat except it's like I'm floating above the scene, watching our family sitting mutely at the heavy timber table through dinner. Pushing food around on our plates. We are four mouths barely eating, four sets of eyes down on our plates, four minds divided, thinking different thoughts. If I could guess our thoughts tonight, here's what they'd be:

Mum: *How much longer until I'm done here? Maybe I should change my name.*

Dad: *How will I keep breathing without her?*

Lachy: *Who will read me stories at night and cut the crusts off my sandwich exactly the way I like?*

Me: *How did we get here? This isn't real. Not us. We are four robots moving cutlery across plates as we've been trained to do our entire lives, ignoring the giant knife swaying over our heads.*

When we clear up from dinner, I head straight to bed. Leave my curtains open as the wind bashes round the eaves and rattles my window panes to get in. It moans and howls like an evil spirit sent straight down upon us from Mount Wilderness.

I curl into a ball on my bed and hug my knees. There are still safe places, like my room, where I am dry, I am warm. The wind cannot get in. The house is still standing, still ours. It has stood for a hundred years without a storm breaking it and it will stand for a hundred more yet.

I close my eyes and think of Drake. Sunlight in his straw-tipped hair. Drake's arms holding me like I was delicate, special; different to the rough practical pats he's given me before. There are the different things we spoke about as we rowed back downstream to the Pa Tree. Words and ideas I hadn't considered, in the same way that I only see the leaves on top of the river, running, flowing, diving, but below that, down in the dark green deep, are the mosses, cool, silent, strong.

Even if the worst happens, Drake had said to me, *there are things you get to keep.* And when he spoke, it wasn't a question, it was a statement. It was Drake saying to me, *these things I know.*

Tell me, he'd said, *tell me what they are.*

And when I'd shrugged, he'd insisted. *I'm going to keep rowing until you tell me. What are the things nobody can take from you?*

I could think of two things. Only two in the beginning.

Nobody can take from me: My house full of my ancestor's footsteps.

The Pa Tree.

Good, good, he'd said. *But there's more. Much more. Nobody can take from you the bare blue sky. You get to keep that always. And the river; the river is yours. What else?*

I had to think for a long time. When the world is ending and the sky collapsing on your head, it's almost impossible to look up and find pretty things. But when I looked hard, really hard, I found them.

My memories? I'd said.

Yes, good.

Our family photos? My brother. My dad. My mum.

And now the world of possibilities in Drake's words opened before me.

Yes, he'd said. *You still have them. But there's more. What about the smell of fresh grass clippings? Swimming in the waterhole at World's End? Turtle races into the river? You still get these.*

The stars through my bedroom window, I'd said.

The smell of the wood fire, he'd said.

My name, I'd said.

Us. You still get us, he'd said, and I could hear the smile in his voice.

You think that's actually something I want to keep? I'd joked.

Too bad, I'm keeping it, he'd said.

Anyway, I thought you wanted to . . . I can't say the word anymore. 'Leaving' is sharp-edged, painful.

Not yet, he'd said. *But now you're distracting me. Tell me what else you get to keep?*

My mind was spent. I could think of nothing else worth keeping.

School, he'd said. *You get to keep school.*

I'd dug him with my elbow and Drake had laughed, making Bridge rock wildly from side to side.

Hey, I didn't say everything you got to keep would be good! If you're busy keeping things, there's bound to be some yucky stuff too.

So then we got to listing all the horrible things I could keep.

Spinach on your dinner plate, he'd said.

Brushing my teeth. Cleaning my room. Getting knots out of Lachy's hair.

Listening to that shark song of Lachy's on repeat until you want to scream, he'd said.

Snow's farts on long car trips.

By that point, we were both laughing.

Ronnie slobbering on your face, he'd said.

Bec's puke-worthy smoothies.

Now, lying in bed alone, I think of more of the nice things I get to keep. The things nobody can take. Things Drake's dad didn't take from him, even after he left. I hug myself in a ball and as I close my eyes to sleep, I tell myself more of these things:

Burnt sunsets from the back deck.

The slide of icy raindrops down my shirt in a storm.

Frost crunching beneath my shoes in the winter.

The bonk of banjo frogs by the river.

The chalky feel of parched earth beneath my bare feet.

Ghost stories and toasted marshmallows round the campfire.

The full moon rising behind Mount Wilderness.

Baby swallows in the spring.

Clear sparkly night skies.

My breath like a long fog on winter mornings.

The wind rattles the shutters and branches skittle across the tin roof as the drumming of the rain begins. I fall asleep clinging to everything I will keep. Everything that is mine.

Sixteen

Two weeks later, on a crisp Saturday morning, the boxes are slotted into the back of the dual cab in neat squares. Dad helps Mum load the last of them into the tray while I stand beside the front fence and watch.

'Well, that's it,' Dad says. His hands hang limply by his sides.

Lachy throws his backpack into the passenger seat.

Mum dusts her hands on her pants and walks towards me. She wraps her wiry arms around my shoulders and squeezes me tightly, holding me to her. I want to cling. Cling and not let go. She holds me for a long time. I can't tell if it's her heart I can hear or mine. Both beating against each another.

When we pull apart, Mum holds me by the shoulders and looks at me, her eyes brimming with tears. 'I'll miss you,' she says, blinking.

I nod. The words are all in my head, in my heart, in my

throat. I will miss my mum. I will miss her like she's dead. I can't imagine life here without her smell of shampoo in the bathroom, her clothes hanging in their wardrobe, the sound of her soft slippers down the stairs, the tinkle of her laughter. I will miss, and miss and miss.

My tears are warm. They roll like waves down my face.

'Are you sure you don't want to come, honey?' Mum says to me. 'It's not too late, is it, Dan?'

I don't hear what Dad says, but I know he would let me go.

'The unit's not set up yet, but we can camp on the floor. There'll be room . . .' Mum says.

I shake my head. I'm still a 'no'.

No, I can't bear to see her unit. No, I don't want to leave my dad here all alone in an empty house.

My one whole heart has been broken into two parts. One half wants to go with Mum, to stop the tears gathering on the bottom lids of her eyes. To let her know that I do still love her, I always will. But the other half has the loyalty of a lion to its pride. And my pride is here. I won't abandon Dad. He might not be crying on the outside, but his waterfalls are inside. And they are gushing.

Dad looks paler, skinnier than before, but he still walks, still eats, still wakes. Still chops wood and drinks cups of tea when I put them in his hand. Still gives me smiles and words, even if they are robotic.

The thing is, I can't tell either of them how I feel, because it's like making a choice. Picking a team. Taking a side. I am team Gillespie. How do you choose when you love both?

Mum gives me a last hug goodbye and then, like a secret note pressed into my hand, she whispers into my ear, where no-one else can hear. 'You'll look after Dad, won't you?'

I blink back my tears and give a solitary warrior's nod. I know my job. Dad needs to be minded. Watched.

And yet I know there is something wrong, very, *very* wrong, about fifteen-year-old me watching Dad. The responsibility of it. I am their child, not their minder. They're meant to be watching *me*, protecting *me*. It's all topsy-turvy. These are *Mum's* choices, but now it's *my* job to make sure Dad is okay.

I could hate her for it. I should. But I don't have the energy. This is a game of survival. I must ration out my choices, my fuel, my energy, to get through. Later we can decide what was fair and what was not, but now my energy needs to go to Dad.

He might never recover from Mum leaving. I don't know if he will. I can't see beyond one day and the next. The end of the week is too far. Does anybody really recover? I think of Bec, sweeping leaves off her roof the other day. The cup of tea. The way she spoke about change. Is it ever okay, even all those years later? So many questions. All new terrain.

I remember reading something from St Francis of Assisi about how to get through really difficult things, and in it he said, 'Start by doing what's necessary, then do what's possible.' It is necessary now for me to stay with Dad, take care of him. Each parent needs a kid and Mum has been kind enough to start us slow. *We'll transition into a new arrangement,* she'd said. It sounds very gentle for what is actually a brutal process. Every second weekend to start, and build up time with her from there. I wish I was okay with it.

Mum lets go of me and I feel relieved that goodbye is over. At the same time, I want to cling to her legs like a baby koala, hang off them like I did when I was little to stop her walking. I want to go back to being the baby in the sling against her chest, which I've seen countless photos of. A Velcro baby, she called me. I want to be cuddled, and fed and not have to worry about survival.

Mum stands awkwardly in front of Dad for a second. His face is an empty plate. Unreadable. Their hug is brief, soft, and when he pulls away, he brushes his cheeks below his sunglasses.

'Good luck, hon—I mean, Nomes,' he says gruffly.

Mum adjusts her sunglasses, blows her nose. 'Thanks,' she says. 'Right, Lach, give your dad and El a quick kiss, and we'll head off. You'll be back on Monday after school.' She gives us a quick smile.

'Wait,' Lachy says. 'What about Snow? Awen't you going to say goodbye?'

'Oh, yes, of course,' Mum says. 'Of course I am.'

She forgot Snow. Snow, who has been with us most of my life. I feel sick to the core of my stomach. Mum *forgot* her. She hasn't even left yet. I want to cry all over again.

'Snowy, Snowy, come hewe!' Lachy calls, crouching down and patting his thighs. Lachy doesn't realise, and it's better that way. Better he doesn't know how quickly love can be forgotten. Lachy is antsy, raring to go, like they're heading off on a family holiday. There are perks to being eight.

Snow wriggles her way out from under the house and bounds towards us, her shaggy tail whipping.

'Snow, sit,' Lachy says, and she sits. He lifts her big white paws onto his shoulders for a cuddle. 'You be a good giwl while we ah gone, okay?'

Snow looks over his shoulders at the car, at the tailgate still down, the ute tray loaded. She begins whining up at Dad. She jumps down from Lachy's shoulders and starts prancing like a pup. Whining, begging, wagging her tail like a frayed flag. She thinks we're going on holidays. Somewhere exciting without her. She yelps up at Mum, her eyes begging.

Mum adjusts her sunglasses, kneels down to Snow's level. Her cheeks are wet. She pulls Snow close, who is whining against her ear, and she whispers something to Snow that we can't hear. Then she stands up.

Snow keeps whining, confused.

Welcome to the club, Snow.

'No, girl.' Dad's voice is stern.

Her whining softens to a high-pitched whimper.

Mum climbs in the driver's seat, Lachy in the passenger seat. All her belongings fit into one ute. Everything she owns in the world, except us.

'Love you,' Mum croaks. One narrow little hand out the window, one wave, and they're driving.

Snow whines, her nose pointed at the ute, but stays by my side. We stand together as the ute gets smaller, leaving fresh tracks behind the tyres.

She's done it. Mum has left us.

The Gillespies

When we watched Nanna's car fly down our narrow drive three and a half years ago, dust clouds kicking up from the tyres, we didn't know it would be our last Christmas with her.

She'd arrived two days beforehand. Then, we were a baking people, a wrapping people, a table-decorating people. On Christmas Eve, Lachy and I had laid our sacks before the tree, hung our stockings over the hearth, left Santa a glass of milk and two cookies on a plate, and for the reindeer a bunch of carrots on the porch. Mum called us all together for a photo. We smiled and she snapped us, the pine tree sparkling with lights in the background.

I stayed up into the late hours with Nanna and Mum. Wrapping and talking, laughing and wrapping, while Lachy dreamt of prancing, and magic and ho-ho-ho.

Christmas morning was slanted sunshine through window

panes and bleary swollen faces. It was not enough sleep, and cups of tea, and Christmas carols and squeals of excitement. Even Snow had a dried bone with a bow on it under the tree.

As the sun rose higher, the day grew dry and hot as dog's breath. No water in the river, just buckets we'd set down for the thirsty wild animals out in the field. Fans *whoop-whooped* overhead. We had a roast lamb for lunch in spite of the heat, set up on the back porch to catch any passing breeze. But flies arrived by the hundred, so we moved our feast inside.

Nanna gave us presents and cuddles. She laughed her high-pitched cackle, tipping her head back so her long white hair fell down her back. She was the only nanna I knew with long hair. *A hippy child*, she said, when I asked her about it. *Can't ever shake the hippy out of me.* Her eyes shone. Mum's eyes were shiny too, because Nanna lived so far away in the city and we only saw her once a year. And that once a year was marked off on Mum's calendar month by month and week by week, the same way Lachy counted down to Santa.

Nanna stayed with us for a week. Always a week. And every evening, after dinner, she and Mum would sit on the back verandah, Nanna's whoops of laughter carrying over the field. I remember her snorting from laughing so hard, and Mum's tears running down her cheeks when she couldn't catch her breath. Nanna cooked us all dinner and I thought it was funny because that was usually a mum job. The thought of Mum needing to be taken care of never crossed my mind, but Nanna took care of Mum in lots of ways. Cups of tea and bubble baths with fresh towels, new bed sheets and hot baked cookies. She bought Mum special things we could never afford, like perfume, and fine seashell chocolates, creams and expensive paints that made Mum gasp when she held the tubes in her hands. Nanna cared that Mum was an artist. She wanted to see what Mum had been painting. I remember her telling Dad, 'She *must* paint.' She said it sternly, like painting was essential to Mum's entire survival and Lachy had giggled beside me.

One day during that last visit, Mum and Nanna were sitting on the back porch bench after lunch with a glass of wine when I heard Nanna ask Mum if she was okay. Of course Mum was okay. She had been humming almost the whole time Nanna was there and nobody who is not okay hums. Humming is a happiness all of its own. I was about to go out and sit with them, make us into three little women, but then Lachy called out for help building his new blocks and I thought I'd help him just to give Mum and Nanna a break. And when I'd finished helping Lachy with the Lego, I went to join Mum and Nanna a second time, except Mum was doubled over with her head buried in Nanna's lap like a little girl, with Nanna stroking her hair.

Before I slunk back inside, I heard Nanna say, 'I just worry, that's all.'

Worry? About what?

'Are you and Dan okay?'

Was she kidding? We were Gillespies. The lucky ones. We were all okay.

Nanna wasn't a Gillespie though. And for all the time she spent worrying about Mum, it was actually Nanna who wasn't okay.

Two months later, she called Mum with the bad news. Cancer. In an organ called her pancreas. There wasn't much the doctors could do. It would not be painful, there was medicine for that, but it would be quick.

Four months after that, Nanna took her last breath. She left us.

I was at home in the living room when Mum's phone rang with the news.

Mum was quiet beside me. Very, very quiet. I'd stolen a glance at her and tears were spilling from her eyes, her nose running. She was biting down hard on her bare knuckle and I knew there would be blood. I wanted to pull her hand away from her mouth, stop her biting herself like that, the way Nanna would have done, but after a while she took her hand out of her mouth on her own and began to whimper.

'I'm sorry,' Mum had said to herself. 'I'm so sorry.'

I'd known Nanna wouldn't have minded that we'd missed her dying. But Mum minded. She minded a lot. It had happened faster than we'd expected and Mum had only gotten to the city twice to see Nanna beforehand.

I would never again hear Nanna's high-pitched laugh or get one of her bone-scrunching cuddles. She would never again cook for us, or tell me stories about when she was young. She couldn't look after Mum anymore, or cook her meals, or bring her nice perfume, or run her bubble baths or ask if Mum was okay. And I couldn't ask her any more questions, either. She was taking anything else I wanted to know with her, to the silent land.

Then suddenly Dad was beside Mum, holding her. She sobbed and he held her, her sobs shaking her body and the sobbing getting loud, louder, until I thought someone was going to rush in and tell her to *shhh, stop it.* But, of course, nobody did.

After that, there were days and days of Mum lying in bed like a rag doll, staring at the walls. Silent unbroken streams of tears running down her cheeks. I went and laid on the bed beside her and held her hand. I felt like there were all these words tangled up in a knitted ball inside Mum's chest and she couldn't say them. In the months and years afterwards, I heard her say some of them.

You told me I could go see my family once a year. One flight a year, you promised me.

I felt sorry for Dad that life got busy and money got tight. But when Mum was saying those words, she was crying hot hard tears and I felt sorry for her too. Because when you lose some things, you can't get them back. It turns out there are certain things you don't get to keep. Things like time.

I'm sorry, Dad would say. *So sorry.*

But no matter how sorry Dad was, Mum didn't seem to get any more forgiving.

Broken promises, I heard her spit at him once. *All our lives, saying one thing and doing another.*

That's when Dad needed to build her the art studio. Why didn't he?

I think Mum broke the day Nanna died. Broke in a way that nobody could fix. She stopped painting. Forgot to eat. To laugh. There was no more swimming in the river. Maybe when your mum leaves, part of you flies away with her and you never, ever get it back.

Seventeen

Snow is still whining as the ute carries Mum and Lachy further away, shrinking from a matchbox, to a grain of rice, to a puff of dust.

I need to watch her leave so that I can believe it. Otherwise, I'll be hunting the house for her, calling out, 'Mum . . . Mum?' Looking for her in the bedroom, down by the river, out on the porch bench.

Inside my chest is an ache like hunger, empty, hollow as a drum. There are no tears. Just me, left behind, my arms limp by my sides.

'Alright, we'd best get on with it,' Dad says, and he heads inside.

I follow him.

There are blank spaces on the walls in the living room. Family pictures of our smiling faces that used to hang there have left big pale empty rectangles on the paintwork, where years of sunlight have faded the paint around the frames. They are missing puzzle pieces from our family.

Still, I travel the house, opening cupboards and making a mental note of what's missing. Her gold-gilded mugs. The gaps in the bookshelves. The faded rectangles on the walls in the hallway where her paintings hung. To be fair, she did leave us some of her paintings. She only took her favourites. *I'll make more,* she'd said, *I'll paint more. Do you want to keep the ones on the walls?* We said yes, all of us. We wanted anything of hers, everything of hers. Hungry, greedy little us. Whatever she would give us of hers, we would take.

I remember our baby photo collections and I race to the living room drawer to look for them. All gone. Those are my pictures too. She didn't even ask me.

Dad is in the kitchen. The kettle is hissing. I head upstairs to their room. Now Dad's room I guess. Open their wardrobe. One side of it is empty. It looks the way I imagine a wardrobe might look if someone cleared all their hanging things in one hurried swoop to leave in the middle of the night. Maybe this is how Drake's dad's wardrobe looked after he left. A couple of coat hangers are pointing at odd angles, and in the right-hand corner a lone dress is slunk like a snake, forgotten. It must have slid off a hangar and been missed. I pick it up, stuff it under my shirt like a thief. Dad will probably want it, but I need it more.

I go to the ensuite bathroom Dad built a few years back. One toothbrush instead of two. Her night cream, missing. Her special perfume from Nanna that sat alongside Dad's cologne, gone from its glass shelf. Dad's cologne now sits tall, and brave and alone.

Everywhere I look, a new stab wound.

How can Mum not exist here anymore, in the only place I've known her? Why did we let her leave? Dad even loaded the boxes into the ute for her. Why? Why didn't we chain the gates shut, kick, and scream and fight until she gave in?

We didn't try hard enough and now she's gone.

There will be no Mum voice in the house anymore to call out 'Hi, how was your day?' when we get home from school. No soothing cool hand on our foreheads in our beds when we have a fever. No white nightie figure waving me off to school of a morning. No soft knocks on my bedroom door, and her face peering around the doorway, her hand extending a chocolate cookie to cheer me up.

She's gone. It feels like death. Like someone just ripped out my guts.

I remind myself of all the things I get to keep, without her.

The sky.

The wind.

The stars.

The river.

None of it matters. None of them help. What's the point of the leaves, the trees, the great wild universe, if I don't have Mum here to share it?

I am a burnt-out tree stump, my stomach hollowed. If I were a colour, I would be grey. Grey, and sick and aching. A hollow pulse beats just below my diaphragm. She has left our memories behind for us. Mum has moved somewhere new, without memories, yet we're meant to keep living in a house full of them.

I can't do it.

I bolt downstairs, clutching Mum's stolen dress under my shirt. Bang out through the front door, past Snow, who is still staring in the direction of the ute, watching, waiting, whining. Past the old wooden swing on the pear tree Mum and I used to push Lachy on when he was a toddler. I run down to the Pa Tree, gulping, gulping for air. My chest is heaving high in my ribcage, but it's not enough. Not enough air. Too many thoughts, the pain in my ribs too sharp. My chest is burning, my heart hurting.

I try to speak to the universe, tell her what I need, but I have no voice for words, only thoughts. Only breaths. Fast and sharp.

Help, universe, help me!

I clutch at my shirt. A swimmy sensation takes over my limbs. My hands and feet feel fuzzy, pins and needles at their tips.

My mouth is numb, fingers closing into fists. My mind is buzzing, like grey ants, grey sweaty ants, and the sound of the river is in my ears, a gargled warbled rush.

Bright white headlights flash at my eyes.

There is a sliding sensation down the base of the tree, knees buckling.

There is no more time or space. Just the Pa Tree, me and the silver rush of the river slipping by.

Then nothing.

Eighteen

Sunlight in my eyes. Wetness on my face. The smell of damp earth. Rushing, gushing in my ears.

I lift my head gingerly off the ground. A pain throbs on the right side of my forehead. I touch my fingers to it and wince. A large bump moons out.

My vision is blurry, but slowly my eyes focus on my surroundings. First, the twiggy gritty earth beneath my hands, and then, further away, the house sharpens into view. White and still against a steely sky. Finches flit down to the river and up into the tree branches, chirping like they always do, like nothing at all has changed in the world.

Only something is moving, a dark figure blurring into shape as it comes towards me. Someone is running. Running fast.

I try to sit up, but I feel dizzy, like I've been on a bad ride at a carnival and might vomit. So I stay on the earth as I wait for

Dad to reach me.

'Elliott!' Dad says. He sounds almost angry.

And then I start crying, right there on the ground beneath the Pa Tree. Soundless noiseless tears. Tears that come from deep inside me, like a volcano that needs to erupt.

My face must say a thousand things my voice can't, because Dad falters as he approaches, then stumbles towards me. His face is carved with concern, his eyes soft. Dad crouches down to me and without a word he sweeps my hair off my face. Then, using the gentlest of hands, he lifts me like a baby into his arms, against his chest.

'It's okay,' he croons. 'I'll get you home.'

And even though I am shaking in his arms, hiccup-crying and shuddering from the force erupting inside me, he carries me up the hill one steady step at a time.

I made a promise only moments ago to care for Dad. Look after him, watch him. Already, I've failed, and he doesn't even seem to have noticed. The father I am meant to protect, the one who shares my blood, my house, my name, is holding me. I am weak when I was meant to be strong. But I am also powerless. The feelings are too big, too deep, too powerful. Like the floods that ravish the river, the grief has washed away everything else. Any decision I've ever made, any plans I had. Things happen to us that change everything. Mum leaving is one of these things. I can't opt out of how I feel. My body is doing it all without checking in with me.

As we near the house, Dad kicks open the gate of the fence and carries me up the verandah steps, through the front screen door, which bangs shut behind us. I can feel his arms quivering from my weight. He carries me straight to the lounge and lowers us both gently onto it, still cradling me. I want to stop crying, but I am gulping and sobbing in big breaths, my snot and my tears staining his shirt as he rocks me back and forth.

We are a little boat out in a wild and dangerous sea. I can't quiet the waves. They splash upon me one after another like they have no end, like the tears are limitless and will never stop falling. Why so many? What do they achieve? Tears from the sky water the earth to grow new things. What do my tears grow? Yet, even if they have no worth, they are a deep swell flowing out of me, onto me, onto Dad, drowning us. And through the waves, words bubble out of me.

'I'm sorry, Dad, I'm so sorry.'

'Don't you be sorry.'

But I am. I'm sorry for him, for me, for Mum, for Lachy. Sorry that I'm being like this. Sorry that he's suffering, sorry that he's having to take care of me instead of me taking care of him, sorry that I didn't go with Mum and spare him seeing me like this because staying hasn't helped Dad, not at all. I've made it worse. And going with Mum would have made her feel better, so I'm sorry that I made a bad choice. I'm sorry that I had to choose at all, that Mum made me choose. I'm sorry I didn't notice things were so bad. I'm sorry that it even got to this at all. I'm sorry I couldn't stop Mum leaving.

And yet all I keep saying on loop, is 'Sorry, Dad, I'm so sorry,' my voice thick with tears between gulps and hiccups.

'This is not your fault,' Dad says firmly. 'None of it. You don't need to be sorry. This is about Mum and me.'

But even Dad must see this is about so much more. Mum dropped a stone into the river and now we are all being swallowed by her ripples.

'This is adult relationship stuff,' Dad continues. 'None of it is your fault.' He smooths my wet hair back. 'I'm so sorry if you've ever thought that. If we've made you feel that.' He keeps rocking me gently in his arms. 'You're going to be okay,' Dad says, even though it isn't entirely clear that I am going to be okay. 'You *will* be okay.'

And I want to be. I wish I could stop the pain, the tears. I need to be better. So I nod. I hope it makes him feel better. I hope it makes it happen.

Next moment, Dad pulls out his phone. He's dialling a number.

I shake my head, clutching at him. 'Not Mum, not Mum, not Mum.'

Because for all that I hate how she's done this to us, I do know, deep down, that she's hurting too and I don't want her to feel any worse. Don't want to hear Dad say, with words like knives: *See what you've done?* The same way he blamed Mum the night they told us. When he said she was destroying us. I don't want this to get worse, I can't handle it. Only better. Only easier.

I keep clutching Dad's shirt and shaking my head, but he ignores me and the phone is answered on the other end.

'I could use some help,' Dad says gruffly.

'We'll be right over,' the voice responds.

I know that voice. It's not the voice of my mother.

A few minutes later, Snow is barking. There's the far-off grumble of an engine and gravel crunching up the drive. Dad lifts me into the crook of the lounge, in the corner, where I sit, my bones heavy with fatigue.

A car door slams shut, footsteps follow. A shadow falls across the front door. And there is Bec, her hair tied up high in a rusty-coloured scarf. Bec, who is magic, who can surely fix anything. Just maybe not this. And behind her is Drake, exchanging soft words with Dad.

Bec's hand is on my back now, warm and strong, making the tears come fresh and fast again. 'You let it all out, honey,' Bec soothes. 'That's the way. Let it out.' She rubs my back. 'Drake, can you get her a blanket? Also the first aid kit. And hit the kettle. Good kid.'

A short time later, a crocheted blanket is tucked around me.

Bec parts my hair and examines my forehead.

'That's quite a shiner you got there,' she says. 'Did you faint?'

I shrug. 'I don't remember. My breathing was fast. Too fast.'

When I stop shaking so hard, a warm mug of tea is pressed into my hands. Drake sits one side of me, Bec the other. Dad is on the floor at my feet, his hand on my knee.

Bec rummages in the first aid kit and puts antiseptic ointment on my head, making murmuring noises. She gives me two paracetamol and a glass of water.

'You swallow that down, sweetheart, it'll help with the pain.'

She rubs my back and the three of us sit there a long time as my trembling settles to a shiver, and then to nothing at all. Around me, Dad, Bec and Drake talk of small things, but their words are just threads of light passed through the air. I watch the shadows creep across the floor, the sky turn from steel to rust and from rust to ash.

My body is tired, old from the weight of the day.

Drake helps Dad carry armfuls of wood inside and, together, they start the fire. It's nice to have a little flame to watch, a fire caterpillar that grows and sends an amber light dancing across their faces.

'Do you want me to call her—your mum?' Bec asks gently once the fire is going.

I'm no longer crying. I could talk to her.

'She'd want to know. She'd want to talk to you. Help you.'

I shake my head. 'She knows.' She's my mother. Surely she felt the earth shift.

The fire is blazing now in the hearth, and I feel so tired I could sleep for a hundred days.

'I don't think she knows this. The depth of it.'

Still I shake my head.

What does it matter? What difference would it make? Would it make her stay? Would she come back only to leave all over again? I wouldn't survive another leaving. I've always prided myself on my strength. Only, it turns out I'm not strong. It's just that, besides Nanna's death, nothing terrible has happened to me. My strength, untested. Now I see how weak I truly am. How fragile. How easily I could shrivel up and die. I am as trembly as fresh-mown grass. One puff of air, one gust of wind, and I'm scattered.

I rub my eyes. They feel tight and puffy, my whole face swollen and welted like a series of bee stings. The ache in my head has dulled, but not the pain in my heart. I guess paracetamol doesn't fix that. I'll have to get used to carrying that around.

Bec cooks us all dinner. Two-minute noodles with frozen veggies and eggs. We don't sit at the dining table. We eat on the floor, cross-legged, before the roaring fire in the hearth as the last light drains out of the western sky. Nobody has thought to turn the lights on and so we are silhouettes against the dark.

After dinner, Dad sees Bec and Drake to the front door. 'Thanks for looking after our girl,' I hear him say.

He shuts the door and walks back towards me. The car engine revs to life, and headlights sweep our living room as Bec turns the car for home.

'*Your* girl,' I say.

The language is important. No more denial. Nothing is *theirs* anymore.

'No,' he says firmly. 'Ours. Always ours. That doesn't change.'

I nod and wriggle under my crocheted blanket. An old one from Nanna, made to keep us warm.

'Want to sleep out here together?' Dad asks.

It's been a long time since Dad and I have slept out.

Dad makes up a bed on the floor beside me using cushions, a blanket and a pillow. Then he goes to the door and calls Snow inside. Her paws are a soft pounding *thud* against the hardwood floor. She greets me with a cold nose, a lick on the hand, a flicking happy tail and a body wagging with excitement. She thinks this is fun. A special night. Dad gets Snow to lie down on her mat near the fire.

'Night, sweetheart,' he says to me. 'Get some rest.'

Our house feels like a husk. How do we ever get used to this? The walls creak. The wind tickles the eaves. Mount Wilderness is on her best behaviour. No storms, no sleet, no rain.

Then, as I settle down to sleep on this too-early too-dark night, I receive a text from Mum.

Hi honey, hope your day has been okay. Lachy and I have been busy settling in, unpacking. Just about to go for a night swim. Will send pics in the morning. I love you. Xx

I stare up at the ceiling in the heavy inky night. I think of Mum, swimming with Lachy, tucking him into a strange new bed with strange new sheets in a strange new room. I want to cry all over again, but my tears are used up. I have nothing left. Where Mum is, I imagine there is light, and warm food and cuddles.

I type out a response to Mum:

Love you too. Tell Lachy I said goodnight. ❤

Then I delete the message. She has absolutely no idea what we've been through. This is what our new lives will be like. She will know only the bits I choose. Is this what she wants? I tuck my phone under the cushions on the lounge where I can't see her name on my screen anymore.

The Gillespies

After the snow had melted off the peak of Mount Wilderness, the freeze had gone with it, and in its place was honeysuckle perfume and new blades of grass sprouting from the thawing earth. Lizards crept out of hibernation and along with the lizards, turtle hatchlings the size of coins, dark and new, swam through the shallows of the river with their webbed claws.

Dad had been promising Lachy a treehouse all year. *Big enough to sleep in,* he'd said. Through the quieter winter months, through frost, and fog and sleet, Dad had worked with chilblained hands, hammering and screwing timber, to build Lachy's place high in the tree. By October, it was complete, with windows and a trail of rungs leading up the trunk for a ladder.

The treehouse was big and sturdy enough to fit us all inside it. We trekked down to the river's edge, to the thick smooth trunk of the forest king, which stretched its arms up to the chalky sky like it was thanking the universe for its existence. And nestled in the enormous tree, embraced by its branches, was the treehouse, perched like an eagle's nest on top of a ship.

We brought with us all the essentials for our stay: pillows and sleeping bags, marshmallows and two-minute noodles, matches and beanies. Lachy, Mum and I gathered kindling for the fire into a pile, while Dad stacked the wood on top, added some firelighters and struck the match. In a rush, the flame stretched like a hungry dragon to the sky, to the brave stars peering out in the last light of the day.

Mum cooked two-minute noodles and we slurped them until our tummies were full. We lifted our heads to the twilit night as the fire licked the stars, reaching, reaching, against a withering sky.

'Tis the time for magic,' Dad said. 'For witches, and moonbeams and the casting of spells. For the making of wishes.'

'Let's make wishes,' Lachy said. 'All of us.'

'Okay,' Dad said, 'But you can't tell anyone your wish or it might not come true.'

We closed our eyes and each made our wishes. I didn't know it then, but I wasted mine.

As the sky grew black and the flames stopped leaping, the stars came out. Light of lights, sparkling, bedazzling. Nothing we make on earth is more brilliant, not even fire.

'What are stars made of?' I'd asked.

'Most of the stars we can see are actually suns from other solar systems far away,' Dad answered. 'Some of the suns we see burning don't even exist anymore, but the light is so far away, and takes so long to travel to us, that we're seeing the old light from the old sun which is no longer there.'

Lachy's mouth fell open. 'But how does a sun die?'

'Well, little man, when a sun gets old, billions of years old, it swells and turns into what is called a "red giant". The bigger sun then sucks in all the planets around it, until it gives one almighty explosion as a supernova and collapses into a black hole.'

'Whoa,' said Lachy. 'Is that going to happen to ow sun?'

'Our sun's a bit smaller than others, so it probably won't explode anytime soon, but it will still get bigger and die eventually, and the earth will die with it.'

'So we'll all die?' Lachy said.

'Every human will die, every single living thing too,' Dad said.

Lachy's face is haunted by the flickering firelight.

'You're scaring him, Dan,' Mum said.

'I'm not scawed,' Lachy said, but he moved closer to the warmth of the fire.

'We don't need to worry, though,' Dad said.

'Why not?' Lachy asked.

'Because that won't happen for around five billion years,' Dad said. 'Something else will get us long before then.'

'You know, what Dad gave you kids was the scientific explanation,' Mum said, 'but artists have an interesting relationship with the universe too. Artists don't only rely on scientific facts. They also consider dimensions beyond what human intelligence can prove. Many artists believe in third dimensions and higher intelligences. Let's face it, there's more about the universe that science *doesn't* yet know than it does know. The universe is full of secrets.' Mum tilted her head back to the stars and sighed. 'I don't think any of us can know what's truly out there, or how it all works. But it sure is beautiful. Full of magic and mystery.' She smiled. 'Actually, tonight the sky looks a bit like a painting called *Starry Night*, only the artist who painted that picture painted it from behind the barred window of his asylum room and—'

'Alright,' Dad laughed. 'Enough of the arty mumbo jumbo. These stars are far better than any painting I've ever seen.'

And Dad started talking about science again. About time travel, and rockets around the moon and black holes that suck in other planets.

I don't remember Mum talking to us about art or the sky anymore that night. A short time later, she kissed us all goodnight and climbed the rungs up to the treehouse to put herself to bed. *She was tired*, she said. Mum was tired a lot.

But we weren't tired, and we stayed up longer than Mum, longer and later. Just Dad, Lachy and I. Dad told us ghost stories, and we toasted marshmallows and when Dad called up the tree asking Mum if she wanted any, she didn't answer. She was probably asleep. I don't think Mum was really into toasted marshmallows.

When it was late and the fire was just a pile of glowing embers, Dad threw dirt on top of it and we all climbed up the tree to sleep. Then we were four bodies sleeping in a treehouse under a great blanket of stars.

Nineteen

Monday night is our first night as a family of three.

I manage to cook dinner by myself. Nachos, which we mostly eat. Lachy manages to bite his bottom lip instead of crying. He also manages a shower and I only have to ask him twice.

I bring Dad tea, extra hot, the way he likes it. In a different mug. No slogan. Just tea. Made with love. Dad plays Metallica softly on the piano and we all sit around watching the fire.

Dad's phone rings beside him and the screen lights up. The words 'Honey (Mum)' flash across it. Dad looks at the screen for a while before he picks it up, puts it to his ear.

'Hi,' he says.

There's a soft murmur on the other end. I can't hear the words, just her pitch.

'Yeah, we're doing okay,' he says.

Even though Lachy's eyes are brimming with tears again.

Even though it's more like we're standing in the aftermath of a tornado, surveying the damage where our house once stood.

'Can I talk to Mum?' Lachy says.

Dad nods, holds up one finger at Lachy.

'Yeah, El made us dinner.' His voice breaks on the word dinner.

Another murmur on the other line.

Dad inhales. 'Nachos. Lachy did a good job of his. He—oh, yeah, sure.' He looks at Lachy. Extends the phone to him. 'Your mum wants to talk to you.'

'Mum,' Lachy says, and he starts crying. 'I miss you . . . I miss you so much. I want you to come home.'

See, kid? See? This is when being eight sucks. This is when you have to feel it over and over, because two nights in a unit with one bird aviary and one night swim isn't enough.

Lachy clenches the phone in his small hand, hunching himself into a ball on the lounge. It hurts to watch him trying to be brave. There are garbled noises on the other end of the phone. I look at Dad. His eyes are glistening.

I hate her for this.

'Why not . . .' Lachy says, starting to sob. 'Why won't you . . . just come home?' Tears spill out of his bewildered little eyes and down his rosy cheeks.

I hate her even more.

I can hear murmuring on the other end. Lots of it, in a

soothing tone.

Lachy sniffs. 'I know.'

More murmuring. More words that mean nothing when she's not here.

'Yeah . . . I have,' Lachy says. His face is white, he's gulping back tears. 'Yeah, I played with Twent and Zach . . . we played tag.'

They speak for a little longer before Lachy says, 'Hang on, I'll ask.' He looks at me. 'El, you want to speak to Mum?'

I shake my head, turning my back on him.

'She doesn't want to,' he says.

It hurts saying no to Mum. I want her more than she could know. But I want her *here*. In the same way Lachy does. In our home, where she should be. If I hurt her enough, she might realise this just isn't worth it.

'Mum said maybe next time, El?'

I shrug.

Lachy bites his bottom lip. Dad gestures to Lachy to hand over the phone to him.

Dad looks at me as he's speaking to Mum. 'It's a very difficult time, obviously. She's taken it hard.'

I almost laugh at that. Does she know I fainted? How broken she left me? Mum seems to care more about herself lately than about anyone else.

'Yeah, maybe next time,' Dad says. 'I'll talk to her.'

I don't respond. No. The answer is no. No next time. No second chances. Why should I, when she isn't giving us any? Why is Mum allowed to decide what she wants to do for herself, but I'm not allowed to decide what I want to do for myself? My face burns with fury.

I turn my focus on Lachy. 'Have you brushed your teeth?' I ask.

I flinch when I recognise my tone. An echo of Mum's. I guess teeth-brushing is my job now, along with dinner. Maybe I have to be like a second mum now.

Lachy doesn't respond.

'Well, go brush them.'

He runs off to the bathroom.

I don't mean to be bossy and horrible to the poor kid. It should be Mum here telling him this stuff, not his cranky older sister. But cranky older sister it has to be. I'm it. Just another job for me to pick up. Add it to the list of all the other ones that are going to be mine and Dad's now that Mum has skipped off.

A while later, I realise Lachy hasn't returned.

'Lachy?' I call out. 'Did you brush?'

No answer. The least the kid could do is work with me.

'Lachy?'

I stomp around the house looking for him. Not in the bathroom. Not in his bedroom. I can feel my rage boiling up again.

'Just because Mum's gone doesn't mean you're allowed to grow furry teeth!' I yell. 'Where are you?'

'Heah.' A small voice, muffled, far away.

I head upstairs to Mum and Dad's room. Correct that, *Dad's* room. When will I get used to that?

'Lachy.' My fury shrivels the second I see him. Lachy is on the bed, on Mum's side, curled up into a ball, cuddling her pillow.

I kneel down beside him. Mum's pillow has wet stains on it.

'I'm sorry, Lach,' I say. 'I didn't mean to be bossy. Did you brush?'

He sniffs into her pillow, burying his face in it. Sometimes I forget how small he actually is. Second grade small. I got to have Mum home until the tenth grade.

'It smells like huh,' he says. 'Huh pillow. She didn't take it.'

I remember Dad saying that when we first got Snow, she was given part of her mother's blanket to help her settle at night because it smelt like her.

'I know this is really hard,' I say, combing my fingers through his curls. 'It's hard for me too. I didn't mean to be mad at you.'

He sniffs. 'I know. It's okay.'

'Why don't you keep her pillow?' I say. 'Dad won't mind. You should sleep with it.'

I sit on the bed. Try to ignore the empty bedside table which should be stacked with her crooked pile of books, her earrings, her glass of water.

'She can't wead me my stowy,' Lachy says, sobbing quietly. 'Now thewe's no-one to wead to me.'

'I can read,' I say. 'We can start a new book? Maybe even one of my old favourites from when *I* was eight?'

He looks up at me. But instead of his eyes sparkling, they remain dull and lifeless. From beneath the pillow, Lachy pulls one hand out.

'I found this,' he says.

It's a piece of fabric I recognise. A soft, thin old nightie. The one that always made Mum look like a ghost when she was waving me goodbye from the verandah on school mornings.

He fiddles with it in his hand, then holds it to his nose. 'If I lie heah like this and close my eyes, it feels like I'm cuddling huh.'

I blink back the fire in my eyes, in my throat. If she could only see him.

'I don't think I want any stowies tonight, El. Thank you anyway,' he says, curling back in to her pillow. 'But I want to sleep heah, on huh side. Do you think Dad will let me?'

'Of course he will,' I say. 'Of course. I'll go tell him.'

I give Lachy a soft kiss on the forehead. 'Goodnight, beautiful boy.'

'Night, El.'

I leave him with his eyes closed, breathing Mum in.

On my way out, I get one last glimpse of him. Small, scrawny knobbly-kneed little Lachy curled into himself.

Tell me, universe, do kids survive this?

Each step I take down the stairs, my heart pounds a little harder, the rage burns a little brighter.

If it wasn't dark, I'd text Drake:

Bridge needs a swim.

I could burn off the rage. But outside it's a dark moonless night and a vicious wind tears through the cracks under the doors.

I head for the kitchen instead, past Dad who is finished on the phone and is sitting on the lounge with his tea, watching the fire, listening to soft music.

There are dishes to wash, so I busy myself washing them. Clanging the crockery in the rack. It's not very satisfying and Dad doesn't seem to notice, but I keep going anyway. I feel like picking up a plate and smashing it onto the kitchen floor. Watching it shatter into smithereens, the pieces skidding across the floor into the living room.

We're allowed to be angry. We don't have to just lie down and accept this.

When Dad comes into the kitchen, I'm drying the dishes. Still seething with rage. At her. At him. At this whole messed-up situation.

As Dad places his mug down next to the sink, I spin around

to face him, still drying a plate. 'At what point, exactly, are you going to fight for her?' I spit at him.

'El,' Dad says sharply.

'Are you just going to let this happen?' I say, raising my voice. *'Are you?'*

'What do you mean?'

I put the plate down, slow my speech for clarity. 'Are you just going to let her leave?'

He rests a hand on the benchtop, as if to steady himself. 'I'm not letting anything happen. Your mum isn't chained here. She's free to make her own choices.'

I nod. I get it now. 'So you're not going to run after her and fix this?'

'Our marriage isn't a broken fence, El. I can't just bind it up, make it work again. It's a lot more complicated than that.'

'Oh, I understand,' I hiss. 'I remember.'

'El.' Dad is firm. 'I can't force your mum to stay with me, much as I would love to. Don't you think I've tried already? You're a kid. You and Lachy are just *kids*. You haven't seen how hard I've tried, so don't you dare make this my fault.'

'You told her,' I say, my voice low, steady, menacing. 'You said one visit every year to her family when she moved here. How many did she get?'

He is silent for a moment.

'How many?' I press.

Dad's eyes are wounded, like I personally pierced them. 'I was wrong not to make that happen,' he says.

'And the art room? Her painting?'

Dad presses his hands against the wooden bench. 'You're right about that. I didn't prioritise it.'

'You let her get sadder and sadder. You didn't even see her anymore. You didn't step in, you didn't try and fix it.' I throw down the dishcloth. 'You let her break and now she's gone. Mum is *gone*.'

'Sweetheart.'

I slide halfway to the floor, barely able to catch myself, catch my breath. He holds me by the arm and pulls me up instead.

'You failed,' I whisper into his shirt. Even though I know it wasn't just him. We *all* failed. It was a joint effort.

And then I sob all over him, the one who failed, and into his arms. I want it to be his fault. Her fault. *Someone's* fault. If there's someone to blame, we have a starting point. A way to fix it. Put it all back the way it was meant to be. The four puzzle pieces back together.

'I know I failed, sweetheart,' Dad says softly and I realise he's crying too. 'Your mum is right. It takes two people to make a marriage work.' Dad sits beside me on the floor of the kitchen, holding my head against his shoulder as we both cry, stroking my hair. 'Nobody owns anyone else,' he says. 'We might be married, but I don't own your mum any more than she owns me.

I can't force her to stay here, married to me, if she wants to fly away. She has to *want* it. And she doesn't want it anymore. Whatever the reason, she isn't happy here anymore.'

'But you promised forever,' I whisper. It sounds childish, but it's true. 'You both promised in front of Nanna and the whole town full of people.'

Dad nods. 'We did. We both did. And we meant it.'

I take a deep breath in. I hate that he is agreeing with me. I want him to fight with me so that I can fight him back and then somehow we can wrestle our way to a solution.

'So now you both need to stick to your promises,' I say.

'Yeah,' Dad says, dropping his hands into his lap and studying them. He twists the ring on his fourth finger. The one she put on there, which he's still wearing. Is she? 'Unfortunately, El, life doesn't always follow the plans we make. You'll learn this as you get older.'

I shake my head. 'No. No, I won't.'

Dad smiles. 'Sadly, you will. At the end of the day, we're all islands and when two people choose to share their journey through life, to walk the path together, that's a beautiful thing. But it has to be freely shared and freely given. Not begged for. Not forced. People are not property, sweetheart, even if they're married. I certainly would never treat your mum like something I have a right to. Believe me, I wish nothing more than for her to come back to me, nothing in the world do I wish more. I wish she'd give me a second chance. But then I look at all the ways I've failed her, like you said, and I realise I don't deserve it. I had my chance. You don't always get a second go. I didn't make her happy in all the little ways, and the little ways add up to all the big ways. You're right to blame me.'

'No,' I say, 'I was being unfair. You're not the one who left.'

Dad takes a deep breath and sighs, long and slow. 'The thing about marriage, sweetheart, or any relationship for that matter . . .' He rubs his eyes. Hangs his head. 'It's woven with years of laughter, and pain, and scars and joy. It was my job to make sure that the tears didn't outweigh the laughter. And I got it wrong, for both of us. Now your mum's hurting; she's hurting a lot.'

I shake my head. 'Not as much as us.'

'Oh, I'd say every bit as much. Maybe you should go see her,' Dad suggests. 'Find out for yourself. You and your mum probably have a lot to talk about. She deserves that much, don't you think?'

Why is Dad being so kind? Where is the yelling and the cursing? He should want Mum to burn in hell for leaving him. Shouldn't he?

'Why are you being so kind to her?' I say. I'm not ready to be nice about this.

'I love her,' Dad says defensively. He bites his bottom lip, then inhales deeply. 'I'll always love her. And when you love someone, I mean really love them, you want them to be happy. Wherever that is and however. Even if it makes you unhappy. So I want your mum to be happy even if it means I'm not. I know you and Lachy want that too.' Dad pushes himself up off the floor and offers me his hand. 'Come on, sweetheart.'

I take his hand and he pulls me up. We finish drying the dishes together and Dad starts singing off-key to Metallica. I'm happy he can still sing.

'I want you to be happy too,' I tell him.

In response to my words, Dad's singing gets more off-key and exaggerated. He starts singing in high notes, then low notes.

He's that bad I laugh. 'You are actually murdering this song.'

'I love that sound,' he says. 'I'd almost, *almost* forgotten what it sounded like to hear you laugh.' And he hugs me. 'We're going to get through this, sweetheart,' he says. 'Of course we will. We're Gillespies.' And he holds out his fist for a fist-bump like when I was smaller.

I fist-bump him back.

'And I'm going to get better at this,' he says.

I raise one eyebrow. 'Singing?'

'Pah! I'm already an ace at that.' He smacks the dish cloth down on the bench. 'I meant at this dad business. For you kids. For all of us.'

When we finish the dishes, I pad to the dark silence of my bedroom. I keep the curtains open for the pinpricks of light from the universe. Snow jumps up on my bed with me. Settles her hefty body at the base of it and we both tuck in.

I hear Dad's heavy footsteps creaking up the stairs. He and Lachy will have each other through the long night. I wonder how Mum is spending her first night alone. Without Snow, or Dad, or Lachy or me. I wonder if she's lying in the dark like me, thinking of all of us.

Twenty

It has been a month. Since she hugged me goodbye, since I heard her voice. A month without seeing her single-dimpled smile, smelling the sweet tang of her perfume, hanging over the bench in the kitchen chatting to her about my day, a month without her too-large bangles on her narrow wrists banging against the table at dinner time, sitting on her bed watching her apply face cream before the bathroom mirror. I am starting to forget things: the way she walks, the sound of her voice, the way she talks with her hands. I am struggling to remember the lines on her face when she frowns, the ones when she laughs.

It's true that it's been my choice not to see Mum, not to speak to her on the phone. Texting is all I've been able to manage. It's also true that I miss her with a pang sharp enough to make me gasp. Some might say it's my own fault for not seeing her, but they don't understand how it feels to be left by the one who's meant to care for you.

I've started skipping school. The talk became too much. Not the talk about Mum and Dad separating. Tamar and Frankie were good about that. Basically, they pretended it hadn't happened, just the way I wanted. It was the other talk. Little things, normal everyday things, that I could no longer stand hearing. Like how Tamar's parents are repainting her house, and the new bedroom she's getting, with the insurance money. Or how Mumma is still pushing the vegan diet on Frankie. Everyone else is recovering, moving forward. And it's all just a little bit too sharp to ingest, like swallowing ninja stars.

The clincher came on Frankie's dad's fiftieth birthday. Which I found out about by accident. From Drake, actually. Because he and Bec had been invited. My heart did this weird little dance in my chest. Surely Frankie had just forgotten to mention it to me? So I sent her a text.

Hey, Drake told me about your dad's party. When is it?

Frankie read my message, didn't respond straight away. My heart skipped a little harder.

When Frankie finally did respond, it was to say,

Oh yeah. My parents were going to invite your family. They just didn't know who to invite, like which one.

What do you mean?

Another pause.

Because of, you know, the situation.

Was she actually kidding me?

The situation?

I sent her a laughing face.

Do you think we have some sort of disease?

No, it's just, no offence, but it's kinda awkward for everyone. Picking which one to invite.

That's when I realised our new family dynamic was making other people uncomfortable. But at the same time that I felt edgy about that, I also understood. It doesn't matter how kind a split-up is, people feel like they have to pick a side. There was suddenly this giant gap between Mum and Dad and nobody knew what to do with it. Whether they could exist in the same room together, or whether they hated each other's guts and making them share a room at a party might result in something ugly. Like what happened with Jude's parents at the school office. How could I be upset with Frankie when even *I'd* felt forced to pick a team?

Besides, I couldn't even imagine being at a party anymore. Laughing, or dancing, or being carefree when a hole had been publicly punched right through the middle of my family.

Frankie had texted:

So should we invite your dad?

If I said yes, *I'd* be the one making a choice. The same choice I expected everyone else not to make. I'd ended up typing:

Invite them both. Let them figure it out.

In the end, no invitation came. The party went on without us. I'm sure everyone dressed up and had fun. It looked like it on socials. And I was glad not to be there, having to pretend at a time when my family is strapped together with tissue paper.

The call to visit the Year Coordinator with Dad happened because I'd missed too many days of school without a medical reason. Dad fumbled through a very awkward conversation about the 'separation' (a cringey clinical word, but I guess better than the 'situation'), and the impact it'd had on everyone, but especially on me.

And the Year Coordinator put me in touch with the school psychologist, who is really very good and very accessible, she'd said. And the same school psychologist—her name is actually Kate, I've discovered—who I am sitting stiffly in front of right now, has just asked me about the 'time-spend' arrangement with Mum.

'The what?' I ask.

'The time-spend arrangement. How you spend time between homes?' she asks, folding her hands in her lap. Kate wears a trim pair of red-rimmed glasses. She has wavy auburn hair, pinned back in a claw clip. Everything about Kate is neat, unruffled, professional.

'I don't,' I say blankly. 'I haven't spent any time with Mum.'

But it turns out my answer is a bit of a surprise to Kate, so that sends her down a determined little rabbit hole to find out why.

And when I tell her why, 'Because I don't want to live anywhere else, ever, or have Mum live anywhere else,' which is the truth, she keeps asking me silly questions.

'I'm just trying to understand, so bear with me,' Kate says, sliding her glasses back up the bridge of her nose. 'Is your plan not to see your mum anymore, ever?'

'Not until she comes home, no.'

'Okay,' she says, entertaining the reasonableness of my stance.

Except I'm not stupid. I know my stance is not entirely reasonable. I just don't care. It's not meant to be reasonable. It's meant to apply pressure and pain on Mum. To make her return.

'And if she doesn't come back,' Kate muses, 'what then? Have you thought about that?'

'No. I prefer to live in denial.'

'I'm being serious, Elliott,' she says. 'Honestly, how are you coping without your mum at the house?'

I blank stare her. 'How do you think?'

'Well, I could guess, but I'd prefer to hear from you about how you feel you're coping, because obviously I'm not you. And everyone responds differently to a separation. No two separations are the same, just like no two people are the same.' She pauses and waits for me to consider this. Why are psychologists so damn patient? Do they ever snap out of frustration and start yelling at their clients?

'Can we just say I hate it then, Kate?'

Anything to shut her up. And I insist on calling her Kate. It's the only bit of power I have left.

'You can say whatever you like. Do you feel the same about school? Do you hate school too?'

'No,' I say. 'Hate's a strong word, Kate.'

Her eyes flash me a warning. She is obviously irritated by my use of her first name. But I bet she's also worried about me shutting down just when I'm starting to talk.

'Well, I'm looking at your attendance record here, Elliott, and something has clearly happened because you were a kid with one absent day in two years. And now . . . lots of half days. A bunch of unexplained absences. It tends to paint a picture of someone who isn't very happy.'

'Yes, I'm not exactly at my shiniest.'

Another thanks to you, Mum.

'Can we talk about why?'

'Can I say no?' I say, my knee starting to jiggle. I check my phone. How much longer?

'Well, you can, of course, but it doesn't help. And that's all I'm here for. I have no agenda other than to help you.'

I look at Kate sideways. 'I think you have an agenda to keep me going to school.'

She considers this. 'I do, you're right. Because that's the best thing for *you*, not for me. So tell me what's making it hard for you to stay here.'

I sigh, pressing a hand against my knee to stop the jiggling. 'Because this is a small town. Families know families. Everyone knows about mine. Everyone feels the need to make a choice. Team Mum, Team Dad. Because people treat separation as a disease, even my friends. Are those enough reasons?'

And when all her stupid idiotic questions make me cry, she doesn't try to stop me. Just pauses and hands me tissues. Asks if I'm okay to continue, which no, I'm clearly not, Kate.

'I can understand why that would be upsetting. It must hurt, truly hurt, to have lost your mum in this way. And so suddenly. But what if there were ways you could soften the blow? I mean, have you thought about going for a visit, even just for an hour?'

I shrug. 'Of course I've *thought* about it. She hasn't been erased from my memory, unfortunately.'

'Your mum is a huge player in your life to lose. And you're a big player in her life. And I'm speaking like this is a game, but it really isn't—none of this is a game. I'm sure you're very aware that this is your real life, with real consequences, because you're the one living them. And I just wonder, if you did go see your mum, what is the worst thing you think could happen?'

'The worst thing? The *very* worst? That she thinks she's won,' I say. 'That I've accepted it. That I'm adapting. And then I lose her forever.'

'Okay, let's unpack that for a second.' Kate thinks for a moment. 'That's a really interesting viewpoint. Correct me if I'm wrong here, but that response tells me that what you're really scared of is losing your mum.'

Do they really pay Kate for this? I hope her salary isn't too high, because we're nowhere near genius territory.

'But it seems to me,' she continues, 'you run the same risk if you don't go to see her. If she can't move home, for whatever reason, and you refuse to see her outside the house, isn't the outcome the same? Don't you lose her anyway?'

I stay silent. This is exactly why I didn't want to come and see Kate. I don't need people to point out what I already know. That either way, I lose.

'Think about it,' Kate said. 'It might normalise life just a little bit if you can rebuild your relationship with your mum. What have you really got to lose?' She balances her hands like a scale, one up, one down. 'A month is a small bridge to build. A year is a lot longer. You lose a lot of things in a year and time is something you don't get back. It doesn't always give second chances. Maybe just take some time to think about that.'

I don't exactly know what Kate thinks I've been doing the last thirty-one days. I've already been taking my time. I've been thinking more than I wanted to think about any single thing in my life ever. I hope Mum has been thinking too. Thinking, and feeling and hurting. I hope Mum has a Kate to tell her she needs to back down too.

The Gillespies

Lachy, Snow and I were straight out of the car, bare feet against hot powdery sand, sprinting down to the edge of the sea. The water rushed against our toes and shot shrieks of joy from our throats. Pippies dug themselves into the sand with their tongues and we dug them back out with our hands, scooping them from the sloppy wet sand just to watch them burrow under again.

Snow barked at the water and bit at the rushing waves, and Lachy and I chased her through the shallows. Snow had only seen the ocean a few times in her life. Like us, she didn't care that she got wet or that Lachy fell right in and got drenched, because it was a summer afternoon and all the world was baked and shiny.

Mum and Dad unloaded the bags from our ute into the little bungalow in the sand dunes before walking down in their bathers, hand in hand, to join us. We built a sand fortress and dared the tide to crumble it. We made Mum a mermaid tail of sand, and when Dad asked for one too, we made him a merman. I took a photo of them both. It is still pinned to my wall.

A whole week we spent by the seaside, and every evening we walked a stretch of the miles-long beach as the sun sank behind the hills, turning the water murky and the sky speckled peach. Mum and Dad held hands, and Lachy ran with Snow, up the beach and down, throwing the ball to her and back to me again.

One night, we sat atop the dunes, Lachy and I sliding down the sand hills over and over until our legs grew too tired. Dad pulled Mum close to him, whispering into her ear as a glow appeared over the ocean. The glow grew brighter, until it burst into light. A bright full moon was rising.

Mum gasped. 'I've always wanted to see this!'

We watched as the moon cast a beam of white light over the rippled waves, making a staircase across the sea that led all the way back to the moon.

In my mind, I stop the memory there, where everything was perfect. I don't like to remember the last night, after Lachy and I went to bed. Everyone was probably just tired, but I felt sick in the stomach when I heard Dad yelling at Mum, and Mum saying that Dad didn't care about her, not really. And when Mum took herself off for a walk in the dark, I hated how my heart fluttered as I shut my eyes and focused on my breathing. Regular, calm breathing. Thinking on repeat, *everyone fights*. And Mum did come back, she always did after they fought. But this time it took quite a while. I know because I hadn't been able to sleep, so I heard her come in. I heard her hit the kettle and pour water. I heard the lounge creak with her weight and, early in the morning, when I woke for a glass of water, she was asleep there, on the lounge, with scrunched-up tissues beside her.

But later in the morning, Mum was up like normal, cooking eggs in the kitchen, and Dad was cuddling her from behind in the way that he does, talking low in her ear as she cooked. And I knew then that whatever their fight had been about, all was well again. They loved each other more than the fight. More than any other thing that could tear them apart.

Twenty-One

It's been three weeks since I first met Kate and I've seen her twice more. She stopped pushing the go-see-your-mum card. Instead, we talked about other things, like getting me back to school regularly. Turns out I was right about her agenda to keep me there. But I guess she was also right that my education is for me, not her or my mum. And I kinda don't want to fail Year Ten and have to repeat it all next year. So Kate organised a break card for me from my classes in case things got too much. I use it when I need to. There's a space for kids on break cards in the library. Nobody asks questions there, so when I need to, I've been disappearing into fantasy worlds to take me away. When you're fragile, social media can feel like thousands of tiny cuts. But reading is safe. It's living someone else's problems for a while, getting lost in someone else's adventures. It's new friends and new places. It helps me forget. Kate and I also made a plan for me to at least arrive at school every day. If I can't get all the way through, Dad picks me up. That feels safe too, knowing I'm not trapped.

It's not that I hate all of school. It's just that, some days, I feel like a moving piece of concrete. I still enjoy English. Ms Myers is still my favourite teacher. One of the things she tells us is that if you expect nothing in life, you'll never be disappointed. Sounded kinda grim when she first said it. A bit depressing, actually. As if I'm never going to have expectations! But, shock of shocks, today I've taken her advice.

Dad is driving. It's mostly a quiet drive, except for Lachy sitting in the back, who is telling me all about the bird aviary, and the pool and his new bedroom. Evidently, despite his suffering, Lachy still believes this is a holiday resort. The kid has been duped. But then I think of how he's been at home, without Mum. Crying his little eyes out until they're two red puffballs. This is no holiday for anyone. Especially not for me. I feel sick in the guts.

How are Lachy and Dad going to cope tonight, without me? It's my job to mind them. But I have more immediate concerns. We're only minutes away from town.

'I'm going to call you tonight, okay, Lachy?' I say, my panic factor sliding up a notch. I twist round to face him. 'You can speak to Mum too. And Dad, I've left the ingredients for the bolognaise next to the stove. Call me if you need help.

Lachy,' I look back at him again, 'I've left you a note in your room, reminding you of your jobs for tonight. Brushing your teeth, showering and practising your reading. And your sounds. Your r sound.'

'El,' Dad says quietly, his hands firmly on the wheel. He shoots me a look. It says 'no more'.

Lachy has gone quiet in the back seat, chewing his bottom lip. Maybe his mind hasn't leapt quite as far ahead as mine. He probably hasn't thought about the quiet house when he gets back; just him and Dad, no Mum, no sister telling him what to do.

We pull up alongside a sprawling complex of white rendered buildings dotted with palm trees and green gardens. A concrete wall curves either side of the driveway, the shrubs along the edge neatly trimmed, a painted sign saying *Country Oasis*. It is like a foreign land, which is too modern, too green, too orderly.

Dad takes a left and swings the ute into a visitor spot out the front. He turns down the corners of his mouth and nods.

'Looks nice.'

I see the place how he might be seeing it. Well-maintained, neat, tidy, urban. The complete opposite of home.

'Wait till you see inside,' Lachy breathes.

But I don't know that Dad will ever go inside. Would he want to? Would Mum want him to?

'And, El, the pool is am-AZING.'

'You said that.'

Tone it down, kid, can't you see Dad's heart is fretting?

I send Mum a quick text:

Here.

She texts back:

Two secs.

I open the car door and pull my backpack out from down at my feet. Dad and Lachy get out too.

I haven't seen Mum since that day I can still barely think about. Leaving day. But suddenly, there are her light quick steps down the stairwell next to the unit entrance. She's wearing a baby pink turtleneck sweater and a pair of jeans. She half runs to the ute to meet me, but stops when she's a couple of body lengths away.

'Hello,' she says to me. Like she's meeting someone new, someone she's not sure how to approach.

'Hi.' I sling my backpack over my shoulder. I don't want to linger.

Lachy lunges at her legs. He does want to linger, so Mum collects him into her arms.

'Hi, little guy.' Then she looks at Dad and her voice is quieter. 'How are you?' she asks.

He nods. 'Okay.' His mouth is a straight, strong line.

Lachy watches them, his eyes flitting from one to the other.

'Come here, you,' Mum says, tickling his ribs. 'How are

you doing, you little rapscallion?' and she scruffs him up in her arms.

'Good,' Lachy says, laughing. 'But I wish I was staying. Why can't I stay too?'

'Lach,' Dad warns. 'We've discussed this.'

'Your turn is next week,' Mum says. 'It's only fair El gets a turn on her own, like you've had. Just to get you both used to the place.'

'I *am* used to it,' Lachy says. 'I love it heah.'

The truth is, Lachy would love any place Mum was. Any place in the world where she could snuggle him up would be a happy home for him.

'Well, I'm *not* used to it,' I say, to save everyone from a Lachy meltdown. 'I haven't even stepped a single toe into the place.'

It is the biggest act of charity to pretend I want to be here. I hope Mum realises what that just cost me. But the truth is, I do want to spend time with Mum alone, even though it scares me. I've missed her so much it makes my stomach tumble.

'Okay, one last cuddle,' Mum says to Lachy.

He squeezes Mum tight around the waist, burying his face into her tummy. 'You ah the best mum in the whole enti-ya wowld,' his muffled voice says through her fleecy jumper.

'And you're the best Lachy in the whole entire world,' she says, holding him at arm's length, smiling at him. 'And I'll be seeing you tomorrow. Then I'll pick you up after school on

Monday and we'll go get a milkshake, okay?'

Lachy pulls away and nods. He's blinking back tears.

I hug Dad goodbye, then Lachy.

'Be brave, kid,' I say, and squeeze him hard.

Then I wave their car off without looking at their faces as they drive away.

Mum clasps her hands together, takes a deep breath. 'Boy, have I missed you,' she says, putting one arm around me as we head upstairs.

I was prepared for hospital-grade white walls, blank bedrooms without a peep of history, without secret nooks or an attic full of stories. Without wild grasses out our windows and mountains breathing down our back doorstep, without the gargle of the river and the freedom of birdsong from birds who live in tree hollows and fall to the earth to die.

Disappointingly, the unit is some of these things. But it's also different to the pictures Mum showed us online. Different to what I expected, which, thanks to the advice of Ms Myers, was nothing. Inside, there's a lounge with a bright crocheted throw. No TV, but Mum's never cared much for TV. Instead, there are bright splashes of artworks breaking up the walls alongside black and white photos framed on the walls.

One of the photos is a picture of Mum and Lachy down by the river, back when Lachy was still in nappies. Mum is holding him on her knee, his chubby feet splashing in the water.

Another is of Mum and me on our seaside vacation from the professional photographer we paid to take photos of us. We are by the water's edge, huge breakers bursting foam into the air behind us. Mum is holding her hat on her head to stop it from blowing off, and she's laughing. I'm looking up at her, my hair blowing behind me in the wind, also laughing. That day seems as though it belongs to someone else now, in an entirely different lifetime. Where did all our laughter blow to?

Mum takes me down a short hallway and opens a white panelled door. 'Your room, mademoiselle,' she says, making a grand sweeping gesture with her hand.

She lets me enter first. A rattan lamp is glowing amber on a bedside table beside a bed with a patchwork quilt. Strung up diagonally across the ceiling from end to end are artificial vine leaves tangled with fairy lights. There's a chic wooden desk with a big, mosaic bohemian-style mirror hanging above it, which I guess is also mine. On one wall she's hung a photo of me when I was little, and on the other, her painting of Crooked River and the Pa Tree.

'You gave me the Pa Tree painting?' I say.

'It's your favourite,' she says matter-of-factly. 'Of course I gave it to you.'

Then I notice a small bookshelf in the far corner. I walk over to it and run my finger along the spines of the books. Mum and I have a thing about books. Old ones, which we love opening up and sticking our noses into. The musty smell of yellowed pages is like magic. She has gathered a collection of the classics she used to read to me in bed: *Black Beauty*, *Alice in Wonderland*, *The Secret Garden*. I pull out *Anne of Green Gables*, with its gold gilt edges, and open its yellowed pages. I stick my nose into it and inhale.

I look back up at Mum and raise my eyebrows.

'I found them at this gorgeous little op shop in town,' Mum says. 'Picked out things I thought you might like. Do you like them?'

The mean part of me wants to say, 'No, I hate them, I hate everything about this place.' But, actually, the room looks like the kind of room someone might show off on social media.

'You did a good job. When did you have time to . . .?'

'Well, I've been here a while now,' she says.

Of course. Seven weeks since we've not been a family. I've been telling myself the unit is temporary. A short-term holiday rental. I call it 'the unit', not 'Mum's unit'. 'The unit' could belong to all of us. Some parents buy a holiday apartment. Others rent one. This could be our holiday apartment. That sounds normal, even if seven weeks is a long holiday. Thinking of it like this is the only way to soothe myself. Mum will get happier, they'll get back together; these things take time. Even if this space looks long term, nothing is forever.

Mum shows me through the rest of the unit. Lachy's room, decked out in space motifs, with a planet bedspread and a universe light projector for his ceiling. Mum's room, with its neatly made queen bed, tassel pillows and patchwork quilt. There are still a couple of unpacked boxes stacked in one corner and her walls are still blank, but her room has a window that looks out over the garden. I pull the curtains back and Mum is at my side.

'Feels kind of like you're in the jungle, huh?' she says.

Mum has somehow managed to find the only apartment complex in town that is set out like a nature park, with little pathways running through the foliage.

'And the best part? I don't have to look after the gardens,' she says. 'They have a gardener here who does all the work. I just pay the rent.'

She shows me the bathroom, which she's decorated with a few succulent plants, and then we move to the kitchen.

'It's only small,' she says, 'but the fridge and the cupboard are stocked, so help yourself to anything. I got those cheese and onion chips you like, and there's chocolate milk in the fridge. I bought pancakes for breakfast too.'

'Mum,' I say. *Stop trying so hard.*

'Yeah?'

'Nothing,' I say.

I notice tears welling in Mum's eyes. 'Tell me you like it,' she says. 'I want that so much. Please tell me you like it.'

'Oh, Mum.'

She looks small and childlike.

'Can I give my girl a cuddle?' she says, opening her arms. 'Will you let me?' I nod, and she wraps me up, her fingers clinging to my hair, her nose breathing me in deeply. 'Oh, I have missed you,' she says. 'There's been a part of my heart missing without you. Part of me, gone. We need each other so much.' She sniffs back her tears. 'I want you kids to be happy here, to visit me. I don't want to lose you,' she chokes.

I hug Mum back. 'This isn't what I want, Mum. None of us do. I mean, it's nice, okay? But it's not what we want.'

'I know, honey.' She strokes my hair. 'I wish it hadn't worked out this way too, but it has. I will always care about Dad and I do hope we'll always be friends. Which is more than most get.'

There are so many things I want to say to her. That she can change the way it's worked out. That she can be Dad's wife, not just his friend. But these conversations only go round in circles, so as an act of generosity, I push my own feelings to one side.

'You won't lose me,' I say to Mum. 'I miss you too much.'

'Thank god for that,' she says, squeezing me tight. 'Because I miss you impossibly.' She laughs and swipes at her eyes. 'Aren't I a fool, blubbering everywhere and I haven't even finished the tour.'

But Mum's not a fool, not at all. I can feel her love for me in every corner of this place, in all the little things she has prepared for me. Even though I don't want any of it.

Twenty-Two

Mum's balcony overlooks a curvy aqua pool, the surface of the water shimmering like silver discs. We take the pebbled path through the frost-bitten air to get there, our breaths making lines of steam.

'This is only for the brave,' Mum said, her teeth chattering.

Blades of a winter breeze cut through our clothes, bite into the bare skin of our feet. I squint through the darkness towards Mount Wilderness. I know where this wind comes from, I know she who breathes it, even if she is hiding in the dark. My towel is clenched to my chest as we reach the pool edged with palm trees lit up by fairy lights. The water is vivid like some magical green potion against a dying twilight. Ghostly steam rises off its luminescent surface.

'Bit different?' Mum says.

I nod. The murky banks of Crooked River are probably

edged with ice crystals tonight.

'It's heated all year round, so it feels like the Bahamas once you're in,' Mum says, her teeth chattering so loudly I can hear them clacking.

I laugh. 'Nothing could be f-further from the Bahamas. It's about ready to s-snow.'

We strip off our clothes on a banana chair. The first stars are peeking out of the frosty night, as the crisp air nibbles goosebumps along our arms.

We line up side by side along the tiled edge of the pool, two bodies quaking with cold. One short squeal, one small splash, and Mum's body is rippling through the water like a silvery fish. She bursts off the bottom like a rocket, pushing the hair off her face and exhaling as she turns to face me.

'It's so warm!' she says, 'Get in!'

My feet are cold stones, so cold they are burning from the icy ground, but I take a breath and dive in after her, my body swallowed by a blurry underworld. A green bubbly silence. My feet tingle back to life, my entire body shivering with delight as I stretch out, carving a path with long arm strokes across the pebbled pool floor. I am a mermaid, the water warm and soothing against my bumpy skin. I want to stay under where it is warm and silent. In this magical between-world, but then air beckons me up. When I break through the surface, my hair is slicked back and I am panting, breathless.

Mum is on her back, treading water with her hands, her tummy and legs floating, her eyes reflecting the fairy lights twined up the trunks of the palm trees.

'I love watching the moon rise,' Mum says. 'I do it every night. Look.'

And I turn in the direction she's pointing. A bright amber glow hovers over the tree line.

'Just a couple more minutes,' Mum says, 'then watch how the stars dim to make way for their moon.'

I float on my back like her and look up at the palm-fringed inky sky, pricked with starlight.

'Why do you think it is we so love the moon?' Mum muses.

'I don't know,' I say. 'We need the sun more.'

'Maybe it's because she's mystical, the stuff of quiet afterlight, and midnight and secrets. Her light is pale, more forgiving than the sun. Nobody ever got burnt by the moon.' Mum spins herself in a revolution on the surface of the water. 'Or maybe we love the moon because when all the world has gone to bed, we can make magic. It's well established among artists that the darkest hours hold the greatest creativity. Did you know that? Look, here she comes.'

We watch as the moon rises, minute by minute, above the treetops, a crooked sliver of a smile dangling beneath the stars.

Our ears and our hair are arctic by the time we stop watching and dive back beneath the liquid warmth, our scalps shivering to life. And in the slow burbly underworld, we dive and swoop, two silver fish darting through a green sea. We tumble and somersault until we're giddy with butterflies, until we're both panting and hunched over the steely edge of the pool, breathless and laughing.

This. This is the mum I want to remember.

'Okay, time to be even braver,' Mum says, looking sideways at me. 'Getting out is always harder. Trust me on that one. You ready?'

We hoist ourselves out of the glow, the warmth, and into the cruel biting breeze, the ground like ice bricks beneath our feet. We half-shuffle, half-run, jaws clenched, bodies shuddering, our limbs stiff with ice until we push through the door to the unit. Mum lets me shower first as she turns the heating up inside, and the shower is steaming, scalding, shivery. It brings me back to life. When I go to my room afterwards, Mum has left on my bed warm fluffy socks, track pants and a jumper. She showers and we make warm cups of tea with chocolate biscuits. Mum plays soft music. I grab hold of these things in my mind, adding them to my list.

Here's what I get to keep:

The sound of Mum's voice.

Night swims.

Chocolate biscuits and tea.

Warm fluffy socks.

Track pants and jumpers.

Hot showers.

Music.

A warm bed on winter nights.

I get to keep them all. Even in the unit, with its smells of other people's dinners wafting into our living room: garlic, and curry and stir fry.

I hear voices rising and falling nearby and I look towards the balcony.

'It's people going down the stairwell,' Mum says. 'Took me a little while to get used to that.'

I can see right into the glow of other living rooms in other apartments. In one, a mother sits on a lounge with a young child. In another, a man stands at the kitchen bench, hunched over something. They must be able to see us too. It's a naked feeling, but nobody else seems bothered or interested.

When we finish our tea, Mum takes both our mugs up to the sink. 'So, I've applied for a job,' she says. 'Teaching art at the community college in town. For adults mostly.' Mum fidgets as she says it. 'I don't know if I'll get the position, but I'm going to give it a red-hot go.'

I'm quiet for a little while, nibbling on my cookie. Mum used to work at our school. I try imagining her in a new job. A new place. Teaching adults, not kids. And I can see by the reckless way she's washing up our mugs that she's pretending not to care. Which means she cares. A lot.

'Well, you're qualified, Mum. You have a degree in fine arts.'

'Yes, but that was a long time ago, El. It's been a while since I've worked. I'm just going to be patient. The right opportunity will come at the right time.'

'You didn't apply for jobs before,' I say. 'Why are you applying now?'

What I mean is, did you have to leave us to get a job? Why couldn't you have stayed with us and made all these changes? Bought new furniture and new bedspreads, applied for new jobs.

Mum stops drying the mug in her hand. 'To be honest, I wasn't in a great headspace after Nanna died. But I wasn't happy before then either. It was only recently that I was able to start thinking about Dad and I again. About what happened to our love, where it went. And I need an income to support us now,' she says.

I've never thought about this before. How does she pay rent for the unit? Do Mum and Dad still share their money, keep the same joint bank account? Or do they have to split it all now? Mum hasn't got a job yet. How is she surviving?

'You and Dad are still sharing money, though, aren't you?'

She waves her hand through the air like it's nothing. 'Yes, yes, we're still sharing, but at some stage I'll need to stand on my own feet. Anyway, that's not something for you to worry about, honey, that's something for Dad and me to sort out in time. We have more important things to talk about than silly old money.'

But the way she says silly old money makes my stomach churn. Money is survival.

Twenty-Three

Mum curls up beside me on the lounge, and tucks a blanket around us. There are things I have decided to ask her while I'm here. Just in case I don't see her again for a while.

'You know when you fell in love with Dad?' I ask her.

'Mmm?'

'Was that a scary feeling?'

Mum thinks for a second. 'It was terrifying,' she says. 'And when I think back on it, there's not much of my life that I planned. I certainly didn't plan to fall in love with Dad, I wasn't even meant to be in this town. I was so young.' Mum smiles wistfully. 'Straight out of uni and full of ambition, full of optimism. I'd been offered my first job at this incredible art centre in the city.' Her eyes shine.

'Why didn't you take it?'

'Well, the centre caught fire the month before I was due to

start work and it was shut down for the next year, so I looked for a stop-gap. Just a job to pass the time. I was offered a decent salary to move to town here and teach art therapy in a healing centre. Little did I know, your Nan Gillespie was among my students. She was softly-spoken, still grieving the loss of Pa. Everyone in the centre was healing from some sort of pain, but I really liked your Nan Gillespie. She was one of my favourites. There was a real vulnerability about her. And one day, your dad came into the class to pick her up. Nan Gillespie showed him what she was working on, and introduced me to her son. Dad kept looking at me oddly and I wondered if he thought I was also a student. So I explained to him that I was teaching the class. He looked kind of bewildered. I guess I *was* very young to be teaching, I was only twenty-one. A baby!' Mum sweeps the hair off her face and puts down her mug on the table. 'After that, Dad would come to class each week to drop Nan Gillespie off and pick her up. I watched how careful he was with his mum, how he never rushed her, the interest he took in her work. She was very frail for her age, Nan Gillespie, and he was patient and protective of her. The three of us would talk and he would make me laugh.

'Then one day, after taking Nan Gillespie back to his car, Dad reappeared in the class. I was just washing out the brushes. I'll never forget how serious he looked, fiddling with his belt buckle, as he asked me if I'd like to go out to dinner with him somewhere. I thought he meant all three of us, and I said, "Sure, I don't know many places in town, but where do you and your mum like to eat?" His face flushed red as a tomato. But to his credit, he stayed there in front of me and clarified that he himself would like to take me out to dinner, if I'd like to go with him. I think that's when I first started to fall a little bit in love with your dad. And then during that first dinner out in a small booth at the back of the hotel, I fell a little bit more in love with him. He was so very real. He was textured, and serious and responsible, not at all like the guys I'd met at uni, who were only looking to have fun. And very soon, I was completely and utterly in love with Dad. The kind of love that was beyond my control. Like being strapped into a rollercoaster ride, all consuming. I couldn't have stopped it even if I'd wanted to. And I didn't want to, because it was thrilling.'

I smile at the thought of my parents being young and in love. 'Were you ever worried that it might not work?'

'Yes, of course I was. Me being far away from my family, far from the only city I knew, I was worried I'd be homesick, and I was. When Dad asked me to marry him, and start a life with him, I gave up that job in the city at the art centre. I gave it all away because the thought of returning to the city, the thought of going anywhere at all where he wasn't, was just unbearable to me. And he couldn't leave his mum. So I left mine. I left my home, my family and my aspirations in the city, and for the first couple of years, I cried a lot. But I was also determined that it *would* work.' Mum clasps her hands together tightly, looks down at them. Her eyes are watery. 'We'd *make* it work. Nobody knows, really, if they're still going to be in love ten, twenty years down the track. Falling in love is leaping into a valley and hope the other person catches you. Loving someone deeply means walking along the edge of your darkest fears, and it means being open to losing them too, the way I lost Nanna, the way Dad lost Pa and Nan Gillespie, the way I lost your dad. There are many paths to losing someone you love.'

Mum grabs a tissue and catches her tears as they fall. Almost like she's used to crying now. She knows how to keep it silent, when to catch them.

'Do you regret coming here, taking that job, meeting Dad?' I ask. 'I mean, obviously you regret marrying him.'

'No,' she says sharply. 'I don't regret any of it. I don't believe in regrets. If I'd not met Dad, I'd have had another life entirely. And that life wouldn't include you. It wouldn't include Lachy. I wouldn't be who I am now, and Dad would be different too. A writer called Robert Louis Stevenson once said, "Everybody, soon or late, sits down to a banquet of consequences." I made my choices. Those choices had consequences and two of those consequences were the most delightful children on the planet. So I'm very happy to sit down with them.'

I realise, suddenly, all over again, how scared I've been

of losing Mum. If she could leave Dad behind, maybe she'd leave us too? Maybe we hadn't made her proud enough or happy enough, maybe she regretted everything about her life, including us. But even though I've spent weeks rejecting her, I can see that her love for me still burns bright.

'Have I ever told you about the night that you were born?' Mum asks.

I know this story inside and out. 'Dad's told me the story,' I say.

'Well, Dad's version of the story is a little bit different to mine,' she says. 'Just warning you. Because the night you were born was the most terrifying night of my life.' Her hands tremble and she clenches them together. 'See, a storm was raging outside and the wind rattled through the house like it was made of bones.' Her voice is tight. 'I imagined the wind stripping planks off the house, one by one. All day I'd carried this ache in the pit of my belly. No pains, just an ache. But you were three weeks off due and I didn't want to be dramatic. If there's one thing Gillespies have never been, it's dramatic.'

I think of how I collapsed by the Pa Tree. Maybe I'm changing the trend.

'Another thing Gillespies don't do is make a fuss.'

I think of the fuss I made the other night with Dad in the kitchen. When I threw every mean thought I had at him. I think Mum underestimates the Gillespies.

'I didn't want to stress your dad out. So I said nothing, and while he was busy outside, I stole away upstairs to run myself a warm bubble bath. Then I soaked in it a long time and I felt better. Weightless, warm, relaxed. The wind whistled through the eaves and moaned through the cracks in the roof, but inside I was safe.' She sits a little straighter, pulling the blanket tighter around us. 'I remember climbing out of the bath, careful not to slip because my tummy was so big and full of you that it could throw me off balance. I pulled on my dressing gown, and I can still feel its soft fleece against my steaming skin.

'The afternoon had grown dark and the house with it. Much darker than it should have been. I remember opening the door to the back deck and the wind gusting in around me, leaves blowing inside. I looked up at Mount Wilderness, who was bearing down on our little house, clouds gathered round her head like a crown. She had become to me a spectre, a mighty wonder who brought us rain, and icy winds and storms that shook our world into submission. I wrapped my dressing gown tighter around me and shivered, trying to keep the wind from biting my bare legs, but the wind did not care for my chills—it had a life and a will of its own. Some instinct inside me trembled. I knew Mount Wilderness was going to throw all her might our way in a few short hours. Maybe you knew it too.

'As the light faded, the storm gathered her strength. The rain marbled big on our tin roof and then it volleyed down.

The first strike of lightning came like a match struck in the darkness. I was adding a log to the fire when it happened.

'The sky growled and suddenly, I felt a pop inside me. A gush. Warm water down my legs. A pain gripped my stomach.

'Mount Wilderness did not care one bit. She was too busy unleashing on us. She did not care that you were coming.

'My body shook with terror and I called out to Dad. Quietly at first, then louder. But the wind and the rain snatched my voice away. The evening was loud, violent, aggressive. And Dad was outside frantically gathering the last of the wood. I yelled until he blew in, arms full of rough-chopped wood. The next pain followed and I leant on the lounge, bent over in its grip as I clutched my belly. Pain followed pain, and then Dad was calling the hospital. *Help will come*, I thought. *Help will come.*

'A fork of lightning split the darkness outside and I felt like it went right through me, the pain was so great. It felt like Mount Wilderness herself had reached down and grabbed hold of my stomach in her fist. I cried out as the storm howled against our roof, our walls, our land.

'That's when I knew we were too late. I *knew*. You were coming too soon and we'd left it too late. Would you be like one of the cold, little lost babies in the cemetery? Come too soon and too far from help?

'No. I wouldn't allow it. I had cared for you so tenderly those last months. Had eaten well, and slept well and stroked you inside my tummy. Nobody had ever loved anything as much as I loved you. We had plans for you, so many plans. Mount Wilderness was not going to take them.

'"To the car," I gasped to Dad, pointing at the front door. But Dad was still on the phone, and another pain seized me. I couldn't move, couldn't talk, could only grit my teeth and breathe. I cried out.

'Dad put the midwife on speaker. "Too late," she said to Dad. "That baby will be born in the car if you leave. The roads are too dangerous."

'I looked at Dad and I'm sure he saw the fear in my eyes, the sweat on my upper lip. We were on our own. No hospital, no midwives, no doctors. Out in the middle of a wild storm with no help. I had never felt so scared. Neither of us knew a thing about delivering a baby, especially not our own.

'But the midwife's voice was calm on loudspeaker, almost bossy. "Dad, I want you to get some towels," she said. "Can you do that?"

'We shared a look at each other. Mute with something between terror and awe. She'd called him "Dad". Which is exactly what he was about to become. A father. And I, a mother.

'"Towels," Dad repeated. Everything the midwife told him to do, Dad did, while I stayed by the lounge, struck by the pains that came thick and fast. There was no break between one pain ending and another beginning. Even if I'd tried to get to the car,

I couldn't have. I couldn't move a single step.'

I watch Mum's animated face, her flushed cheeks, telling me this story, and I realise that this is a new story. I haven't heard this one. Not this way.

'I was on all fours, like a cat, on the living room floor before the fire, terrified you would be born sleeping as my body started making noises. "Sounds like she's pushing," the midwife said.

'I shook my head. "Too soon," I gasped. "Too fast." The midwife must have heard me, because she responded very sternly. "Nonsense. Babies come when *they're* ready, not when we are. Now, Mum, I need you to listen to your body. Dad, get ready to catch this baby."

'I remember someone bellowing like a wounded buffalo, and realising that someone was me. The wild animal I'd become. There was a splitting pain, then, suddenly, no more pain. Just a tiny, naked little baby on a towel on the living room floor. One minute inside me, the next minute out.

'Dad wrapped you in the towel and lifted you to me, through my trembling legs, and I held your wet, warm, skinny little body to my chest as I knelt back on my knees. My body was shaking so hard I could barely sit up, so I slumped sideways against the lounge.

'"Do you want to check or will I?" Dad asked.

'"Check what?" I was numb. Not exactly sure what had just happened to me. I wondered if maybe I'd been in some sort of accident.

'"The baby," Dad said.

'"Oh." I'd just had a baby, that's what had happened. Our baby had been born. "You check."

'Dad came around to the front of me, peeled back the towel, moved your umbilical cord out of the way and his eyes welled up. He looked into your face as he spoke. "Why, hello, little princess."

'"A girl?"

'Dad touched your face. "Not just a girl, *our* girl. The most beautiful thing alive." Tears were falling down his cheeks.

'Then there was no more lightning. There were just red and blue lights flashing outside and the clomping of shoes through the front door. There were two paramedics checking you, checking me, cutting your umbilical cord, taking us in the back of their ambulance to the hospital. And you lay alongside me, blinking in the light. Tiny little you, the centre of a world of drama. Very much unlike a Gillespie.'

I laugh, choking back a tear. 'I think I might still be very much unlike a Gillespie,' I say. 'Still a drama queen.'

'And don't you ever change,' Mum says, pulling me to her in a one-armed cuddle. 'It took me weeks to process your birth. The speed of it, the terror, the shock, how wrong it could have gone. I didn't get to enjoy those first weeks. But I got to enjoy the weeks that followed.

'The thing is, your birth was so much like life. Things happen—unpredictable twists and turns—almost like our lives are plotted to a script we don't get to read. And that script is full of surprises and shocks, and none of us know if there's a master design behind any of it or what's coming next. None of us truly know where we start, or where we end or what we endure in between. But that's where *you* began, my dear Elliott. That was your opening page. It was pretty darn spectacular.'

I realise now that I've only ever heard Dad's stories. And as much as I love Dad's stories, they're one side of the coin. They are his view, his version, and I took them for the only version. I took them for truth. I've never really heard what Mum saw, or felt or did. And I don't think I've ever really asked. Two people can tell different versions of the same story and both be right, both be wrong. Like the colours of a rainbow, the truth is split across a spectrum.

'Dad is a hopeless romantic,' Mum says. Almost like she's read my mind. 'But his stories about us aren't how I felt. They're not what I lived. A lot of people in Crooked River have had tough hard lives. Look at the graveyard, littered with babies, children, young women and men. They died out there over the years—from exposure, from swollen rivers, falling trees, accidents, infections, too far from hospitals.

'When Dad first showed me his world at Crooked River, I fell in love with the land. The majesty of the mountains, the chill wind that blew off their snow-capped tops, the way the snowflakes floated from the slate sky in winter and the crackling of the fire in the warm hearth inside. Back then, I didn't know what the land would take. I didn't know the cost of its beauty, or the cost of becoming part of Dad's world. When Dad took me picnicking up the top of Mount Wilderness one spring afternoon, we looked down over the patchwork earth and Dad got down on one knee and asked me to marry him. The sun was warm on our faces, the ring sparkled in its light, the whole world sparkled. It was a beautiful sun-drenched world. And I said yes. I loved him, so I said yes. It didn't matter that we were so young or that we'd barely known each other six months. He didn't lie to me; Dad never lied. I knew marrying him meant living in his house at Crooked River. He made it clear that he could never leave. Not with the history, not with Pa there. Pa knew the cost of Crooked River, though. He'd been married before.'

I look at Mum and frown. 'Before Nan Gillespie?'

'Yes.'

'To *who*?' This is a ridiculous piece of information. 'Who else was Pa married to?'

'I thought you knew?' she asks.

I shake my head.

'It's not really my story to tell, but it's no secret.'

'Are you sure?' I say. A sick feeling unfurls inside my stomach like smoke. It writhes and snakes around inside me. It feels like betrayal.

'I can only tell you what I know,' says Mum. 'It may not all be true, honey. This is just what I've heard over the years.'

I close my eyes. Steady myself to be unsteadied. Lately, life seems like a whole lot of unsteadying.

'Before Nan Gillespie, before your dad was even born, Pa married a lady named Rose. From what I understand, Rose was very smart. She was strong and she challenged Pa. A lot. There were some big fights. Loud fights. There must be some truth to it, because after she and Pa had three babies and all three of them died, she left Pa. Which wasn't an easy thing, back in their day. It's not even an easy thing to do now, but back then, women were expected to get married and stay married.

'To be left was devastating for Pa. He begged Rose to stay. She said no, life with Pa had been too much. She'd lost too much. To him and the land. Three babies was enough. So Rose moved back to town. She chose what she needed to do to survive. Which might sound selfish, but it takes serious guts to put yourself first, especially when doing so will hurt someone else. And, oh boy, did it hurt Pa. I've seen their letters—he kept them all through the years. He wrote, begging her to come back. She couldn't, wouldn't. And Pa, it seemed, couldn't leave the land and follow her to town. The Gillespies grow roots in that place. And Pa, he grew a bit older, a bit wiser, before he met Nan. Fell in love again, except Nan Gillespie shared his love of the land. Not long after Pa and Nan Gillespie got married, Dad was born. Strange, isn't it?' Mum strokes my cheek with the back of her fingertips. 'If Rose had stayed with Pa, you wouldn't even exist. We wouldn't be here having this conversation right now.'

I try to rearrange the Pa in my head with this other version Mum has just given me. I like *my* version better.

'Why are you telling me this?' I say. My eyes well with tears. 'I love Pa.'

'Of course you do. Sweetheart, Pa was a lovely man, and he's very much worth loving. But we all have histories and stories that make us. Nobody knows them all, except ourselves, and real stories are rarely clean and tidy. They don't follow a straight course on a map. But when Pa's first plan didn't work out, life opened another one. And because of that, a whole new generation was born. Because of that, life made way for you and Lachy.'

I don't like where Mum is heading with this.

'I don't want a new plan for Dad. New kids, or a new wife, or new anything. I just want us. The way we are. The way we were, I mean.'

Mum gives me a soft smile. 'I love your Dad, El. I'll always love him. He's part of my story. You and Lachy are made of him. But I can't keep travelling along a life path that is no longer feeding me. I'm thirty-seven now, not twenty-one. Nearly half my life is behind me, hopefully the other half stretching ahead. Our lives on earth are nothing more than a blink in the dust of eternity. We need to spend our time here wisely, with the people who make us the best versions of ourselves. I know leaving my marriage seems like a foolish thing to you, I know it does.' She looks at me for a response, but I look away. 'You and Lachy see us as Mum and Dad, but actually we're more than those titles. We're people, Dad and I. Two very different people, it turns out, both wanting different things. Always have wanted different things, I suppose. Dad's happy on the land. He could live by Crooked River all his life. Dad has no need to travel or explore the world. He's content where he is.'

'I'm content too. We live in a magical place. Have you forgotten how lucky we are?'

'Oh, honey.' Mum tucks a strand of hair behind my ear. 'I haven't forgotten. Yes, we've been very lucky, but life's not just about luck, it's also about needs. Very different needs. Dad's a practical man—fixing fences, chopping wood, managing floods, and fires and storms. He was exciting when we first met, so very different to me. I was a city girl. I'd grown up with books, and museums and art galleries. I had dreams of all the travelling we'd one day do. Trekking far off places around the world!' Mum sighs, and smiles, staring off at some vision of her life only she can see.

'Dad had different dreams,' she says. 'He dreamt of a life on his family's land. Dad showed me all around his world, invited me into it, and we swam in the river, we ate wild plums from the Pa Tree, we rode on his quad bike. We climbed Mount Wilderness and drank local wine, watched the sunset from the back deck. And it was all magical. I fell for the limitless star-spangled sky towering with cumulus cloud and the smell of the wood fire. It was like living inside a storybook. *His* storybook. We accomplished all of his dreams, and I wanted to show him mine. I wanted him to explore art galleries with me, go for high tea in the English gardens of a castle, climb bridges and sky scrapers. When I learnt later that Dad had no interest in art galleries and he hated the crowded cities, I hid my disappointment. It wasn't his fault. He isn't wired to appreciate art or big, old sandstone buildings. He can't change who he is. He shouldn't have to.

'But one day I woke up and realised that I had changed who *I* was. What *I* loved. I had given up all my dreams to be what Dad needed, and I no longer knew what was left inside me. Who even was I, outside of Dad, his land, his house, the mother of his children? I had surrendered everything that made me sparkle, everything that gave me purpose. I came to Dad as an artist. That's who he fell in love with, and who I loved being, but over the years, I became a hollowed-out husk. The cocoon left behind after the chrysalis has emerged.

Where was the butterfly? Nobody should give up on the butterfly.'

Mum clasps her hands together in her lap. She takes a deep shaky breath. 'When Nanna died, I realised how much I'd lost. Time I could never get back. Promises Dad had made about trips to the city, time with my family. It wasn't his fault we couldn't afford it, but his mum had been looked after by us, he'd spent all his time with his mum and mine was gone. She'd died all alone. I'd let that happen without stamping my foot down and demanding what I needed. You and Lachy also missed out on precious time getting to know my family. I let that happen. I am as guilty as Dad is. I'm also guilty of not always knowing what I needed, but I know now.' Mum looks up at me, her hands still clasped in her lap, prayer-like. Her voice is steady. 'I need something different for myself. I have to honour that feeling inside of me, right here . . .' She touches her breastbone. '. . . which says this is the right thing. It wounds me deeply that what's right for me hurts the people I love the most. I want you to understand how much I have hurt for you, El.' Her blue eyes are clearer than I've seen them, prettier than I've ever noticed, pricking with tears. 'Do you know that?'

If I dig really deep, I do know this.

'I hope one day you can understand.' She is whispering as she clasps my hands in both of hers. 'This was not a choice I made lightly. In choosing me, I am choosing *you*. I'm choosing to be the best version of me so that you can have me for the long haul.' A tear runs down Mum's cheek, and she lets its silver track stay on her face. Unhidden. 'You and Lachy will always be ours. Half mine, half Dad's. We both made you, raised you, and we'll keep doing that, it's our job. It's all we care about. But Dad and I need different things. I've invested a big and important chunk of my life with Dad, and him with me. But we're not each other's people anymore. We haven't been making each other happy for a long time. We've been existing, side by side, maybe as friends, but not as partners. Life has called each of us to different beginnings. And life is all about beginnings. It's the grandest adventure of the spirit. It's what we're born for.

'So I want you to meet life where you need it to meet you. If you can't see a track through the forest, slash one yourself. Even if the track is scary and the destination unknown. I want that for you. I want you to go through life choosing yourself, El, because trust me, nobody else will. And one day, when you're older, I want you to remember me telling you this. *Choose yourself.* You don't need anyone's permission but your own.'

Mum cuddles me and tells me how much she loves me, how much she wants me always in her life. And we sit in silence a long time, sipping tea on the lounge.

That's when I know this is not going away. Mum leaving is permanent. This is forever. I will join the club of kids who split their time between two homes. Yet somehow my lungs are still working. I am still breathing. And Mum is beside me, still holding my hand.

Twenty-Four

A week later, I wake in the dark. Dad's house or Mum's? Dad's. Definitely Dad's. Only I'm shivering and disoriented. I must have kicked my blankets off in my sleep. The night is a dark cloud that warps my vision. I don't know the time, I know only that my mouth is dry as a camel's in the desert and I won't sleep till morning if I don't water it. So I roll out of bed, put on my slippers and head out the door.

A glow is coming from beneath the kitchen door. When I open it, the light is bright in my eyes. I squint, blinking, shielding my face.

'Dad?' I mumble.

He jumps in his seat at the dining table, holds his hand to his chest. 'You scared me, sweetheart. Don't creep up on me like that.'

I pour myself a glass of water, finish it. Pour another.

'I wasn't creeping.'

As my eyes adjust, I notice he has a bunch of papers sprawled across the table. There are figures scrawled down them in lines.

'What are you doing?' I ask. Dad's wearing a beanie and his fleece dressing gown. 'It's so cold in here, you should go to bed.'

'Yeah, I was just crunching a few numbers,' Dad says. His ears are burning red, his eyes bloodshot.

'Is everything okay?'

'Yeah, I was just looking at a few different things.' He slides the papers together into a neat pile and stands up.

'What's even the time?' I ask.

'Too late, and I'm going to bed.' He kisses me on the forehead. 'You go back to bed too. Night, sweetheart.'

'Night.'

I leave the kitchen before Dad, put the glass of water next to my bed and climb into my blankets. I go back to sleep, but my mind is uneasy and I rattle between dreams without getting any real rest.

It's a dull, cold morning when a car pulls up to the house. I hear the crunch of tyres on gravel as it approaches, Snow's three-bark warning. I recognise the four-wheel-drive as it parks out the front of our gate. I recognise the two people who get out of it. The first is pushing black-framed glasses up the bridge of his nose, a black beanie pulled low over his ears to match, and the other is holding a baking dish covered in aluminium foil.

'Hiya,' Bec says as I open the front door. 'How you doing, sweetie?' Her breath comes out in small clouds of fog.

'Good,' I say. 'What's going on?' I look at the dish in her hands.

'We didn't call; we're a bit rude like that. I was just wondering if your dad's around? I'm hoping to borrow a hammer drill. And this . . .' She lifts the tray in her hand. '. . . is my down payment.'

'You don't need to pay—'

'Shush. I don't take without giving.'

Just then I hear footsteps in the living room behind me. I duck my head behind the front door and there is Dad, a towel wrapped round his waist, hair wet, dripping ringlets down his chest.

'Umm,' I say quietly, 'we have visitors.'

'Oh.' Dad backs out of the living room.

'You guys want to come in out of the cold?' I ask, opening the door to full extension.

'Please. It's so bitter out.' Bec follows me into the kitchen and rests the dish on the counter just as Dad comes back wearing trackpants and a fleece jumper. 'You like chicken lasagne, right?'

'Oh, ah . . .' Dad shakes his head. 'You really didn't need to—'

Bec holds up her hand. 'It's not charity. It's payment. See, we're in a bit of a pickle with a cabinet we need to install at home,' she says, 'and I was just wondering if we could borrow your hammer drill.'

'Yeah, of course,' Dad says. 'But you didn't need to bake for us. We're fine.'

'He always this ungrateful?' she asks me.

I hit the kettle. 'Mostly. Cuppa?'

'I won't say no to that,' Bec replies, rubbing her hands together.

I know Dad probably wishes she'd just leave. He's not one for small talk. But I'm going to teach him a few lessons about entertaining the neighbours.

I make us all tea, and we sit in front of the fire talking about the snow dusting the top of Mount Wilderness, and when the river might drop. We dance around everything except the fact that Mum is missing. And Lachy, who is having his weekend with Mum.

When Dad takes Bec outside to show her how to work the hammer drill, Drake and I head to the front of the house. The sky is the colour of salt, hung low with cloud, the air like needles against our skin.

'Want to go for a quick wander?' Drake asks.

'Nice day for it,' I joke. But a thrill bubbles up inside me. If he asked me to go for a quick wander in a pouring rain, I would want to be with Drake. I would still say yes.

I grab a scarf, a beanie, and then we head out the front door.

'Snow,' I whisper under the house. She opens her eyes, lifts her head, and I can hear the swish of her tail as she wriggles out from under the latticework. 'Want to go for a walk, girl?'

Her tail swishes and she barks, once.

We head off in the direction of Mount Wilderness, her snow-caps brilliant against her green grass, the earth underfoot crunchy with frost. Snow limps along beside us.

'Poor girl, she's a bit stiff in the winter,' I say. 'Arthritis must really suck.'

Snow keeps up with us mostly. She's just a bit slower, takes her time stopping every so often to sniff at a fence post or a tuft of iced-over grass. It's only when we follow an old goat track winding along the river's edge, that I realise we've lost Snow. I turn back to look for her, only to find that she has stopped to rest on a shale rock, panting.

'Come on, girl,' I say patting at my knees to encourage her. She doesn't get up. 'Don't be so lazy.'

Snow huffs and looks away from me. Clearly, she's done. Not going any further in the cold. We backtrack to meet her and sit beside her on the rock, which is cool but not ice-addled like the earth.

'You know the hammer drill was an excuse, right?' Drake says, smirking.

'What do you mean?' I say. 'Bec's not trying to hit on my dad, is she?!'

'No!' Drake doubles over laughing.

'Oh, thank goodness. I can't take any more shocks.'

'She is checking in on him,' he says. 'Seeing if he's okay. Which is slightly different to hitting on him. Mum told me that after Dad left, she had two big surprises. One was the people she thought she could count on who didn't check in with her. The second was the people she expected nothing from who stepped in with food, and chocolate, and tea and support. She wanted to be the second kind of person for your dad. But what I meant was, *I* was the one who told her to come over and ask for the drill today. I wanted an excuse to see you.' He grins and looks away from me, like he's suddenly shy.

'Oh.' It feels like a small fire has been lit inside me. Could Drake like me like *that*? Could he really? I'd started to believe I'd dreamt that afternoon in the grass. 'Well, that's kinda nice of Bec. And of you. You are a good egg, Drake,' I say. 'A very good egg.'

Drake squints. 'Yeah, you're not a bad egg yourself. In fact, you're looking more like a bear than an egg, with those pompoms.' He flicks the pompoms on top of my beanie. 'A very cute bear.'

I look away, because I can feel my face flushing, but thankfully Drake changes the subject.

'How's your dad, though?' he asks. 'He's looking a little less than cute. He looks a bit . . .'

'Like death?' I say.

'A shade more alive than that.'

'He's improving. Eating again. He actually sang off-key rock to me the other night, so that's a good sign, I guess. The day Mum left, he was pretty ghastly. Not that I can talk.' I grimace at the memory of Drake in our living room. Watching me at my worst, at my ugliest, my weakest.

'For what it's worth, I think you're doing well too. You've even been to your mum's.'

'To "the unit". Let's just call it "the unit". Not Mum's.'

He nods. 'So how *was* "the unit"?'

I screw my mouth to one side. 'I wanted to hate it.'

He laughs. 'Of course you did. Elliott hates anything new. And did you?'

'Unfortunately, no.'

He laughs again. 'What a shame.'

'She had it looking pretty great. And we went for a night swim together, which is the first time I've done anything like that with Mum in forever.'

'Wow.'

'Yeah,' I say. 'She's applied for a new job too.' I pick at a loose bit of shale beside me. Something felt just a little bit off about the way she told me.

'That's great,' Drake says. 'I guess she needs to cover the rent.'

'Yeah.'

I remember Dad's face last night when he was crunching numbers in the kitchen. The red flush that crept up his neck when I found him there. Almost like he'd been caught out doing something wrong.

'Hey,' I say. 'When your dad left, what did your parents do about money?'

'Man, El, I have no idea. It was so long ago. I just know they sold their house and split whatever they got from it. A while later, Mum bought the land here. Why?'

I bite the inside of my cheek, unsure if I should tell him. It was probably nothing.

'I might be overthinking things, but last night—I mean really late last night, I'm not sure of the exact time—I got out of bed to get a drink from the kitchen and the light was on. Dad was sitting at the table with a calculator.' I suddenly remember the detail about the calculator. When I was half asleep, I didn't really register that but it feels important now. 'He had sheets of paper in front of him, a pen in his hand and he'd written down all these numbers. Which isn't a dad thing to do. Dad doesn't budget, he doesn't number crunch. Especially at night.'

Drake wraps his arms around his knees. 'Do you know what they're planning to do about divvying up their bank accounts and things?'

I shake my head. 'Too soon for that. But Dad will keep the house. I mean, it's not an ordinary house, it's our history. Maybe Mum will take her car and Dad will give her some money to help her until she gets a job.'

Drake nods. 'It's possible, I guess.'

A whirlwind of panic twists through my stomach. 'It's not just "possible". Dad wouldn't give up the house. Nobody could make him.'

'Of course,' Drake says. 'I wasn't saying he'd have to.'

We sit in silence for a while. I hate that Drake knows more about all of this than I do. I feel like I'm in a dark cave and every so often someone shines a spotlight on the roof of the cave and shows me something awful. Look at that spider over there. It could be dangerous. Maybe not, though. Oh, look, over in that corner, a diseased bat! It could bite you! Who knows if it actually will, though.

'You know,' Drake says after a while. 'Your dad was probably just doing up a new budget. Now that he's running the house. Maybe he was trying to figure out how to help your mum too. I mean, who used to look after the money, and the bills and stuff?"

That's the Drake I like. The sensible practical Drake who assumes nothing.

'Mum,' I say. 'It was a mum job. Bills, the business account, invoices, Mum did all of that. That makes sense.' The tornado inside me whittles out.

I lay back on the rock beside Snow, put my hands behind my head and study the chalky clouds in the broody sky. A light wind moans over us from Mount Wilderness and I shut my eyes to listen to it. Then I feel Drake lie down on the other side of Snow, so I roll to face him and when I open my eyes, his are already open. Watching me.

'I'll always make sure you're okay,' he says. 'No matter what happens. You know that, right?'

I look into his eyes and he looks back into mine like he's making me a promise. I replay that afternoon with him under the Pa Tree, before all this with Mum and Dad started. Him brushing the hair from my eyes. The feeling of his lips on my forehead, our hands knitted together in the sunlight.

'Me too,' I say. 'Even if you want to go off to . . . wherever.'

He props himself up on one elbow, grinning. His eyes are shiny. 'You don't mean that.'

I bite my own smile away. 'I'm trying to. I'm trying.'

'Oh, what?' Drake says, looking back up at the sky. He stands suddenly and laughs, hands outstretched. 'You are kidding me!'

I look up to see small white flakes drifting softly down. Then I am laughing too. I am on my feet beside Drake, holding out my palms.

'It's snowing?!'

I look over at Mount Wilderness and I can no longer see her top. Just a hazy cloud covering her, and soft snowflakes floating slowly towards us, drifting with the breeze.

'I haven't seen snow for years,' I say, looking around at the river, the trees, the far-off hills. In all directions, as far as I can see, snowflakes are falling. A rare gift from Mount Wilderness.

'That!' Drake says, pointing at me.

'What?'

'That look you've got right now. The wonder of it. That's what I love about you.'

We both fall silent at his words. He adjusts his beanie so it's even lower on his face, coughs, goes back to looking at the snow gently drifting around us. It feels like we're inside one of those glass globes, in a magical trembling forest. I reach out for Drake's hand, as snow lands in ice kisses on my skin and melts. Drake gives me his warm palm.

'I'm going to confess that I really like your hands. And I like them most when they're in mine.' I throw my head up to the sky. 'And it's snowing. It's actually, really, completely *snowing*!' I say, grinning.

'Come here, you.' Drake picks me up under my arms and spins me around like a kid.

'I want to make a snowman!' I say in his ear.

'We might need a little more than a dusting for that,' Drake says, putting me down.

'Let it snow, let it snow more!' I yell at Mount Wilderness.

Drake puffs out his chest dramatically. 'I command thee to make it snow more. Elliott the Great demands it!'

But Mount Wilderness doesn't listen. She never does.

On our way home, through a world of white-laced trees, Snow walks between us and I don't care that she's slow or that she needs to stop and rest, because I don't even want to get home.

At school, Frankie and Tamar often tease me about Drake. Frankie says, *Seriously, you're going to marry him one day. I know it in my vegan bones.*

Am not, I say.

Yet today, the thought of being tied to Drake forever isn't entirely unpleasant.

Even if marriage isn't always forever.

I bend over and give Snow a ruffle as she walks beside me.

'How's our girl?' Drake says.

I squint at Drake through the falling snowflakes. '*Our* girl?' I grin. 'Our girl is great.'

I want to keep walking until our hands are chilblained. I don't care how cold it gets, how cruel and hard the wind blows, I want to stay out in the wild with Drake where the talk is easy and my blood is warm with magic. Let us stay locked in this place where nothing hurts and the earth is white with wonder.

Because in a world where everything is being divided, it feels like something new is just beginning to join.

Twenty-Five

'First, it was the river,' I say, as I tell Lachy a story in bed that night. His eyes are closed tightly shut. 'The drumming of it, the rushing, shushing, gushing. The icy sting against our feet, walking, poking, peering. Boats made of sticks and leaves, racing each other to a watery death downstream. Fish and turtles, waterfowl and eels, startled deer and foxes.'

His eyes unclench and I pull the sheets tighter up around his shoulders.

'Then it was the river, trickling, shrinking, cracking, drying. Waterholes, and quartz and smooth coloured stones. Finally, there was the dry. The bare dull bones of the riverbed, crunchy and parched. Treasure hunts for sticks, and stones and broken bones.'

Lachy is quiet now, his breathing softer, more regular.

'After a very long time of the riverbed, a storm came.

Riding like a witch over Mount Wilderness, casting bolts of lightning and sheets of rain. But this wasn't any old storm, Lachy, this was the storm of storms. The drought-breaker. It spread over the house like a blanket, turning all the land black, and then it let go. Water stolen from across the years, it let it all go.

'We were safe inside the house, you and I. Our noses pressed against the window pane, we watched the howling world outside. Clothes, buckets, branches, all blown sideways. Your eyes were big as two moons. Do you remember? You might have been too small.'

'No, no,' Lachy nods, his eyes again two moons. 'I wememba.'

I take his hands in mine and squeeze them. 'We hadn't seen rain in years. Not proper rain. Not like that. Do you remember us yelling through the house? Squealing and dancing as the rain hammered on the roof? Do you remember the noise? It was the roar of a jet engine. It drowned out even our screams. We ran circles round the living room and Dad picked Mum up and kissed her. Then he opened a bottle of wine. "I was saving this for something special," he said. Do you remember, Lach?'

Lachy nods, his eyes shining. 'I wememba. Dad said it was special because the tanks wuh full again.'

'That's right, but not just the tanks. It was the river again. The river and us.'

I tuck him in, pulling the blankets all the way up to his chin, the way I used to love when I was his age.

'Tell me anotha stowy,' he says. 'Please, just one moah.'

'Tomorrow night.' I kiss him on the forehead and leave.

'El,' he says, as I'm turning out the light.

'Yeah?'

'Will we always have the wiva?'

I hesitate, but only for a second. 'We get to keep the river.' I smile at him. 'Night, Lach.'

He smiles then, pulling the doona tighter around himself as he curls on his side to sleep.

A knife twists in my stomach. It is in this moment I know that I would do anything, no matter what it took. I would fight, no matter how dirty. I would unleash a pack of hyenas and hunt down *anyone* who tried to take the river from us.

Twenty-Six

No longer weeks, but months. Months away from that awful day when I couldn't breathe. Lachy and I have merged our weekends, and now we spend time with Mum every second weekend. Lachy also spends every Wednesday night with her, but I prefer to stay in the one house through the school week. It's less disruptive and means I don't have to drag all my stuff from house to house.

I chop carrots, potatoes, pumpkin. Sprinkle them with herb salt, drizzle oil like the instructions say and slide them into the oven on a baking tray. Next it's the roast chicken.

An hour later, the house is thick with the scent of herbs. I made this. All me. I am old enough to make food for my people to gather around at a table.

Thumping feet cross the living room into the kitchen. 'What is that *smell*?' Lachy says.

‘That, kid, is called dinner. Also known as cooking.’

He scrunches up his nose. ‘I know what cooking is,’ he says. ‘But what is it?’

‘A roast.’

‘Ooh, I love woast,’ he says.

‘I know.’

I let myself soak in the happiness of this one small thing. Gratitude. It’s something I focus on every day. Ms Myers has been teaching us to find the small moments of happiness in each day, gratitude in small things. *Be careful, it might spoil your entire world view*, she says. *You may even be happy!*

This is one dinner. On one night. But it says something to me. I can choose for things to get better. I can make it better.

I pull out an old pillar candle from the cupboard, where we store them for the bad storms. Set it on the table. Light it. Make gravy to pour on the chicken. Ask Lachy to set the table for me. He hums a little tune to himself as he lays the cutlery. When I’m finished serving, we sit down.

‘Wow, El,’ Dad says.

I don’t expect him to bow in gratitude to me. He and Mum have cooked tons of meals I never said thanks for. Actually, I probably complained about them. But I was kind of hoping for a few more words than just ‘wow’. Still, small things I am grateful for.

We’re almost finished eating when Dad rests his knife and

fork together on his plate like we're in a restaurant, laces his hands together and says, 'There's something I need to talk to you both about.'

Lachy looks up from his plate, his mouth full.

'I don't exactly know how to say this . . . but we're going to have to sell the house.'

There is silence. I hold my fork mid-stab. No-one moves, not even Dad, who is watching us. Lachy stops chewing, his eyes wide. The air around us turns to soup.

'No.' The word is strangled, half-formed, in my mouth.

Dad bows his head. 'I'm sorry, kids.'

'No.' My voice is firmer now, taking shape. A solid, red jagged shape. 'This is our *home*.'

And what I mean is this is not just a house. This is the wood beneath my feet, and the walls with my fingerprints on them, and the roof that keeps me dry when the rain thrashes down, and the bathroom with the blue light when the sun is setting that I used to think was a spirit. It's Crooked River, and turtles, and trees, and Drake and the Pa Tree. It is us. The Gillespies. The place that holds our laughter, our memories, the only place we've known.

'I know, El,' Dad says. 'I know it's devastating. And you know I wouldn't make this decision lightly. It's just, we can't afford to stay.' He pinches the bridge of his nose.

'Of course we can.' I press my fork hard into the table, push my chair back. Lachy jumps beside me. 'We'll find a way to afford it,' I say.

Dad shakes his head. 'I've looked at it every which way. It's not possible.'

'Everything's *possible*,' I say. 'You just have to want it.'

Dad shakes his head. 'Not this. The house needs too much work and work means money. When we sell up, all those problems become someone else's. We'll get to buy something simpler. Smaller. We'll start fresh. Make new happy memories in a new place. People do it every day.'

'I don't want new memowies,' Lachy says, his voice pitching high. 'I like ow old ones.'

'Dad,' I say. 'Dad.' I slide down to the floor. 'No, Dad.'

Dad sighs. 'Please, El, don't do this to me.'

Again, I am bucking the Gillespie trend. But I can't not be dramatic about something so horrific.

'Tell me you're joking,' I whisper. 'Please tell me.'

Dad sighs. 'Get up, please. We're all going to do what needs to be done, El. I know it's not easy, none of this is, not for any of us. But I've had to make some hard decisions so that we can keep eating and surviving. And your mum agrees with me. So we've chosen an agency, we've signed a contract. Your mum signed it too. We've both realised it's the only real way forward. We were meant to tell you together on the weekend, but I didn't want you to overhear anything before then.'

'You were going to hide it from us for days? You didn't even consult with us!'

'El,' Dad says. 'This isn't a vote process. This is about economic survival. This is adult stuff, requiring hard-headed adult decisions.'

Every negative word Mum has ever said about the house comes rushing back to my mind. 'Mum hated it here, she'd sell up in a minute. But not us, Dad. We don't hate it. Gillespie House even has our name on it. It's in our blood.' I press my hands together and literally start begging. 'Please, Dad, please call it off. Please, before it's too late. Please don't hurt us, not like this. It'll kill us, it really will.'

'El, please,' Dad whispers, and he wipes his face with his napkin. 'A house is only as good as the people in it. We love it here because we've built a life here, but I promise you we'll build a new life. Without all of us here, Crooked River isn't the same anyway. You know that.'

He's right that it's not the same here without Mum. And sometimes I've wondered why I even want to stay without her, but I do. I still want it. And I know he does too.

He stands to leave, but I won't let him. So I get up off the floor and meet Dad at chest level, my eyes locked up to his. Mum and Dad may have given up, but I haven't. I have not given up on this family. This place. Everything that is ours.

'You sell our home and you sell everything.' My voice is low, steady, proud. 'I will *not* let you.'

He looks down at me, his eyes sealed. 'Unfortunately, El, it's the adults who have to be big enough to make the tough decisions. Please trust us to make the right ones.'

'No.' I shake my head firmly. 'No, no, no. I don't trust *either* of you to get things right anymore. Not since everything went cuckoo. Mum is not in the right state of mind to be making big decisions like this. You aren't either. Selling our house is not doing what's best for anyone. Not unless you've both gone totally insane.'

Does he think because I baked a roast dinner that I've recovered? That I'm fine now, so he can rip these floors, this very house, this river we love away from us too? And it will all just be fine, because time heals everything?

I promised Lachy. I promised him the river.

Rage builds inside me like a kettle boiling. Quietly at first, then gathering noise, like a flash flood down the river, collecting logs, and stones and trees in its path. Until I am kicking my chair and throwing my dinner plate across the room, where it hits the wall with a crack and slides down to the floor. Until I am screaming and yelling words I can't understand, because a monster has taken hold of my body and I cannot control it. There are Dad's hands upon my arms as I thrash, and animal noises bellowing through the house which must belong to me. There is nothing except a black flame raging from my soul, a terrifying monster that won't quiet.

I float to the ceiling and see the scene from above. A demonic spirit has invaded my body. Twisting, and writhing, and turning and yelling, hair across its face. Still, Dad holds onto me. Lachy is rigid in his seat, pale as snow, his eyes round with the witness of trauma.

When the monster leaves, I am back inside my body. And my bones, my muscles, every bit of my skin is burning, pained, tired, spent. There is only heaving, and sobbing and violent shaking. There is 'Shhh, sweetheart, I'm so sorry, sweetheart,' in my ear. There is wet dripping on my arm from someone else's eyes. There are limp limbs and a sore throat. There is a weak slumped body held in strong damp arms. Here on the floor where I was born that spring night so many moons ago, there is vomit. Here, the walls who first protected me now watch me shatter, in this place where time doesn't heal, it only destroys.

Twenty-Seven

Dad puts Lachy to bed and says he wants to talk to me. My eyelids feel like coins and I can barely keep them open so I wait for him in my room, with its shelves full of trinkets. Jars of river stones, quartz, crustaceans. Magic things collected from the years and the moments.

I slump down on my bed like a weighted blanket. Limp and heavy. I have forgotten to let Snow in, but I don't have the energy to go back out and open the door for her.

Dad comes in and shuts the door behind him. He sits on the edge of my bed.

I blink slowly, my eyes thick, lids heavy.

'This is another adult conversation,' Dad says. 'But I'm telling you because you deserve an explanation and you're old enough to hear it.'

'So tell me. I can help you fix it.'

Dad sighs. 'Sweetheart, it's not that simple. I need to help your mum restart her life. I can't keep everything and I can't afford to buy Mum out of her share of this place. I'd never get a loan from the bank.'

'Mum won't take half the house, Dad,' I say, shocked that he would even think that of her.

Dad wipes a hand over his face like I'm a tiresome child. 'It's hard for you to understand, El, but it's not about her taking the house. Mum needs to be able to start over, financially.'

'She's got an interview for a job,' I say. 'She's starting over.'

'That's not enough. I don't get to keep everything we own. I have to pay Mum out a share of our property so that she can go buy something else. It wouldn't be fair for me to keep the house and she just holds onto her car. Renting the unit is fine for now, but she needs to find a more permanent house for you kids. You all deserve that, and anyway, it's the law. People have to divide their money when they separate.'

I sit up on my elbows. 'You mean selling our house is just about money? About coins and notes?'

'Not just that. This house needs more work than I can give it. Mum was right, it's falling apart, there are literally termites eating the back deck, working their way around to the front. I haven't had the time or the money to fix it. This house is falling apart faster than I can mend it. The thing about old houses is that they're money pits. And I just don't have the money.'

'But Pa's ashes are here,' I say, disgusted. 'He's here forever. You can't sell his resting place. That would be, like, sacrilegious.'

'I know. He's where he wanted to be. But we can't hold onto everything, sweetheart.'

This is the man who told me, all my childhood, how lucky we are to be part of something greater than us. A history, a people: the Gillespies. And now he's ready to toss it all out for a bit of money? He's not even going to fight for it?

I feel like I'm living in one of those terrible dreams you wake from but can't shake off for hours. Dad's spirit has wandered and left a husk of a man in his place.

'Yes, we can. We can hold onto this. There are some things we get to keep.'

'We have to adapt, Elliott. And if that means selling the house, we'll have to sell it and rebuild. We'll learn to love a new place. So long as we have each other, we'll be okay.'

'That is a defeatist attitude, Dad! There are other ways to help Mum, we just need to think of them. Think outside the box, like you always say. Lateral thinking, or whatever it's called.'

'You know, Elliott . . .' Dad shifts his weight on the bed, and looks out my window. 'Sometimes life calls us to be turtles. Tough shells on. Carry our home within us.'

'No.' I think of Mum's new home and I want to scream. She has done exactly that. One new home is enough. I refuse to have two. 'You don't understand, Dad. Why can't you understand this?' I want to shake it out of him. The apathy. This listless version of the strong man I knew. 'Dad, when you wake up, you'll realise what you've done and it'll be too late. All of it, too late. Gillespie House will be gone. It won't be ours anymore. And your regret will mean nothing, because someone else will fall in love with our quaint little house, and our clear river and our wild plum trees and we'll never get it back. No Gillespie has ever sold the house. That's how special it is. Turning our backs on it now is the worst betrayal we'll have ever committed.'

But nothing I say can change Dad's mind. The contract is signed. The deal done.

Twenty-Eight

Monday morning, I wake to my alarm. Snow watches me get dressed from my bed. Wags her tail a couple of times. I head to the kitchen for breakfast, but Snow doesn't follow, so I double back.

'Come on, girl,' I say, patting my knees.

She looks at me with her big brown eyes, but doesn't make any move to get up.

'Snow,' I say. 'Get down.'

She blinks a number of times, but still doesn't move. I go to the bed to help her down. My bedspread is wet beneath her. She has wet herself on my bed.

'Get up, girl,' I urge. 'Come on.'

She whimpers lightly and a shiver ripples through me.

'Dad,' I say, my voice trembly. 'Dad!'

Heavy footsteps down the hallway. Snow bows her head,

but doesn't get off the bed. Just looks up at me with helpless eyes as our secret sleep ritual is discovered.

Dad opens my door. 'What's wrong?' he says.

Fear creeps over me like a poison vine.

'What's she doing up there?' Dad says, then lowering his voice, 'Get down!'

'No, Dad, stop,' I say. 'Something's wrong. She's wet the bed. Something's really wrong.'

Snow whimpers again.

'Snow,' Dad says gravely, 'get down, girl.'

She drops her head, resting it on her paws. Dad wipes one hand slowly over his mouth.

'Right,' he says. 'I'm calling the vet. Damn it.'

I forget about school, and the English essay due in class today, and the lunches to pack and the fact that I still haven't woken Lachy. I lower myself down on the bed alongside Snow, right next to her wee and I don't even care because my stomach is gripped in a fist.

I think she knows, she heard. She knows what Dad is planning to do with the house and the idea of it is killing her. Gillespie House is all she's ever known. How will old Snow get used to somewhere new?

I stroke her head. Snow rests her chin on her paws, shutting her eyes. I can hear Dad on the phone to the vet.

'Snow Gillespie . . . Thirteen years old . . . No, she can't stand up. Has lost control of her bladder . . . How much is a house visit?'

I take the day off school, wake Lachy. He sits one side of her in his pyjamas, stroking her head, and I sit the other.

A car finally motors in, the engine running outside. We hear a woman's voice greeting Dad, followed by light footsteps through the living room.

'Down this way,' Dad says.

Then the vet is standing at my doorway, her auburn hair piled on top of her head in a bun. She is younger than I expected. She smiles at Lachy and I.

'I take it this is the gorgeous Snowy beast I've come to see?' she says.

I nod, edging aside to let her near Snow.

'Hello, beautiful girl, how are you?' she says gently, feeding Snow a couple of liver treats, which she takes. 'It's alright,' she croons, 'my name's Susie and I'm just going to have a little look at you, precious.'

Snow wags her tail weakly, two times. Susie holds a stethoscope to Snow's chest, presses her fingers into the sides of her belly, pushes down on her hips, taps her legs and paws with a little hammer.

'Her tummy's quite distended. That means swollen,' she says to Lachy and I. Then to Dad she says, 'That's not uncommon at her age. Dogs develop growths, but they can be more serious when they're internal. How has her appetite been?'

Dad looks at me and I shrug. 'Normal?'

Honestly, none of us have really paid much attention. We haven't even paid much attention to our own appetites.

'I remember seeing food left in her bowl last week,' I remember suddenly.

'Is she the sort of dog who normally wolfs down every morsel?'

I nod. My eyes start to water with what that could mean. Why didn't I question why she'd left food in her bowl when I saw it? I saw it with my own eyes.

Don't let this be the day, universe, don't let this be the day. Do. Not. Let. This. Be. The. Day.

'Dad, mind if we have a quick word outside?' Susie says.

And that's when I know. I know. I pat my beautiful Snow's head over and over, my eyes filling with tears I can't blink away. I don't want to hear it. Can't bear to hear it.

Snow nudges me and licks my hand. I smile at her through my tears. I don't want her to be sad for me. I need to be brave for her. Brave for Lachy.

'What do you think she's saying to Dad?' Lachy whispers.

I shrug.

'Why ah you cwying?' he says.

'I'm not.' But it's very clear that I am.

The vet returns with medicine in a treat, which Snow eats.

She explains to us that Snow is in pain.

'Dogs don't show pain the way we humans do,' she says gently, patting Snow on the head. 'The way a dog shows pain is by being tired, by not being able to move, not eating, not being their usual happy selves. My guess, from having a feel of your beautiful girl here, is that the nerves in her spine have been compressed by tumours and she can't walk anymore. She doesn't seem to have any sensation in her legs. Which means she also can't control her bowels or her bladder anymore. She might have a few accidents today, okay? You'll need to be really kind with her, because she can't help it. So I'm going to get a doggy diaper from the van, and that should help with that. I'm also going to give Snow some special dog medicine. It'll make her a bit more comfortable. I'll come back in the morning,' she says, looking at Dad.

He nods, his lips pursed in a straight line. Then he walks the vet out.

My mouth is hanging open. Tears falling. I can't stop them anymore. I can't even be brave. Why is that too-kind vet coming back tomorrow? Why? I want her and her sweet words to stay away from Snow.

After her car drives off, Dad doesn't come back inside. So I leave Lachy in charge of Snow and go hunting for him. I find him out on the verandah. Down on his knees, shoulders slumped forward. Dad is shaking, his face in his hands. He stays like this a long time, unaware that I'm behind him. Then he reefs his phone out of his back pocket, holding it in a tight grip to his ear. He is still hunched over.

'Nomes?' he says, his voice breaking. Dad is sobbing, great big gulps and shuddering breaths. He can barely talk. 'It's Snow.'

And that's all he says. I watch his body doubled over in pain.

Dad still has the phone pressed to his ear, his head so low it's almost between his knees on the hardwood floor of the deck, his breathing ragged. After a while he gathers himself.

'In the morning,' he manages to say. 'It's the kindest thing we can do.'

Snow is everything good and new. Snow is when I was little, and when Mum and Dad were happy and when Lachy was born. She's all our best memories.

There is a burning ball inside my stomach. A ball of fire. There is no place of comfort, no place I can outrun it.

I don't care, I run anyway. Down the hill, my breaths white puffs over the bitter frosty earth. Away from the house, all the way to the Pa Tree. The burning moves from my stomach up to my chest, higher and higher to my throat. Higher still, until it is bursting out through my mouth in great big sobs, and out through my eyes and down my cheeks, rushing like the river. I am burning alive, all the way through, writhing with the pain of it.

I'm losing everything. Everything I love. My family, my first friend, my house, my river. I'm even losing our stories. I forget what it means to be a Gillespie.

Twenty-Nine

Dad digs with his shovel. All afternoon, he digs Snow a neat resting spot beneath the Pa Tree. Every few shovels, he wipes his nose. When he's done, he stands beside the hole, one arm resting against the handle of the shovel. I stare into the deep rectangle he has made for Snow. Dad puts an arm around me, and we lean against each other. Looking out across the river.

'Mum's staying the night,' Dad tells me. 'To be with all of us and Snow. She doesn't want to confuse you kids—she's not coming back, okay? This is about Snow.'

I nod, grateful that we get one last night, all of us together.

Mum arrives and makes us separate beds on the floor in the living room around Snow, who is on her own mat. Dad builds a fire and chocks it to last the night. We go to sleep listening to the wind rattling the window panes, and we wake in shifts through the night to check on Snow, pat her, reassure her. We will get her through this. We will care for her.

By morning, Snow's breathing is shallow. We watch the feeble sun rise and cast a gentle light on her fur. She is an angel dog, glowing. But she can no longer lift her head, only her eyes. Dad carries Snow outside. Beside the hole is a blanket and Dad lays her down gently onto it. Snow blinks slowly, almost in gratitude. I am glad that her fur is still thick and it keeps her warm.

I dread the sound of the vet's car as it ambles up the drive. I look down at Snow and pat her head gently. The lights have gone out in her eyes. Susie speaks gently, softly, as she crouches down beside Snow on the crunchy earth. Explains to us what it is she has to do.

Lachy clutches at my hand as Susie shaves a small patch of fur off Snow's leg. Tells us now is the time to say goodbye.

'Goodbye, Snow, yoah my best fwiend eva,' Lachy says.

Mum leans down, kisses her forehead, strokes her head and whispers into her ear.

Then it's my turn. I can barely breathe.

'Goodbye, Snow,' I choke. 'You're our girl. Always ours,' I say, and I kiss her beautiful head for the last time.

Then Dad cradles Snow's big head in his lap, and we each lay a hand upon her fur.

'What a good girl you are,' Dad says. 'Such a good girl.'

And then the vet injects something into Snow's leg and Dad

is the last thing Snow sees. She closes her eyes, her head falling gently to one side.

The vet says sorry to us, like it's her fault Snow is gone, and then she leaves. She leaves us with our girl whose spirit has parted from her joyful body forever.

And we are four broken hearts beside a perfect little grave by the river. We are whispered words, and tears and cuddles. Then we are eight hands wrapping her up in the blanket and lowering her blanket into the grave. We are legs standing above a deep hole, four faces raining. We are hands on shovels, and small spadefuls of dirt onto the blanket, taking turns as we bury our own.

That night in bed, Lachy cries out for Snow. Mum says she'll stay until he falls asleep.

'I miss huh,' he says, 'I miss huh so much.'

'I know,' Mum soothes. 'We all do.' She strokes his face. 'We all loved her.'

'I loved huh the most,' he sobs. 'Maw than anyone.'

'I know,' Mum says. 'Snow was loved so very much by all of us. What a lucky girl she was. Not all dogs are as lucky as Snow.'

Lachy's face is shiny and swollen, his hair sweaty in the cold night. Dad on one side of him, Mum on the other.

'I promise it won't always hurt this much, sweetheart.

It'll get better.'

I bring in a glass of water for Lachy as Mum makes soothing shushing noises. In between sobs, Lachy tries to talk, but he can't get out even one syllable now. He is writhing and moaning.

Mum brings warm wet washers from the bathroom. She wipes Lachy's face, the back of his hot neck, his forehead, one smooth stroke at a time. Dad unbuttons Lachy's pyjama shirt and Mum wipes down his chest to stop him from choking.

I go to the window and tear back the blinds. A cold silvery moon looks in on us. I sit back down on the bed beside Lachy and grip his hand in mine until the trembling stops.

'We are born of the river people, Lach,' I tell him in a trembly, unsure voice. 'Of flash floods that burst the banks and carry things away downstream. Of droughts that leave the earth with cracked open sores.'

Dad clears his throat. 'She's right. Our people are *strong* people,' he whispers. 'Remember the big storm that blew off the roof?'

Lachy is shaking and still inhaling sharply, but he's quiet. He nods.

'Well, our people are stronger than that.' Dad wipes his eyes briskly with the back of his hand. 'And we'll heal in time. Because the blood in our veins is a river. It runs inside us. We'll always have the river in our blood.' Dad taps Lachy's chest. 'And we'll have Snow in our hearts. No-one can take that.'

Dad turns away as a tear slips down his face.

When Lachy is calm and sleepy, Mum and Dad kiss him goodnight and leave his room. I can hear them murmuring outside his door, like old times, except it's different.

Lachy's eyelids are thick and swollen.

'I want you to close your eyes,' I say gently.

Lachy doesn't ask why. Just closes them in relief.

'I'm going to play a game with you,' I say. 'It's called The Things You Get to Keep, okay?'

He nods.

'I'll go first. Now there *are* certain things you get to keep that nobody can ever take away. I'll give you some examples.' I start lightly. 'We get to keep sunshine in the mornings. And dew on the grass. We get to keep making pancakes on Sundays for breakfast.'

'I like that,' Lachy says.

'We get to keep building Lego forts,' I say. 'And playing card games.'

He opens one eye. 'Do we get to keep building tweehouse cubbies?'

'Good,' I say. 'You're getting the hang of it. Yes, we get to keep that.'

'Even when we sell the house?' Both his eyes are open now.

I have momentarily forgotten about the house. Since Snow got sick, everything else has been pushed aside.

‘Well,’ I say. ‘We’ll be able to find a tree somewhere, right? Trees are always our friends. And they’re in parks and backyards everywhere. So one way or another, we can still build cubbies.’

Lachy smiles. ‘Good. Do I get to keep my wunners with the lights in them too?’

‘Yep. Nobody’s taking them away.’

‘And my bed with the wolf sheets?’

‘Absolutely, kid.’

‘What about my collectible wocketship?’

‘All yours. You also get to keep your friends. Braeden, and Harry, and Trent and Zach. You still get to play with them.’

‘I get to keep my wock collection,’ Lachy says. ‘And my pet wock.’

‘You get to keep Mum and Dad,’ I say. Then I scruff his hair. ‘You get to keep *me*.’

His eyes sparkle at that.

‘And you know what else, kid? You get to keep your memories of Snow. I do too. Snow was ours. Nothing can take that away from us.’

I bite my lip to stop myself from crying as Lachy tears up again.

‘I’m keeping Snow foweva,’ he says.

‘Me too. And forever is a very long time,’ I say.

Thirty

A *For Sale* sign goes up on the house. It is clean, white, bright. A second one sits high and proud on the road where I catch the bus. It has a big picture of the front of the house, showing off the wrap-around verandah and the Pa Tree down to the left. A picture below of Crooked River, clear, sparkling, the sky above it gleaming and cloudless, Mount Wilderness perched in the backdrop, behaving herself. The house looks cleaner, brighter, than it really is. I think the photographer has used filters. You can't see the white flecks of paint peeling off the timber, or the leaning part of the fence that needs fixing, because even though Dad's a fencer, he hasn't had time to get to ours. Even the picture of the kitchen is taken at an angle that just misses the chink in the floorboards from where Dad dropped his 'Stress Less' mug. I hope anyone who comes to look at the house is disappointed. They should sue the real estate agent for false advertising.

Stately manor. The words make my ribs ache. I have read the ad online about a hundred times, hoping desperately it won't get much interest. *Unique property! A parcel of land this size will be snapped up! For the first time in generations, you are invited to view the Gillespie landholding. This is a reluctant sale by owners seeking a fresh start.*

Since the ad went up, I've found it hard to swallow, to taste. I can't feel anything but a deathly sick ache in my ribs. What if the parents of some brat from school buy it and that kid ends up living in my house? I don't think I could stand it.

This very moment, as I'm riding the bus to school, someone could be walking through my house, looking at Snow's grave, falling in love with my river. They are selling what is mine. The bedroom I have slept in all my life is online for anyone to see, the kitchen I make the Elliott Special in on Sundays, the verandah where I've sat with Mum countless times watching the sky turn gold and the rain fall in sheets during a storm. It is *my* river sparkling in all its glory they're showing off with five different photos. My Pa Tree. They may as well be selling my heart, my lungs, my kidneys. The hollow sick feeling hounds me.

But then I wonder, why am I so attached to our place? Isn't it just dirt, just water, just wood, and paint and window panes? What's the point of any of it if my family is split in two and can't make memories there anymore?

It all hurts. It's not just a 'landholding' like the ad says.

It's the resting place of my Pa, of Snow. It's my past and my future. I've always thought one day, far off when I'm a mum, I would take *my* kids up to the waterhole to swim at World's End, the way Mum did with me. And I would take them kayaking up the river the way Dad did, until I was old enough to do it myself. No amount of money could be enough to convince me to sell it.

Gillespie House, anchor in the storm.

In the wind, rain, sun, dry, wet, fire, flood.

House that we've defended.

House that has sheltered and protected.

We are her people.

The day of the open house inspection, the house is gleaming.

'It looks so good, why don't we just keep it?' Lachy says.

He doesn't understand that everything needs to be divided. One person doesn't get to keep it all. Dad hasn't explained it to him. It's not something he should have to worry about.

'Come play Snap with me, kid,' I say to distract him.

When the time comes to leave, to let other people drive up our drive and walk through our front door, sift through our bedrooms, pry through our souls, Dad says, 'I know this is hard for you, kids. It's hard for me too.'

He thinks we've accepted it.

'I'm going down to Drake's,' I say. 'I can't stand this.'

Half of what I said is true.

Dad drops me off at Drake's before taking Lachy into town for a milkshake.

Drake meets me around the side of his house. 'You sure this is a good idea?' he says, patting Ronnie on his broad head. Ronnie shuts his eyes in delight.

'If I'm going down, I'm going down fighting,' I say.

'Alrighty,' he says. 'Ronnie, boy, let's go.'

We run down the embankment to the river, dirt flying up behind us, skidding out from under our shoes.

Bridge is waiting patiently. Trusty and ready as always. I untie her from the rope, and we drag her down to the river. I climb in first. Next Drake heaves Ronnie on. Ronnie is scatty, his nails scratchy, paws dancing against the poly surface. Bridge rocks, wobbles.

'Whoa.' Drake is knee deep in the icy water as he steadies Bridge with his hand. 'It's alright, boy,' he says to Ronnie. 'Calm down.'

Drake jumps on, the last of us to board, and Ronnie promptly sits down on his lap, panting, tongue lolling out one side.

'Let's do this,' I say.

It's all on me to get us there. Elliott versus river. Upstream against the current. We've never been so heavy, and I've never been more alive. Because we have a plan—I'm not just going to lie down and take this.

We hide around a bend in the bank, out of sight of my house. Just Drake, Ronnie and me. Waiting, waiting for any cars that might approach down our drive. Maybe none will come? Maybe people don't want rambling old houses that need work?

But after a time, we hear the rumble of an engine. Ronnie cocks his ears.

'No,' Drake says to him.

The noise grows louder until a navy SUV comes into view, puttering slowly up the drive and rolling to a stop near the front door.

Ronnie growls.

Drake grabs him by the collar. 'No,' he says again, sternly. Ronnie quiets.

I peer above the bank of the river just in time to see the passenger door of the SUV open and out steps a lady with a broad-brimmed dark hat. She's wearing tight jeans, suede boots and a long cardigan. A man gets out the driver's side and walks towards the house. He is tall, lean, polished, wearing a collared shirt beneath a knitted checked vest. He has thin greying hair and the rims of his glasses glint in the sun. Polished man and hat lady look up at the house.

'Nope,' I whisper to Drake. 'They definitely don't belong.'

We watch as a suited man, the real estate agent probably,

steps down off the verandah and shakes polished man by the hand. The agent opens the front door and the couple are swallowed inside.

'Maybe the problem,' Drake says in a low voice, 'is that you can't imagine anyone else in your house.'

I look at him. Is he dim?

'Yes, Drake, because nobody else *does* belong in my house.'

That shuts him up.

We wait. I imagine polished man and hat lady peering in cupboards in our kitchen and opening doors to bathrooms. Sticking their heads inside my bedroom, the soles of their shoes scuffing against my floorboards, their faces peering out my window to catch glimpses of Crooked River, if you get the right angle. My heart is sick with thumping by the time they emerge, hand in hand.

They head down towards the Pa Tree, and their voices carry to us on the light breeze. Ronnie whines in their direction, but Drake pulls on his collar to quiet him.

'Wait,' Drake whispers.

'It's very quaint,' hat lady muses. 'Historic.' She says this last word like she's taste-testing it, deciding if she likes it.

'It's certainly homely,' he says. 'And that mountain backdrop—it's breathtaking, honey.'

'Yes, I feared you might say that,' hat lady says.

My heart is beating so loud, Drake must be able to hear it.

Do not fall in love with it. No, no, no. It's not yours to love.

Drake's hand grips my arm. We lock eyes.

'Could you see us here?' polished man asks hat lady.

No way. I won't let you see yourselves here. Not for a single moment.

I give Drake the nod. Now!

'Ronnie,' Drake says. Ronnie cocks his head at Drake and whines. 'Go!'

Drake lets go of Ronnie and Ronnie pelts up the bank of the creek. He skids to a stop a couple of metres shy of polished man. Then he backs up, growling. Snarling at the couple.

Ronnie knows they don't belong here too.

Polished man steps in front of hat lady, pushing her behind him. 'Get back!' he says.

Ronnie barks once. The growl that follows is menacing and low. Even from here, I can see Ronnie's lips pulled back across his teeth.

Polished man and hat lady are frozen like statues. The estate agent comes running down the hill, then stops and searches the ground. He picks up a stick and marches with it towards Ronnie.

'Scat!' says the estate agent, lifting the stick towards Ronnie. 'Scram, you mongrel!' Then to polished man, with his stick still raised, he says, 'I'm so sorry, I have no idea who owns that dog.'

Ronnie creeps forward towards the estate agent, teeth still barred, growling. He's always been a brave soul, our Ronnie.

‘Definitely not from here,’ the real estate agent says, backing up himself now. ‘Must . . . must be a stray. The fences here are secure—the vendor’s a fencer, so you can be sure of that.’ He gives a tight smile, before turning his attention back to Ronnie, who is slowly stalking towards the agent, lips trembling.

‘I’m going,’ Drake says. He scrambles up the bank, as we’d planned, his hair a tangled mess. I told him to go full wild today. Raggedy clothes. Tarzan-like.

‘Ronnie!’ he says.

Ronnie stops still.

‘Ronnie, come here.’ Drake pats his knee. Ronnie looks sideways at Drake. ‘C’mon here, boy.’

Ronnie wags his tail limply, still bailing up his prisoners.

‘Ronnie. Now.’

He abandons his mission and runs full pelt at Drake, right into Drake’s knees, where he stands guard in front of Drake.

‘Sorry,’ Drake says to the three stunned strangers. ‘Escapes all the time! He’s a bit of a crazy mutt.’

Ronnie keeps his stance, guarding Drake from the intruders.

‘It’s okay, boy,’ Drake says, then to the couple, ‘He’s used to break-and-enters around here.’

The real estate agent dusts himself off and looks at Drake in disgust. ‘You’ll want to keep that dog on a chain. If he hurts anyone, you or your parents will be liable, you understand?’

‘Got it,’ Drake says. ‘My sincerest apologies.’ He grabs

Ronnie by the collar and runs with him down the bank, to me.

'Liar!' I hiss. '"Sincerest apologies"!'

We hide in the hollowed-out bend of the creek until car doors slam and an engine starts. Then we watch the couple, who considered for one brief moment that this might be their new paradise, drive away.

We are unable to stop our laughter.

'Mission accomplished,' Drake says.

'Do you still think she can see them living there?' I say.

'I very much doubt it,' Drake gasps. 'I think we took care of them! And I must say, the entire plan was genius.'

'Why, thank you, thank you very much,' I say. 'So that's one down. How many to go?'

We wait to find out.

It turns out there is only one other car to arrive, about half an hour later. A shiny red sports car with a gold badge on its bonnet. The kind of car that doesn't belong at a house like ours. A man in a black business suit steps out, clicks the car locked and lights glow on it. He adjusts his tie in the reflection of the car window, then walks up to the house, brushes his feet on our welcome mat, opens the door and lets himself inside. He doesn't spend long at the house. When he comes out, he scans the land briefly. Looks up at Mount Wilderness, asks a couple of questions to the estate agent which we can't hear. He talks to the agent for a little while, then he, too, is gone.

The open house is over. I can breathe again.

We survived.

I turn to Drake. 'Thank you, thank you, thank you,' I whisper.

It feels like a win.

Drake hugs me. Holds me close. I'm aware of his chest against my cheek, his heart pounding beneath my ear. It's not an unpleasant sensation.

Thirty-One

One afternoon the following week, Dad is on the phone to the real estate agent. He has the phone on loudspeaker.

'You might want to move on it pretty quickly,' the agent says. 'Big players move fast, you know what developers are like. He's looking at a couple of different blocks in the area for subdivision potential, so the state of the house isn't an issue. Obviously, we have to be upfront about the termites, which is going to be a killer for most people, but for him it's not an issue. The good news is he's likely to pay above market value, the big bucks, and he did comment to me that your property was well placed. Which it is. But if you blink, you'll probably miss your moment.'

Dad hesitates, before saying, 'Yeah, okay, thanks. I'll talk it over with Naomi.' He doesn't sound like someone who is about to win the lotto.

When he finishes with the estate agent, Dad puts the phone down on the table, spins it around a few times.

I walk into the kitchen. 'What's a subdivision?' I say.

Dad jumps. 'El, I didn't know you were here.'

'Where'd you think I was?'

Dad shakes his head. 'At Drake's. I don't know.'

'What's a subdivision mean?' I press.

Dad raises his eyebrows. 'Well, I guess, ah . . . basically, it means when someone divides land into smaller parcels. Kind of like what happened years ago on the other side of Crooked River.'

'Like where Drake is?'

Dad is staring past me, still spinning his phone on the table.

'Dad?'

'Sorry, what?' he says.

'You mean like how the block of land was cut up where Drake lives?'

'Yes, sweetheart, like that.'

'And what's a developer?'

He scratches under his chin. 'Listen, El, I might need you to save your questions for later. I need to call your mum.'

'Tell me first,' I say. 'Tell me what a developer is.'

Dad sighs. 'Listen, I don't want you getting all worked up about this. I haven't even discussed it with your mum yet. But a developer is usually someone with the skills to divide land in a way that's legal.'

I think for a minute. 'Why would they divide our land up?'

'Money,' Dad says. 'Smaller blocks are popular in the new estates.'

'But we already have a house here. Would they cut blocks around it?'

Dad's eyes glaze over. It's the same look he got when I was ten and I asked him if Santa really squeezed down our flue on Christmas night.

'New houses is what people want, El. Not old places that need a lot of work.'

'Wait. You mean they'd *bulldoze* our house?'

The thought is horrifying. Our house, our heritage and any evidence of it, bulldozed. Erased. Gone, like it never existed. I could never come back to visit, or even look at the place I was born. I would walk past and see new people smiling in the tiny yards of their new homes inside their small picket fences, listening to Crooked River trickling by with no idea that they don't belong here. That this is meant to be ours.

I am in a state of numb mute shock. I cannot think anything but darkness. My thoughts, dark; my vision, dulled; my appetite, gone.

I go to bed that afternoon and can't get out again. I lay there like a limp ragdoll. No shower, no dinner. I sleep and wake to the knowledge that a light inside me has flickered out.

Something has died that I can never get back.

Morning comes, and still I cannot eat. Cannot see. My eyes have lost their sight.

Mum comes, Mum goes.

Frankie comes to see me, and Tamar, but I can't speak to them. Tamar talks about how her house got ruined in the floods, but they don't understand. This is different. I stare at a blank void nobody else can see. That blank void is my future. With Mum off on her own and our home levelled to the ground.

Drake texts me to go walking with him:

We'll go all the way to Mount Wilderness.

Walk right up to her peak.

I don't reply. My fingers are as limp as the rest of me. I can no longer feel a thing.

Drake comes over. Still, I can't talk. Can't feel a flicker of anything. I hear Bec with Dad outside.

'Some losses really are hard to bear,' Bec says. But her voice is from another world.

I wait for more bad news. That's all we seem to get lately. Someone is leaving, someone is dying, something is lost. The fight is lost. I've lost everything I live for.

Cars come, cars go. Faces come, faces go.

Mum is at my door. I don't remember when I last saw her, only that her face has been in and out, her hands have been on me and off me. I don't know what day it is, what time, how long

I've been in bed, when I last ate, or showered or slept.

Mum creeps into my room. Rests a hand on my forehead.

'El, Dad and I are worried about you,' she says. 'Really worried.'

I keep staring blankly ahead. I can't do anything else. There is no spark of life left within me. Nothing that can stir me back.

'We've been talking,' she continues. 'And you know, in a lot of separations, one parent keeps the house and the other one buys something new.'

I am in a waking coma. I can hear the words, but nothing in me can respond and nothing wants to. People's words are just shadows flitting by.

'This property is so big, almost everything we own is sunk into it. That's why Dad's selling it, honey.'

I'm not an idiot. I know this. Mum and Dad have always been cash poor, but our place is worth a lot. To them, it's worth money. To me, it's worth every single memory I've ever made. Every thought I've ever had is tied up here.

'We all need to start over,' Mum says gently. 'I need a little place of my own one day for you, and Lachy and me to live in. I'm not in a rush, but I can't afford to rent the unit forever. Do you understand that, honey?'

I don't care. I don't care. I don't care. About anything. Take what you want. Take it all.

'We have to reorganise the money. Divide some things.

Honey, I know you're heartbroken.' She holds my cold floppy hand in hers. 'I hate seeing you like this. El, can you at least nod to show me you understand?'

I nod. I understand. Of course I understand.

Ever since that ordinary evening when they told us they were separating, I have been understanding. Watching as my life has been divided into lots. Piece by piece, pulling something out from under me. First my mum, then my weekends, then Snow, then my house, and now they're going to bulldoze the lounge room I was born in, my entire existence. Divide our place into a Lego-land of identical matching houses. People will probably start queuing to go rubber tubing down our river. Clogging the edges of the bank with their plastic rubbish and fast-food wrappers. The turtles will have no peace. The Pa Tree will be knocked flat. They'll cut down that many trees to clear space for new houses that the swallows will disappear.

'Dad and I have discussed a sort of idea,' Mum says. 'A sort of compromise, you might call it. And it's just an idea at this stage, but I wanted to run it by you.'

I don't care. About ideas, compromises, breathing, eating, sleeping, anything. I can still see the bare barren earth flattened, with hundreds of people milling around polluting our beautiful river. I stare straight ahead.

'Honey, Dad's been looking into what the developer was going to do with the land. And it takes a long time, but it's *possible*—not definite, but possible—that if we go through Council to get the right approvals, Dad and I could divide some of the land up ourselves to sell.'

Mum holds up a hand as if she expects me to protest about selling some of the land, to fight her on it, but there is not a trickle of fighting spirit left in my blood. I don't care. Can't she see? I'm not here anymore. Do as you please.

'Not all the land, just some of it. A good chunk of it. And that would mean Dad could keep the house for you and Lachy. It would also mean less work for Dad, having less land to maintain. Sweetheart? Sweetheart, look at me.'

'What did you say?' My words are thick, my mind a murky bowl of confusion. It is playing tricks on me and I'm not sure what is real and what is imagined.

'Oh, honey.' She pulls my head to her chest. 'I don't want you, or Dad or Lachy to lose this house if there's another way. You know I don't. If there *is* another way to do this, we're going to explore it, okay?'

I look over at the doorway and find Dad leaning against it. A smile is tickling the corners of his mouth. He looks sort of happy. I don't understand.

'What do you think?'

'I don't understand.'

I look from Dad to Mum, working together to save this place for us even though they couldn't save their marriage.

Even though they're planning separate lives.

'I've already contacted Council,' Dad says. 'And we've organised to meet with a town planner to prepare our application. We're pulling the house off the market, El. Neither of us felt good about that developer guy, or his plans. He didn't have any kind of feel for the area. He was just looking to make a quick dollar. This place is worth more to us than that.'

The freeze in my chest begins to thaw. To soften like the snow on Mount Wilderness in the spring.

Then suddenly I can feel again and I am crying. Crying, and crying and crying as Mum and Dad sit either side of me and hold me.

There is one more thing I get to keep.

Thirty-Two

Mum has a professional name. She was offered that job teaching art at the community college and she is known there as Ms Gillespie. I don't know if Mum will always be a Gillespie, because before that she was a Hansen, but today she is still Naomi Gillespie. And she has asked me to join her art class.

Mum parks the car out the front of the lowset timber-clad building with the words *Community College* out the front. The light is fading, the sunset casting a golden halo over the college, leaving the sky glowing.

Inside, our footsteps are echoey on the hard floors. The studio is a cool open space that smells of turpentine and paint, and has big windows letting the light fall softly across the floors. Outside the windows, the soft green fronds of ferns curl like fingers waving in the afterlight. Easels and stools are arranged around the room and Mum directs me to an easel near to where her own stands, facing the class.

The studio has a quiet sacred vibe, and Mum turns on a playlist I've not heard before. The music is haunting, and as the light outside turns from golden to amber, the students trickle in. Older ladies with white wispy hair and brooches pinned to their jackets. Younger women with red spikey hair and spacers in their ears. Older round-stomached men with gold-rimmed glasses and collared shirts take up easels alongside younger guys with mullets, and undercuts and eyebrow piercings. It makes me think of how Mum began teaching here all those years ago.

The last pair to enter are an older lady with short-cropped hair streaked orange and a man about Dad's age with a beard and thick black glasses like Drake's. The lady is hunched over and her thin veined hand grips the man's forearm as though she is scared she'll fall without him there. He helps her to a seat with a rail around it, giving her a smile before taking the easel and stool next to her for himself. I look at that man and he reminds me of how Mum described Dad being once. I hope this is the sort of person Drake will grow into.

Mum directs everyone in the class as to which paintbrushes are required for the evening, where the palettes are, the water jars, the paints. She speaks with her chin up and gestures to help her newer students find what they need. Mum talks to the class about things I've not considered before. Art as meditation, art as therapy, art as expression. And then she talks about artists I've never heard of, like Monet, and Renoir and Rembrandt.

About the brushes we each have in front of us and the techniques we'll be using tonight.

I think back to that night when she told us that she and Dad were separating. The way she was back then, tears spilling down her face, pulling her knitted jumper over her fingers as she spoke, almost begging me to let her go. How thin and sad she was.

Watching her now, my mother the artist, her eyes shining, her cheeks glowing, projecting her voice around the room, her clothes fitting a little more snugly . . . my heart feels like it's a little bit on fire. Sometimes I forget to paint, because I'm too busy watching Mum stroll around the class, stopping to examine someone's work, offering a comment or helping them make a sharp brush stroke here, a flick there, painting the outline of a tree or a shadow.

'Brilliant,' she says to an older man, who is hunched over his painting. Everyone turns to look. 'See how the texture has added depth to your work?'

All these people, most much older than Mum, watch her as she moves around the room, nodding their heads as she speaks, absorbing her every word, asking questions, copying her. And I wonder if living at Gillespie House, Mum had maybe felt like a swan in the desert. And now she has found herself a pond and she is paddling, she is graceful, she is alive again.

The morning after art class is my birthday. Mum takes me out to high tea in town, where our tea is served in fine English china, with tiny cakes, and scones and dumplings paraded out on three-tiered china towers. The cakes are more pieces of art. It seems sinful to chew on them.

'Can we really afford this?' I whisper to Mum. 'It looks like something served to royalty.'

'Sometimes the finer things in life are called for,' Mum says. 'Just sometimes.'

Dad picks me up from town afterwards and drives me back to the house. Gillespie House, where Dad has always been and probably always will be. Where Lachy runs out to cuddle me, bouncing on the spot about the birthday surprise he and Dad have organised for me while I was with Mum.

Because I, Elliott Gillespie, have turned sixteen. And now, at sixteen, I belong to a people who have two homes. One wild home by the river, with history, and space and spring swallows nesting in the eaves. And one trendy unit in town, surrounded by palm trees and splashed with photos and colour, with a heated pool we can swim in all year round, even under the stars on a winter's night.

'Sit down,' Lachy tells me, dragging me by the hand. 'On the lounge.'

'Yes, sir,' I say.

'Close yoah eyes,' Lachy orders me.

I do as I'm told.

'You weady, Dad?' he whispers.

There's some scuffing, and whispering and footsteps on the creaky boards. And then a weight is pressed into my lap.

I open my eyes. It is a warm, wriggling, shivering little puppy, black as midnight, with big, droopy green eyes looking up at me.

'What?' I say, laughing. 'What is this? Whose is this? Is she ours?'

'He,' Dad says. 'And yes.'

I hold him to me, touching his big panther paws and smoothing the loose folds of skin on his wrinkly forehead. He licks my hand and wags his tail.

'Ronnie will eat this little guy alive,' I say, lifting him up.

'Not for long, he won't, because this guy's going to be a giant,' Dad says. 'But Lachy had eyes only for him. Biggest pup in the litter. Happy birthday, El.' Dad gives me a kiss.

'We've never had a boy dog before,' I say.

'His name's Soot,' Lachy says. 'I alweady named him.'

I smile, and pat the pup's soft downy head. 'Hi, Soot. Hi, little boy.'

After I finish unpacking my overnight bag in my room, I head down to the Pa Tree with Soot.

What do you think of him, Pa? I cradle his soft body in my arms as he gnaws his pencil-sharp teeth on my knuckles. *Kinda goofy, huh?*

I feel something deep inside me. Beyond this house and this land, beyond where Mum lives and where Dad lives. I am them. And I am everyone who made them. One small part of a giant patchwork quilt.

How many people are walking the roads, the rivers, the grasses of this earth by accident? I will never know. But I do know this: I will always be a Gillespie, and I will also always be half a Hansen. There are two stories that make me and there will be two houses that home me.

I grab hold of a branch hanging listless in the dull afternoon light and lean against it, Soot in my arms. The trees are still my friends. I close my eyes and hear the river gurgle. I came good on my promise to Lachy. We get to keep the river. Always, the river. I watch the water rush-rushing downstream, in a hurry to get to Drake's place. Drake won't be here forever. His plans are different to mine. Who knows if *I'll* even be here forever. Forever is a very long time. And I've only lived sixteen years.

I pull out my phone and text:

Rowing partner required.

I wait a moment for my phone to beep.

Is the lady seeking to go up or down?

I smile as I type my response.

Surprise me.

Before Drake can surprise me though, I surprise *him* with our new furry friend.

'He looks like a little Ronnie,' Drake says, and we fuss over him.

Drake helps me into Bridge and rows us upriver. Soot is snuggled on my lap as I watch our house disappear behind the bank. Quaint and old worldly, all alone on its hill in the afternoon light. Crooked River has never gargled so sweetly, the water never looked so clear and sparkling, the grassy banks greener. Our weeping willow is hunched over the water, full of pride and bright new plumes. Mount Wilderness is sharp-edged against a spring sky. She sits like a god, mighty and majestic, her white caps dwindling. The water in the river is shallow and we reach a point upstream where we can't go any further. It's not rained in a while. Soon there will be no more rowing and swimming, only splashing. Then there will be drought, and only walking. None of it, ever the same.

This is our world. And we came one signature from losing it.

We turn around and head back downstream. Drake parks Bridge down on the bank and we lie together under the shade of the Pa Tree while Soot sniffs around the trunk. Spring sunshine warms the dry grass, basking the land in gold. The air is alive with cicadas and insects cheeping. Swallows flit in the branches of the Pa Tree. Drake says something funny and we both laugh like the spring will never end, and nothing terrible will ever happen to us again.

Today is a happy day, a birthday, a new puppy day.

Drake leans over and says, 'Happy birthday, El.' And then he kisses me. On the lips. And I kiss him. And then we are two bodies tumbling through the grass, our hands on each other, kissing and playful, until I'm sort of breathless and Drake has dried blades of wheatgrass all through his hair.

'Looks like I found a real Tarzan after all,' I say, smiling up at his wild locks.

He looks down at me and traces my face with his fingers. His eyes are dazed.

'You know how I talked about leaving here?' he says, suddenly serious. 'I won't do it, Elliott. Not ever. I'll never leave you.'

I think of Mum. Her dreams of art galleries and big cities. How she let it all wither and die to be with Dad.

We don't own the future with anyone. All we own is ourselves in the now.

'You need to leave.' I smile up at Drake. 'You, and your crazy wild dreams and your crazy wild hair need to leave. Your education isn't here, and you can't give that up. But you do need to promise me one thing.'

'Anything,' he says. 'Anything at all.'

'You will never forget—our river, me, this . . .' I hold my arms out to the sky, and the Pa Tree and the wheatgrass encircling us.

'No matter where else you go or who else you meet, you'll remember us, like this.'

He smiles into my eyes. 'I'll remember always. Even if I get to ninety-nine and a half.' He touches my lips with his fingers, bends down and kisses me again.

I never want this to end. I want to hold onto the day I turned sixteen. Live it over and over. Because not so very long ago, I felt like all the world was dying. And now, small buds are unfurling in the spring and rising from the earth towards the sun. And I realise that endings are only ever new beginnings.

When Drake takes Bridge back to his place downstream, I lean against the Pa Tree and watch him go. He turns back before he rounds the bend, smiles at me, lifts one hand in a wave. I take a photo. Capture the exact moment.

I don't go back to the house. Not right away. I lean against the tree, hugging my ribs. The feeling of his fingers still tingles on my face. I can still feel his mouth on mine.

Universe, I whisper. *Thank you. For one more thing I get to keep.*

Soot is splashing along the rocks at the edge of Crooked River, licking at the flow of water. He sees me watching him and prances back towards me, past the stone that now marks Snow's last sleep. Soot doesn't know time existed before him, or that any other beast has called this land hers.

Lachy runs down from the house towards me and Soot bounces up to meet him. Lachy keeps running, Soot by his side, until he reaches the Pa Tree.

'Did you show him?' he says. 'Did you show Soot where Snow is?'

'Not yet,' I say. 'Do you want to show him?'

'Me?'

'Yeah. Snow was your dog too.'

Lachy stands a little taller. 'Yeah. Yeah, she was.' He scoops Soot up in his arms and carries him to the spot where Snow lies. 'You need to know something, Soot,' Lachy says gravely. 'You don't know Snow, but we loved huh very much. And she's buried here.' Lachy crouches down and lets Soot sniff the stone. 'Right here, she's buried.'

'Say that again,' I say.

'What?' Lachy looks up at me.

'Buried. Say it.'

'Why?'

'Just say it!'

'Snow's buried here—oh!'

'You got it!' I say. 'You got it, Lachy!' I pick him up, Soot still in his arms, and spin them both around. 'You got the r sound!'

'I did! I did! I did! Burrrried. Buried, buried, buried!'

And like a pair of maniacs, we both run up to the house, yelling, screaming for Dad.

'Dad, I can say r!' Lachy shrieks. 'Dad! Dad! Rrrrrr, are, her, buried!'

Dad comes racing round the corner to meet us. 'What's wrong? What happened?'

Lachy is panting hard. 'I can say r. Rrred, race, right! I can say it!'

'Oh, wow,' Dad grins. 'Good for you, buddy. You mastered your last sound!'

'Can I call Mum?' Lachy says. 'Can I tell her?'

'Of course. You can call Mum anytime, you know that.' Dad pulls his phone from his pocket and hands it to Lachy.

Then Lachy is dialling as fast as his eight-year-old fingers can. 'Mum, Mum, Mum, guess what!' Lachy says. 'I can say it! I can say the r sound, listen! Rrrrun, run, run. Rabbit. Rrred, race. I can say r!'

I can't hear what Mum says on the line, all I can hear is a high-pitched sound like a squeal. And I am smiling beside Lachy, and Lachy is jumping around with the phone pressed to his ear, and Dad is laughing at us both. And in this moment, I know that no matter what happens from here, we get to keep laughter. We get to keep joy.

The Gillespies

I can't go back to the beginning. I can't change what we were or fix what was broken, because life doesn't always give second chances. Only endings that give way to beginnings, as one door closes and another opens. But I do have now, this very moment, and here's what I see. Here's what we are.

We are three faces peering up towards the top of Mount Wilderness. Her snow caps have melted, but the air is still thin and sharp in our lungs like ice crystals. We are three pairs of boots putting one foot after the other, straining up her steep grassy climb. We are three breaths panting and three sets of fingers clutching at rock ledges and hands linked to pull one another up where the track is crumbly. We are sunshine bright on three faces and three voices floating high above the world.

'Come on, don't stop.'

'How much further?'

'Higher, higher.'

We are explorers of a great and sometimes terrible place. And when—after stumbles, and falls and scratches—we reach the highest peak, we are gods, looking over a world unrolled as a blanket at our feet.

At the summit of Mount Wilderness, the sky is ice blue and scattered with cotton-puff clouds, caressing the purple ridgeline of faraway mountain ranges. We can see to the end of forever here, to places we have never yet been, over golden mountains, and suede valleys and sparse stretching tablelands.

'Whoa,' Lachy breathes. 'Just whoa.'

We stand there in silence, us three, breathing quietly, absorbing the colours, the depths, the textures into our vision. Etching photographs in our minds. We do not know when we will be here again. That's the thing I've learnt. We do not know when anything will be again. We know only now.

'Can you find us?' Dad asks after a time.

'What do you mean?' Lachy says. 'We're here.'

Dad laughs. 'I mean the other us. Home.'

I search out Crooked River first, a thread of mercury snaking across the patchy emerald land. I find the bend where it tracks the small patch of land I fought for, to our house nestled between the hills, and the trees and the long shadowed wheatgrasses. Those who have never known the love of a place cannot possibly understand, and for them I feel both sadness and envy. For they will never know the pure abandon of losing themselves within it, nor risk the loss of themselves without it.

'There!' I say, pointing. 'We're down there.'

Lachy follows my finger, and then jumps on the spot. 'I can see it, I can see it!' he says, stretching his own grazed finger before him. 'That tiny little dot there is us! That's our house!'

'It is,' Dad says. 'And if you look just beyond our house, a little further down the field . . .' Dad takes hold of Lachy's finger and points it to where he means. 'Right there, in that spot where you can see that yellow patch of earth, and all the way along that line, that's where the new road's going in. And here . . .' He moves Lachy's finger again. '. . . in that little patch that looks brown, that's where they're building the new houses.'

As Dad traces out the new subdivision, my stomach sinks. New people and new homes will creep onto our land, but I say nothing, because the truth is, not everything can be kept. No matter how much we want to hold on to the way things are, change comes to the land, and to the people and to families. History tells us this is the way of life. And maybe one day the whole of Crooked River will be filled with homes, but I don't live in one day. I live in today. And today, I stand atop Mount Wilderness and feast on the sky, on the mountains, on the rivers, on the valleys. Nobody can own the earth's beauty. It's a feast for everyone.

I take a photo and send it to Mum.

In spite of everything, all the sadness since, I feel sure it will still make her smile.

Dad lays out a picnic rug and I help him unpack the cheeses, the dips, the crackers, the strawberries. Today is our first picnic as three. Though I guess we used to have picnics as three before Lachy was born. And one day we will probably have picnics as four, and maybe five and six and more.

But today we are three sets of hands reaching for crackers and pouring soft drink into cups. We are a babble of chatter and laughter ringing out over the valley far below. And when Lachy pulls out his pack of cards, we are three sets of hands sliding cards to each other across the rug and clutching them to our chests.

Dad leans over to see Lachy's cards, but Lachy presses them against his chest. 'I've got this, Dad.'

Dad musses Lachy's hair. 'Big boy now, huh? Don't need your dad anymore?'

Which makes Lachy pounce on Dad, and then they are two tumbling rumbling bodies atop the highest peak of Mount Wilderness.

I sit back and watch us. The Gillespies. The lucky ones.

Because we have learnt now, all of us, about need, and want, and pain and grief, and we have held on.

Acknowledgements

What They Told Me is a deeply personal story about the experience of a teenager going through parental separation. Having experienced my own marriage ending whilst raising my five daughters, and working as a lawyer in family law, I obtained some unique insights into what is often a poorly-recognised grieving process happening right across our country. Every day, parental separation indiscriminately impacts kids and their parents when their entire lives are upended. Every day in my work as a solicitor, I would meet with parents in the midst of what I can only describe as the tornado of their lives. It is a harrowing time, a highly emotional time, and that's just the adults.

What about the kids? With fifty to sixty thousand Australian children experiencing parental separation each year, I felt compelled to explore what it might feel like to be a child caught in the midst of a parental separation over which they have no control. Social sciences evidence that children aged seven to fifteen years experience the most significant challenges following parental separation, and yet whilst the stigma of parental separation is lessening, I could find few books for my own children where parental separation represented the central conflict in the story.

Every separation is unique, and the family courts in

Australia recognise the rights and the needs of the children as primary. This means sometimes the children will live with Dad, sometimes with Mum and sometimes with both, depending on the set up each parent has and the ages and needs of the child. Unfortunately in my work as a family lawyer, most cases involved at least one parent who could not be reasonable, and a high proportion of these cases ended up fighting it out in the family court system for two to three years. Thankfully, the majority of parental separations don't end up in court. Contrary to popular stigma, there are many fair, reasonable and kind separations in the real world. It is a myth to believe that parents will always hate one another after separation, or seek to punish one another or alienate the children (though, sadly, that does occur in a minority of cases).

As I started writing *What They Told Me*, I had no idea what Elliot's story would be—whether her parents were going through a nasty, embittered separation with blame-throwing, or one where they were trying to be child-focused. I just let Elliott tell me her story, and what she told me of her experience, I pieced together into *What They Told Me*: a unique story of what is an everyday reality for many Australian families going through the division and upending of every certainty in their lives.

It seems fitting to start by thanking Chad, my ex-husband and the father of our five daughters. To his credit, he remains to this day a firm friend, an ally, a co-parent, an admirable man and someone whose company I can still enjoy. Every day I am immeasurably grateful for this.

Thank you to my incredible agent, Clare Forster from Curtis Brown Literary Agency. You have encouraged me, book by book, sourced new options for me, and always made yourself available for discussions and advice when I am in unfamiliar terrain (which is often!).

To Lorae, my amazing editor third time running, we pulled off another one! I have absolutely enjoyed working alongside you; you are gentle, professional, astute and very forgiving of me when things haven't gone to plan!

To the team at Scholastic Australia . . . our third venture now and your team continues to amaze me. What a well-oiled machine Scholastic is. Your commitment to quality literature, getting books into kids' hands and championing a love of literature in schools is commendable.

To my fellow lawyers from Tony Cox Lawyers—Tony, Jess, Tani, Shelley, Mel and Hamish—thank you for sharing your knowledge with me, a few years of your time, a few years of laughter, and questions, and thoughts and answers. Law is a tough profession mentally and I admire all of you.

To those of my friends and family who have come to me during your own family law matters, thank you for trusting me with your pain, your most vulnerable selves.

For Chris and Tracey, who lost their beautiful Ronnie beast in 2023. When I wrote Ronnie from the start, I saw your gorgeous boy in him.

For Leah, Rob and Sharon, your friendship and loyalty through both my stable and my tumultuous years has been a far greater comfort than you could possibly know. Thank you for loving me warts and all. And for giving me your truth, your honesty, always.

Nix Hamilton, my dear childhood friend, and the one who is forever cheering me on when I say I just cannot write this novel, I will be first in line at your book launch when your first novel is published. You deserve so very much to be heard. But above and beyond that, a lifetime of thanks from me, for being my friend.

Kerrie Gee, for thirty years of friendship! Is it possible? We must celebrate. We have seen each other through far too much in life not to! Thank you for your unswerving love and guidance.

To Shelley, who travelled with me through my marriage separation, and I with her through her own, it is difficult for those who have not been there to understand, but I would not have survived it without you. Thank you.

Mum and Dad, you helped me in every possible way from the moment I was born, through every trial and tribulation. You taught me what unconditional love is.

As always, for my girls, Mia, Zara, Sophie, Heidi and Lacey, who teach me at every stage of life what it means to be loved and fallible, to be a mother, to be a daughter, and how we love one another over and over again as we each change and grow.

Finally, Jamie. My husband. The one who makes me feel precious, and beautiful and utterly loved. Everyone deserves to have someone like you by their side. I truly am the lucky one.

Also by Hayley Lawrence

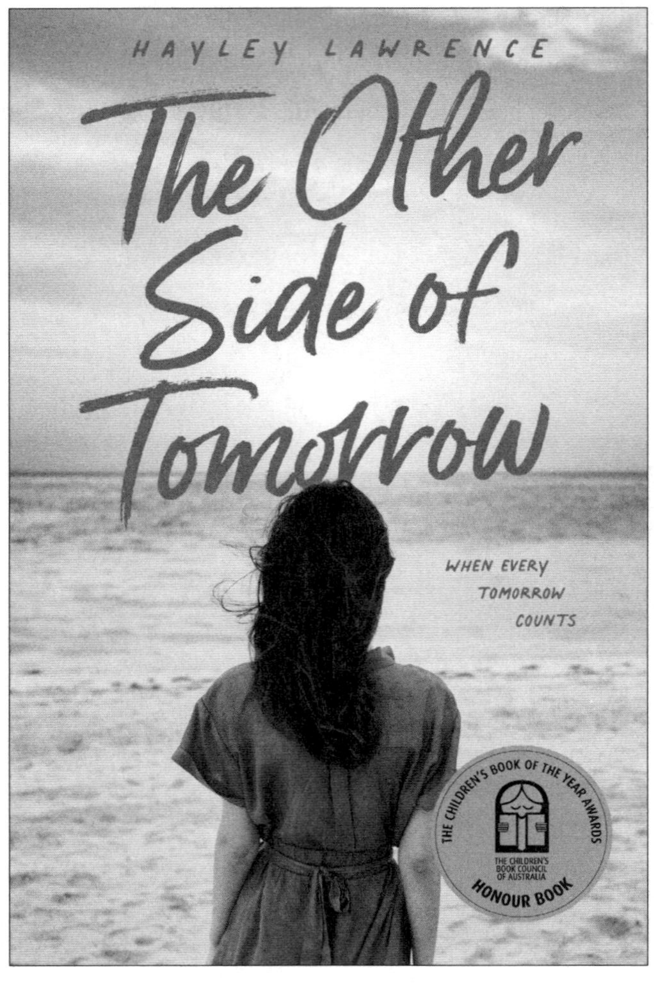

Out Now

The pretty girl? The scarred girl? Or the girl who survived?
SKIN DEEP
HAYLEY LAWRENCE

About the Author

Hayley Lawrence has been writing since she learnt to hold a pencil. She is currently a lawyer in coastal NSW where she lives with her five beautifully wild daughters and writes novels. Hayley's work is haunted by the stories she encounters as a lawyer, through her daughters and in the incredible people who lay their souls bare to her. Hayley's novels have won fellowships, been shortlisted for *The Australian* Vogel's Literary Award, longlisted for the Sisters in Crime Davitt Awards Best Young Adult Crime Novel and recognised as Notable Books and as 2023 Honour Book for Older Readers in The Children's Book Council of Australia's (CBCA) Book of the Year Awards. Find her online at www.hayleylawrence.com.au.